GNOSIS

Boris Mouravieff

Boris Mouravieff

GNOSIS

BOOK THREE
The Esoteric Cycle

STUDY AND COMMENTARIES
ON THE ESOTERIC TRADITION
OF EASTERN ORTHODOXY

Translated from the French by Maneck d'Oncieu
with the help of E. and S. Witkin,
and edited by Robin Amis.

PRAXIS INSTITUTE PRESS

Praxis Institute Press,
P. O. Box 375, Newburyport,
MA 01950, USA
Tel: (508) 462 0563 Fax: (508) 462 2340
and
China Hill, Brightling Road,
Robertsbridge, East Sussex,
TN32 5EH, UK

Printed in Great Britain by
BPCC Wheatons Ltd., Exeter

9/02

Cover design by Lance Hidy,
diagrams by Martin Gordon.
Praxis Research Institute gratefully acknowledges
the contributions of a supporting team of
translators and editors.

First published in French by
les Éditions du Vieux Colombier,
collection La Colombe, Paris, 1965,
then by les Éditions de La Baconnière,
Neuchâtel, Switzerland, 1972
English edition first published 1993

British Library Cataloguing-in-Publication Data:
A catalogue record for this book is
available from the British Library

Library of Congress catalogue card number:
91-226573

ISBN 1-872292-12-7

'JESUS SAID TO THE SADDUCEES: YE DO ERR,
NOT KNOWING THE SCRIPTURES,
NOR THE POWER OF GOD.'

(Matthew xxii: 29; Mark xii: 24.)

CONTENTS

FIRST PART: THE WAY

SECOND PART: THE TRUTH

THIRD PART: THE LIFE

symbolic and hieroglyphic. The Lord's Prayer examined in the light of its context. Our supersubstantial bread. The architecture of the Paternoster. The road that the faithful can follow by means of the Lord's Prayer. A glimpse of the first hieroglyphic meaning of this prayer. The birth of Jesus and the meaning of the Immaculate Conception in Eastern Orthodoxy. Mathematical relations which bring into relief the value of the global work of Jesus Christ compared to that of an ordinary terrestrial man.

PUBLISHER'S INTRODUCTION

This is the third and final volume of a work that addresses many needs, but deals particularly with one little-known question expressed in the idea that: '*Christianity has not been tried and failed, as claimed, but it has been found to be too difficult and has never been properly tried.*'

This statement, of course, could be true only of a Christianity of effort; one which requires people to *try to be Christian*, not one that assumes that anyone can be a Christian without the need to make effort: it is true, in other words, of an ascetic and mystical Christianity — in the sense used in the Eastern church — a Christianity that is experiential in content; for where there is no effort nothing can be said to be tried, and where there is no experience nothing can be known to have succeeded or failed. This idea, then, refers to a Christianity that is ascetical; ascetical precisely in recognizing the two ways of life and two states of being described by St Paul when he said of the first: '*Envyings, murders, drunkenness, revellings and such like: of the which I tell you before, and as I have also told you in times past, that they which do such things shall not inherit the kingdom of God.*'

And of the second state he said: '*But the fruit of the Spirit is love, joy, peace, longsuffering, gentleness, goodness, faith.*'[1]

Boris Mouravieff's *Gnosis* restores to the 'public domain' this spiritual tradition that depends on special knowledge, demands both experience and effort, and leads to real changes in people's consciousness and hence in their lives and their state of being. And detailed studies of the early Fathers of the Church reveal that at one time Christianity did have such a tradition of conscious transformation; the direct equivalent of the spiritual forms of Yoga in India or the Sufi doctrines in Islam, although for more than fifteen hundred years this form of the Christian tradition has never been generally tried or even known about by the average Christian. Mouravieff tells us that it was hidden from persecutors and sectarian disagreement around the third century AD, and that, as a direct result of this, although it survives in unwritten form in certain monasteries of the Eastern churches and in partial form in certain texts little known to Western man, its existence has in general been forgotten by the Christian West to this day.

Yet today, as in the past, wherever this teaching is rediscovered it meets the needs of many of those who sincerely wish to be Christian, yet have found it very difficult to transcend their own weaknesses; have failed to become Christian in action as well as intention; even to begin to live a Christian life as Christ and His apostles lived it. This forgotten tradition, then, provides guidance for those Christians whose zeal outstrips their abilities and who are not satisfied to bear the name Christian without being

1. Galatians 5: 21–22.

able to act as Christians; it awakens sleeping hearts which have not entirely forgotten what it means to wake. Such people will understand that if it is not true on the individual scale that Christianity has never been tried, it is entirely true on the scale of society as a whole; that Christianity for most of its two thousand years has never been properly tried outside the cloister, the hermitage, the catacomb, and the hidden places of those mystics who shun publicity.

Quite a few years ago, in his book *Lost Christianity*, Jacob Needleman hinted that there exists or had existed a different Christianity, a form of Christianity that was more demanding and more difficult to understand, but also more functional, a 'working Christianity' in the sense that it taught something that could actually be achieved. But at the time the book was written, this question appeared to him almost unanswerable. I say 'almost', because even then the old books existed, books once built as 'bridges' by servants of higher powers to help people cross again from one river of Christianity to the other, to the living river: the mystical Christianity which Christ called the *living water* — but man's thinking had in the meantime changed so much that few people at that time could understand such texts. Yet even one or two decades ago the information that would make this ancient reservoir of living water accessible was available to the English-speaking world only in abstruse translations of certain texts, most of which had been translated and presented only as curiosities, translated according to modern rules of exegesis not intended to reveal the practical meaning, and so used by those who lack the practical experience or specialist knowledge needed if the practical implications of the text were to be revealed in translation.

This situation is still partially true, but in the years since the publication of Needleman's book — and beginning before it was written — some new translations of early texts or of commentaries on those early texts have emerged, while others have become better known, and there also seems to have been some small growth in the understanding of the highly technical language involved, as well as an increasing number of attempts — at varying levels of success — to explain these ideas in terms that modern man will understand. New bridges are being built.

Here, in volume III of this great work, *Gnosis*, Boris Mouravieff is most clearly revealed as the author of an outstanding example of such a text, a major bridge between past and future, and as such as being far more than a mere scholar of esoteric curiosities. In this third volume he clearly fulfils his promise to reveal the hitherto unpublished essence of the Christian esoteric tradition, making available in 'plain language' material that has only been handed down orally or in symbolic form for millennia. Here too, he actually reveals how the symbols can be read: how this material can be used to expand the hints given by him in the earlier volumes into a full expression of the tradition.

The best evidence is in the results of his work. When this book *Gnosis* is read slowly, attentively, and repeatedly, and in conjunction with persistent efforts at self-observation, the ideas of the text, which at first appear intellectual, begin to change: they come alive, sometimes as we are reading them we see the things they describe occurring right then in our lives, and this gives real meaning to the ancient Gospel idea that we earlier linked to the 'second river': to that 'living water' that Jesus promised to the woman of Samaria: a river of new life. The way he describes what occurs within us begins to become a way of seeing what happens. The changes he describes as happening as a person evolves begins actually to occur visibly within us ... all in the context of a 'different Christianity'. In Volume I, Boris Mouravieff claims to be authorized to publish material previously only available in oral form. At the same time, the text presents itself in a neutral way, so that all in all, then, it is up to the individual, as it has always been, to decide on the truth of such statements according to some inner sense. But by the time one is well into Volume II one should be quite sure of this, though unable to prove it to others.

Later in the book the author claims to give a 'complete' exposition of the tradition ... and emphasizes that only a complete exposition will be effective. Such claims must be treated with care, yet again, if *Gnosis* is read several times, slowly and with sufficient attention, results must lead to conviction ... and the point of this introduction is to inform all readers of the book that, as hinted at earlier, some readers are already finding such results. Yet we must also understand what Mouravieff means by 'complete': in volume II he refers to the fact that for a long time the tradition has been so thinly represented that some elements have not survived to the present time. The historical record bears this out, with many references in existing texts to works that are no longer in existence; so *of course* the book *Gnosis* does not contain all the Christian esoteric teachings ever given. Unpublished writings by the author make it clear that the book does not even contain everything taught in his course at Geneva University in the sixties. So what kind of completeness is he claiming? Close study makes it seem that he means that the books contain a complete method: a complete prescription or rather a complete series of prescriptions by which different types of individual can progress on the way.

Again, if we imagine, as so many do, that in recovering ancient teachings Mouravieff proposes a return to ancient ways — to the ways of mediaeval Russian Orthodoxy, for example — we will discover that this is not so. The book points not towards a return to a forgotten past but to a future yet unknown. Careful reading reveals passages which make it quite clear that he drew on the past only to awake a 'different future', that although drawing on ancient knowledge he is proposing a move toward entirely new solutions for new times, for the Time of Transition, as he calls it, and for the coming Era of the Holy Spirit. At the same time, in this final volume he reveals keys which have been hidden for centuries, including the keys that will enable the hard-working student to read the ancient language of mathematical symbols that encapsulate so much of the special knowledge of the esoteric tradition.

'Since then, the revolutions that have successively brought us steam, electricity, mechanization and atomic energy have transformed the face of the world, and habit as a substitute for happiness has disappeared during these upheavals. This means that although we hear people claim happiness with growing fervour in the feverish atmosphere of our times, we find ourselves in a void. If a few 'last of the Mohicans', with their outdated mentality, raise their voices to call for a return to the 'normal' state of things, in their naïve sincerity they appear like medieval knights leading a cavalry charge against armoured cars!'[2]

A NOTE ON LANGUAGE

In volumes I and II of this book we have translated the French word *psychique* as 'mental' in order to avoid what Mouravieff would call the 'phenomenalistic' connotations given to the word psychic in contemporary English. In Volume III this is no longer supportable: it is necessary here to introduce the idea of a 'psychic Love' that is more than purely physical love, and to describe what is called in French the *plan psychique* as a 'psychic plane' to conform to the author's descriptions which now clearly extend beyond the boundaries of what we commonly know as the mind, although they have only a little relation to the concepts of the psychic normally considered in contemporary thought. We beg the reader's indulgence for this change in conventions.

---

2. Chapter XX, p. 185

AUTHOR'S INTRODUCTION

(1)

At every great turning-point in history, Man is the central problem. Because of this, it is easy to understand that, in the time of transition in which we find ourselves today, between the Cycle of the Son which is coming to an end and the Cycle of the Holy Spirit which is beginning, there is an imperative need for the *new Man* — strong and enlightened — capable of resolving the two great problems on whose solution the future of humanity depends:

1. To make the organization of human society rational and effective on a global scale;

2. To create conditions which will offer a maximum opportunity to seekers who wish to develop their Personality and so reach the Second Birth.

These problems, which are obviously interdependent, have already been discussed in the first two volumes of this work. Different elements of this *Gnosis* have been studied and divulged by degrees so that the willing disciple may gradually grasp how important these two problems are. We will develop this by considering:

—the rationalization of the political, economic and social organization of human society in an *esoteric sense*, which must lead to the general Resurrection; i.e. the incarnation at one time of all the souls attached to our planet;

—the teaching of the revealed *Gnosis* to form an elite of men and women of the new human type, who will be formed from individuals of all the different historical civilizing types and all their specific subdivisions.

(2)

In spite of the difficulties that have come from the failure inflicted on John the Baptist and Jesus, and in spite of twenty centuries of history marked by intolerance, cruelty, ineptitude and collective madness, humanity, without enthusiasm but according to the nature of things, is reaching its unification. It appears, however, that this budding unity can only be maintained and consolidated if there is a rational and harmonious regime on a global scale, and to establish such a system will require artisans of sufficient calibre.

Only a social order formed on an esoteric basis will provide the Statesmen who will be needed tomorrow, men capable of confronting the problems arising from the organization of life in an Era characterized by a super-abundance of sources of energy — an Era where man will be liberated from his servitude to work which is the automatic regulator and safety-valve for the frenzy of mankind.

In other words, in order to regain the initiative that it has lost to the *Machine* it has created, human society must give birth to a new aristocracy, a *Nobility of spirit and service*. This must happen in the same way that, in times gone by, the Intellectuals took the place of a medieval knighthood that had become decadent.

(3)

To solve the problem of Humanity depends on a positive solution to the problem of the individual Man, and we will approach our study of the esoteric cycle of 'Gnosis' in this order.

This means that our efforts will be oriented towards the practical application of esoteric Knowledge — both for the new Man and for the new humanity as a whole. This is to help those who are predisposed to this kind of work and who burn with the desire to reach the Second Birth. Having assimilated the *exoteric* and *mesoteric* cycles of the Doctrine sufficiently, they must now be ready to serve the Cause joyfully, and to subordinate all their own interests to this end. The latter condition is imperative; if the disciple does not observe it, he will make no progress in the esoteric domain but will find himself locked in a vicious circle full of dangers.

To Burn and *to Serve*: this is the motto of the Knight of the new Era. It should be engraved in fiery letters in his heart, and be constantly present in his mind.

(4)

We must emphasize that in the end, at the time of the general Resurrection, the human elite will be formed of polar couples.

During the Time of transition, it is understood that *Gnosis* must resolve the problem of the *New Man* by progressively introducing the rule of the *singular romance* which must replace the *free romance* normal to the previous Cycle and abolish all vestiges of polygamy.

Thus, Man's problem today comes back to the *Androgyne*, which is the highest condition of human Consciousness, which crowns the efforts of the disciples and triumphs in their Second Birth.

In this *Introduction*, we will put forward certain rules allowing us to determine the attitude that should be adopted during these *esoteric* studies and in the practical work they contain. These will help the disciple who has reached the measure of this level of teaching to better gauge his abilities and make sure that he is consciously engaged in these studies, for it is better for him not to venture too far than to have to retreat later on and run the risk of an imbalance in the psyche.

(5)

These general rules are dictated by the very nature of the work to be undertaken during the esoteric cycle of Gnosis. When successful, this work leads to the Initiation which consecrates the deep transformation of the disciple, who is first called upon to *put off the old man*,[1] then to put on the *new Man*.[2]

The danger of psychic imbalance arises from a lack of commitment in the Work or from a lack of will: in fact, it often happens that the disciple manages to put off the old man but does not succeed in putting on the new. His failure may be because he overestimates his strength, but also because of the incompetence of his teacher; and this incompetence is sometimes coupled with unwillingness.[3]

The propositions that follow are not considered from the angle of worldly motives and reasoning, but from the point of view of the *perfect*,[4] who already belong to the new world, at least in principle and in spirit.

(6)

The first point to be remembered by those who aspire to be initiated into the *singular romance* has to do with patience.

On the esoteric plane, patience and perseverance are not measured by months or years, but by decades or even lifetimes — that is, by a succession of incarnations.

It is important to realize that esoteric practice differs in a hundred ways from what we usually imagine it to be. We repeat: no-one can attain the only vivifying, true, *objective* Love without extensively modifying their Personality and its 'psychology'. And this *objective Love* can only be attained here below in its complete and vivifying manifestation at the time of the second Birth, by a work that is *useful to the Cause*, accomplished through sustained conscious efforts.

---

1. Ephesians iv: 21, 22.
2. Ephesians vi: 24.
3. Vol. I, pp. 51–53; Vol. II, pp. 181–184.
4. Corinthians ii: 6; Philippians iii: 15; Colossians i: 28; iv: 12; James iii: 2; I John ii: 5; Clement, Eusebius, Origen, Irenaeus, *passim*.

The way of access to this Love is pointed out to us by Love itself. We must always keep in mind this fundamental notion: that Faith, Hope and Knowledge (*Gnosis*) are the successive stages of a progressive Revelation of Love.

If one or other of these is insufficient or completely lacking at a certain stage, it cannot be obtained at the following one. In other words, without *Faith* in one's heart, it is impossible to attain *Hope*, in the esoteric sense, and without Faith and Hope, *Gnosis*, the living Knowledge which finally gives access to Love, remains forever inaccessible.[5] Lastly, it is necessary to know that Faith, Hope and Gnosis together form what the Tradition calls *courtly Love*.

Courtly Love is therefore the precursor of objective Love.

(7)

I f it does not contain *Gnosis*, human love, including that which contains Faith and even Hope, cannot attain the level of courtly Love. This is because the void left by the lack of *Gnosis* from the Absolute II is immediately filled by the intervention of the Absolute III. This intervention is normal, and is generally desired by the common run of men, but it is undesirable for disciples of esotericism: it generally leads to marriage, with all the different worries and 'considerations' which result from this and provoke successive deviations in the imperfect disciple, dragging him into the closed schema of a vicious circle. As for relations outside marriage, which do not offer the Absolute III the same guarantee of stability as marriage, they provoke even more pronounced intervention in different forms.

Courtly Love is the raison d'être for the couple of polar beings: for the Knight and the Lady of his Dreams; without it, their polarity remains spiritually sterile and they fall back into the common condition. Its practice, however, demands sacrifices and 'exploits'. These are *tests*. For those who surmount them, the salutary effect of *Gnosis* is doubled: when it is enriched by experience, theoretical knowledge becomes living knowledge.

In the Middle Ages, the Knight and his Lady, who considered themselves spiritually ONE — in our terminology, polar beings — did not venture into marriage. On the contrary, they parted, accepting the risk of never meeting again and knowing that if they did not triumph over a hard test, their love would degenerate, losing its meaning and its marvellous power. They knew that, by separating from each other for an *exploit*,

---

5. Vol. I, pp. xviii & 253, Vol. II, *passim*, particularly pp. 61–62 and 247–250.

they stood the chance, while a premature marriage would be reduced to nothing.

Today, as in olden days, courtly Love remains, by definition, the indispensable condition for the success of a supposedly polar couple who aspire to the *vivifying Love* which is our Lord-God.

There is no exception to this rule: it applies to all, beginning with the couple of young and just polar beings; and it is even more obligatory between two polar beings who meet at a mature age, when life has already burdened each of them with a karmic load. In such cases, the first *sacrifice* demanded is the renunciation of a physical relationship, and the first exploit consists in the methodical liquidation of the respective karmic burdens, keeping in mind that the big or small 'Gordian knots' which make up these burdens must be untied, not cut.

If the presumed polar beings ardently and effectively undertake some esoteric work in the same direction, useful to the Cause, the moment will come when they will be purified. Having become courtly, their Love will assume all its objective force, and in the purity rediscovered in this way, they will finally be convinced of the reality of a polarity that they had felt intuitively. There is no possibility of error at this stage.

At this moment, the Second Birth will unite them forever in the midst of the vivifying Love; and death, finally conquered by this, will lose all semblance of catastrophe for them.

(8)

The courtly Love of the Knight and the Lady of his Dreams will immediately place them on the fourth step of the *Staircase*, where their exploits and sacrifices will hasten their advance, provided that *Gnosis*, having been sufficiently assimilated by them, produces its fruits. The time they need for this end will be given them; but they will remain on the fourth step only if they burn with Love. Otherwise, in spite of a promising start, they will not be able to attain the desired goal. If, on the contrary, they make some progress in their work, they will observe as they advance on the fourth step that *Love changes its place* in their physical body, their psychic body and their spiritual body, all at the same time.

In order to help the disciple who wishes to study the present volume of 'Gnosis', we will repeat once again that courtly Love can be effective only if it is based on a *Gnosis which is lived*, for only a *lived Gnosis*, one that has been acquired through experience and has gone down into the heart — one joined with Hope that is founded on Faith — will ensure that the Knight will have the discernment which will prevent him from going astray in the jungle of purely human reasoning and feelings.

(9)

This having been said, we must not forget that courtly Love is the common attribute of the Knight and of the Lady of his Thoughts, that is, of supposedly *polar* beings. At the same time, it is also the meaning of, and the instrument of work on, the Fifth way: the sublime esoteric way which, in the midst of the conditions of this world, will enable the couple to acquire the attitude which will be characteristic of the world to come, the approaching Kingdom of Heaven, and, from the time that they meet, to live here on earth *like the angels in Heaven.*[6]

This is certainly an exploit, and it is not given to everybody to attempt it with a chance of success. But the Fifth Way does not exclude the four other Ways described in the first two Volumes of 'Gnosis'. The great error in the esoteric domain, which, as in all the others, leads to failure, is to embark on an enterprise which is above a man's capacities. The Tradition warns us about this very exactly, as has been made clear earlier. This overestimation of his strength by the disciple is a classic snare that the General Law lays for us, and many people of entirely good faith get caught in it when they could successfully have followed one of the four other Ways which do not force the disciple immediately to pass through the Trial of Fire.

This is why Saint Paul said: '... *he that giveth (his virgin) in marriage doeth well; but he that giveth her not in marriage doeth better!*'[7] This 'doeth better' is commented upon in the Tradition as one of his references to the Fifth Way.

(10)

We have spoken at length on the particular esoteric significance of the regenerating force of courtly Love. To conclude this *Introduction*, we must draw the reader's attention to the esoteric task and the importance of couples who are not truly polar, but who work sincerely by following one of the first four Ways:

1. On the individual plane, they contribute towards the growth and progressive development of their own Personality;

2. On the general plane, through reproduction, they contribute to the realization of the conditions necessary for the general Resurrection.

Because the general Law is stronger than they are, they must avoid defying it so as not to provoke the Trial of Fire too early.

---

6. Mark xii: 25.
7. 1 Corinthians vii: 38.

It is for them that the Apostle said: '*Deprive ye not the other, except it be with consent for a time, that ye may give yourselves to fasting and prayer; and come together again, that Satan tempt you not for your incontinence.*'[8]

---

8. 1 Corinthians vii: 5.

GNOSIS

Volume Three
FIRST PART
THE WAY

CHAPTER I

(1)

The problem of the organization of human society — a rational and effective organization on a planetary scale — is now of immediate concern: tomorrow it will become urgent. Yet, until now, nobody has given any real thought to this problem. It is unrecognized by governments and universities and generally ignored by the press.

Because of the evolution of human society, this problem impresses itself on our minds without the need for any initiative from government, because this evolution accelerates every day, in every domain, to make the norms of past centuries obsolete.

Several times in the first two volumes, we have called the reader's attention to the delay in man's moral progress compared to his rapid technical progress. Today the material means needed to rationally organize the political, social and economic life of humanity are no longer lacking. What we lack is the key to the underlying significance of it all.

When we raised the problem of the new Man,[1] we hoped — as we continue to hope — for the advent of such men in every domain of human activity. It is urgently necessary that they should take over from the statesmen of the old school, who, apart from a few rare exceptions, do not have the moral means — the knowledge and experience — to meet the needs of the time of transition through which we are now passing. In the long run, a situation like this can form a powerful brake on the natural evolution of men and of things, and it may in the end threaten the very existence of the human species.[2]

Today, statesmen of the old school give us ample proof of their inability to rationalize and balance the life of humanity as a whole; that is, to transform the incoherent mass of peoples and States into a homogeneous organism.

In pronouncing this categorical judgement, we are not simply giving way to a desire to criticize at any cost. Of course, there are certain statesmen, responsible for international affairs, who are individually capable of effectively contributing toward a happy solution of the problem we have just raised. But the responsibilities of their role do not allow them to risk innovation. We must not forget that they are ministers, not prophets. Far

---

1. Boris Mouravieff, *Le Problème de l'Homme Nouveau*, in the periodical *Synthèses*, nos. 126–127, Brussels, 1956.
2. Cf. 2 Peter iii: 7.

be it from us, then, to criticize them harshly, for we must recognize that in the domain that concerns us they face insurmountable obstacles[3] ...

However, these considerations change nothing objectively, because the great problem exists and urgently demands a solution. But it is necessary to emphasize that the essential technical means by which we can arrive at this solution also exist today, and that those that are still lacking will be acquired with no further delay. But as well as material means, *creative imagination* and *courage* are also necessary, and these are both missing.

In the meantime human society, tormented by suspicion and fear, lives in a precarious equilibrium maintained by terror. This forces it to orient all its efforts toward destructive actions in order to increase its security.

What is lacking in governments is a *planetary consciousness* which can unite and embrace the individual consciousness of nationalities and States. These are the organs of expression of the particular *historical civilizing types* that exist today.[4]

(2)

We can compare the current world situation, in its scale and significance, to the one that existed at the time of transition between the Middle Ages and Modern Times. What characterized this period was the progressive disappearance of feudal parochialism and its replacement by a nationalist consciousness, a uniting force that acts within the limits of the State. This political process has already been the object of another work of ours, entitled *The problem of super-state authority*.[5] The reader may refer to this[6] if he wishes to explore the question further, or if he wishes to study the role that the United Nations Organization must play. Here we will simply recall that in Europe the passage from feudalism to the centralized national State was not effected by means of a Congress of Barons or Counts — a kind of miniature UN — but through an appeal to the national consciousness of statehood. The *new Men* of that period, who possessed this until then unknown State-consciousness, showed themselves capable of bringing that time of transition to term by establishing the modern State. In France, the principle artisan of this undertaking was Richelieu, and in Russia, Ivan III and Ivan IV were mainly responsible. On the other hand, in those cases where the nation did not produce Statesmen with a modern national consciousness that was able to dissolve the separatist spirit of the feudal lords, the State ended in ruin, despite the flourishing appearance

---

3. The translator here had: '*are obliged to conform to the politics pursued by their governments*'. (Ed.)
4. Cf. Vol. II, ch. XIII, *passim*.
5. Boris Mouravieff, *Le problème de l'autorité super-étatique*, Paris-Neuchâtel, La Baconnière, 1950.
6. As yet only available in the French.

that certain elements in the country were able to maintain. We can use Poland, with the high standard of individual culture that existed in the ranks of its aristocracy, as an example of the latter. Similarly, in spite of the creation of many leagues and alliances, ancient Greece never managed to create a homogeneous State like Ancient and Modern Rome.

On the planetary scale, this process of political unification appears analogous to the unification of feudal fiefs into a nation. But here, as always, analogy is not similarity.

(3)

History knows only two ways of realizing political unification: *imperialism* and *federalism*. In our days, we cannot seriously think of employing the first method, but nothing stands in the way of a rational and organic unification of the human species in the framework of a world federation.

We often hear that it takes a federalist to create a federation. This expression is attractive, but it is not universally true, and it has no real force unless the word 'federalist' is used in a collective sense, or unless it refers to *prophets* instead of *ministers*; that is, *Individualities* and not simply *Personalities*.

A *College of Prophets*, possessing objective consciousness, well-versed in Savoir-Faire, and with the moral means that even the most gifted and cultured *Personalities* lack, could orient human efforts toward a rational organization of the globe.

(4)

We have emphasized that analogy is not similarity, particularly in the situation we are studying. But we have yet to discover if, taking account of the above considerations, we can find a formula that will ensure the *organic* coexistence of peoples and States throughout the world, and guarantee true peace, sheltered from the usual hypocrisy and chimerical fabrications, and in which everyone will get what is due to him.

Nations, like individuals, clamour for liberty; and it goes without saying that without liberty, no one can live, in the complete sense of that term, that is, can *develop in peace and in dignity*.

The transition from feudalism to the modern State, crowned by the French Revolution of 1789, was carried through under the banner of the ideas expressed by the triple formula: *Liberty, Equality, Fraternity*, which has conquered the world.

Yet, strange as it may seem at first, today this formula appears out of date: after a long period of glory in which it enflamed hearts and aroused men's passions, it now seems only a shadow of itself, drained of its substance and incapable of reviving the same enthusiasm it aroused in the past.

To understand this phenomenon better, we will study the manifest historical meaning of the three terms in question, and see where they have led human society after having served it during a whole heroic period.

At first, the idea of liberty was generally seen from a legal point of view, and this meant that people conceived it as a right. Shaken in 1789, and faced with conservative resistance, it immediately took on the dynamic character of a military demand. Since then, by grant or conquest, liberty has been permitted within the limits defined by law or by treaties and conventions.

(5)

L iberty, as we know it, has been criticized more than once. For example, it has been maintained that the 'emancipated' have not usually been granted the means to exercise the rights accorded them. The whole procedure is then without meaning, and hardly more than a theoretical conception. This is, in fact, liberty for a chosen few and not for all, in other words a return to the aristocratic or oligarchic principle under a democratic facade.

It is also said that the principle of Equality is purely imaginary, since Nature in all its manifestations is founded on a diametrically opposite principle, which also applies to the human species: that of inequality. In reality, the proclaimed equality is generally reduced to the equality of citizens in the eyes of the law, and even then the facts do not always support the theory.

Of course, it would be absurd to expect something perfect in the imperfect world in which we live, so it would be more realistic to look for *transient value* than for perfection, as everything changes with time, and even the meaning of ideas may change.

The formula *Liberty, Equality, Fraternity* is a battle-cry. As such, it contributed greatly to the accomplishment of the transition to contemporary History in modern Times, but with the decolonization which is now happening before our eyes, it is losing all topical interest and so has lost its historical significance.

The present situation requires a new formula, a call not to war but to a rational organization of life in the framework of the liberty which has already effectively been won. In this perspective of the future, the motto *Liberty, Equality, Fraternity*, seems outmoded and even illogical.

Today as yesterday, *Liberty* has an aggressive sense, *Equality* is shaky, and *Fraternity* is enveloped in a framework of pompous declarations. This does not mean, however, that we should relegate this motto to some limbo of the mind. On the contrary, it is possible to revive it, even gloriously, if we reconsider it in the anagrammatic spirit dear to antiquity and to the Middle Ages. Indeed, as a watchword it would be more appropriate to the present and the future if it were read backwards, that is, in the following order:

Fraternity, Equality, Liberty.

Let us suppose that, through some marvellous procedure, the great principle of Fraternity becomes a universal reality. What repercussions would this have?

In the first place, violence in all its forms would be rejected as immoral. Fraternity would gradually heal individuals and peoples, whether they suffer from an inferiority or superiority complex, and it would definitely condemn that vestige of the tribal mentality that is known as racial prejudice.

The practical application of the principle of Fraternity would not change the face of the world at one stroke. Misbehaviour, abuse, weakness, and incomprehension—that plague of the human species—would continue for some time to come. But even if it did not immediately change everything, Fraternity would change our attitude toward the excesses and weaknesses that exist in our political, economic and social life, so that they became less and less frequent.

The proclamation and glorification of the principle of Fraternity would not be chimerical acts, but on the contrary would represent a very realistic enterprise that historical evolution approves and demands. Judiciously applied, this principle would prevent some 'powers of this world', and certain industrialists and financiers who only worry about their own interests, from getting the peoples involved in war. Besides, racial prejudice being stigmatized, if the conceit of some people is diminished they will no longer offend the pride of others, and a natural equilibrium will thus be established.

Rooted in the consciousness of peoples and States, the great principle of Fraternity would be the best and only real guarantee of Equality on both national and international planes, and in both social and political fields. Would Liberty not then seem the logical consequence of this new state of things?

It therefore seems evident that the primary element in the national and international legal systems of today and tomorrow should no longer be Liberty, but Fraternity, which, in the historical evolution of human consciousness, forms the cornerstone of the individual and social morality of civilized peoples.

7

II

(1)

A ll this seems very beautiful, the realistic reader may say, but how can we make the principle of Fraternity into a practical reality, so that it becomes an active force in the customs of peoples and States?

Let us try to answer this question.

First, it is important to understand that we have no intention of studying or discussing different political theories, for whether we profess capitalist or communist ideas, whether we are 'liberal' or 'reactionary', the brutal fact remains that technical progress has drawn people out from their former isolation: enclosed in a world whose limits have suddenly shrunk, they are being led mechanically toward unity.

Unexpected and still misunderstood, this new fact entails new requirements for peoples and States. Threatening cataclysm, it demands from man an urgent and radical re-evaluation of values, notably the abandonment of worn-out standpoints and of methods that do not work. From this point of view, Marxism and Capitalism are already part of History, since technical progress has led to a unity which already clamours for the adoption of new forms of coexistence between peoples and States.

And here, we recall again that the feudal State ceased to exist because the national consciousness was stronger than provincial consciousness, although it did not eliminate the latter. This gave birth to States whose central power was strong enough to impose order and peace within a country. Having understood the call of the times, geniuses like Richelieu anticipated and prepared the way for the evolution of the elite. This explains why the unity of the French people was established only in the following century, by a constituent Assembly which abolished feudal privileges and proclaimed the sovereignty of the nation, the separation of legislative, executive and judicial powers, and finally, the access of all citizens to public office, and their equality before the law.

Originating from a newly conquered and bitterly defended Liberty, these rights were no more than the subconscious expression of a Fraternity restricted within the framework of the nation.

This was the process of transformation that interests us.

At present, in spite of certain disturbances we are aware of, on a worldwide scale the elite are approaching a psychological condition which may be compared to that which animated the deputies of the constituent Assembly in 1789. In all the four corners of the world, these men belonging to the elite know in their inmost heart that the present world regime, with its watertight compartments between States that are full of mistrust and jealousy, has lost its *raison d'être*.

The divine principle of Fraternity, which once transformed the feudal States into national States working through the human subconsciousness, continues to work on the minds of men. Today, however, it is operating on the consciousness of the elite on a higher plane and on an international scale.

However, the UN has not yet become an organ which is able to faithfully express this principle. Indeed if we consider the great metamorphoses which are taking place at this world-wide juncture, and contrast them with the weakness of the transformations which are supposed to correspond to them in the modern system of international law, we cannot help noticing a marked discordance between, on the one hand, the structure and works of the UN, and on the other, events and the precipitate march of time. Recent events only serve to emphasize this fact, since the United Nations Organization should not only dress wounds, but should effectively prevent bloodshed.

We have already pointed out that the Organization's weakness is the direct consequence of a basic internal contradiction. This lies in the fact that although the charter was proclaimed in the name of *peoples*, the realization of its contents was left to their *governments*: this is not the same thing.

(2)

On a limited scale the population of the multinational States presents an analogy with that of the population of the world seen as a whole, and the history of these States provides us with valuable examples. The first is that they show that application of the principle of *federalism* can — and does — lead to positive results. Conversely, the negative principle that previously governed ancient Poland, with the *free veto* and the constitutional right to begin civil war under certain conditions, led to the ruin of the State. We might properly compare this anarchic kind of national regime with the international law of the past century, which gives full recognition to the 'right of conquest', a formula which is anarchic in principle and based on the balance of opposed forces ready to act at any moment, a balance that is fragile in its nature and adds up to no more than the right of the strongest.

The new international legal system developed from the United Nations Charter is still in an embryonic state and ineffective. This is because we always look for solutions of the problems on the interstate plane when it would be better to look for them on the supra-state level — just as one combats provincial rivalry by appealing to the highest national authority.

If we compare humanity as a whole to the population of a State, with the individual in the same place in both examples, we must recognize that, proportionally, these states of the present time are analogous on a global scale to the fiefs of the Middle Ages. This comparison led to the appearance of the UN as a kind of *governmental* organization, like an imaginary conference of feudal lords, with no real power.

It would be inane to try and apply the principle of imperialism to unify humanity today — not to mention the fact that this idea involves the creation of *police states* and *Gestapos* of all kinds. The only other possibility is to try to discover under what practical conditions we would be able to apply the unifying federalist principle. History gives us a few convincing examples, especially that of multinational States: first, the old Helvetian Confederation whose sovereign cantons later made up a federated State, and in more recent times, the Soviet Union.[7]

The question then is whether one can be inspired by these examples of federalism which have stood the test, of time in the first case, and of invasion in the second, so as to solve the problem posed by the present lack of international judicial order.

It is necessary to note that modern legal thought is not oriented in this direction. The search for a source of authority over separate states should not tend toward the establishment of a *statelike* superstructure; this would be senseless, and would only create a vicious circle. The search should be simply transferred to another plane, abandoning state or inter-state planes and turning toward the very source of public power: the *popular vote*.

III

(1)

Without losing touch with realities, how in practice could one introduce the question into the general framework of the United Nations, granted that the latter must eventually become universal? Can the example of those multi-national States with a federal constitution be imitated on a world-wide scale, and in what way? Could the parallel Swiss or Russian bicameral system be introduced in the UN? Would this make it more effective?

It seems clear enough that, alongside the present general Assembly of States, the creation of a second general Assembly — that of Peoples — with the precise function of expressing the principle of human Fraternity, would modernize the international legal system and give it uncontested authority. Possessing equal rights, and going into session at the same time and in the same place, these two Chambers together would form the

---

7. The forced federalism of the Communist Soviet Union has since disintegrated, but the United States may well serve better as a working example. (Ed.)

supreme Assembly of the United Nations, similar to the Swiss federal Assembly or to the Supreme Council of the USSR.

This would re-establish the proper balance between the traditionalist principle, expressed by the Assembly of States, and the innovative one centred on the People's Assembly. For although each delegation comes to the present general Assembly with a definite mandate from its government, from which it cannot depart, the representatives at the general Assembly of Peoples would not be bound in this way. They would probably form groups. These would not necessarily be based on their belonging to some particular State or group of States. On the international plane, an Assembly of this kind would then be a true organ for the expression of world-wide public opinion and of the principle of human Fraternity.

Separately, according to this idea of modernization, each of the two Assemblies of the UN could only make *recommendations* as at present. On the other hand, their combined vote during a joint session of the *Supreme Assembly of the United Nations* would naturally be decisive.

(2)

However, all the differences between the States cannot disappear in a single stroke: we must let Time do its work. We may, perhaps, begin by convening *parliamentary* delegations to the People's Assembly; and almost imperceptibly we would reach the point of holding direct elections with proportional representation.

The essential point is that the structure of the UN would then be in harmony with the new rhythm of political and social life characterized by a continually greater interpenetration of affairs within and between states. This would be accompanied by the growing influence of economic and social factors on truly political questions, and in general by a progressive interpenetration of the factors and influences which together make up modern public life — national and international. A structure like this demands real Liberty, not one that is conditional or controlled, but one founded on the principle of Fraternity, and blossoming in a climate of effective Equality.

Logically, this is the only possible way of organizing human society according to the natural flow of its historical evolution.

(3)

But even if it won the *votes of individuals* all over the world, it seems improbable that this formula could be put into practice under the present international regime. The spirit of governments is always conservative, even with a government formed after a political or social revolution. So it is doubtful that the General Assembly of the United Nations, the assembly of all the States, would risk modifying the Charter in this direction according to the provisions of its Article 109. We must admit that this prudence is in a certain sense understandable, as extremist tendencies in the first Peoples' Assemblies could exacerbate the present international tension and cause it to explode instead of reducing it.

A high standard of intellectual culture, even if reinforced by vast experience, would not be sufficient to control the situation. We can ensure the success of the transformation we envisage only on the basis of *Love*; and especially *love of our fellow men*, something that is unknown to men who still do not know exactly what it means to *love one's neighbour*.

This is why Statesmen of the old school will not even be able to begin this debate. The new international politics can only be conceived and led by *New Men*—the *Prophets* we mentioned at the beginning of this chapter. But in the meantime, it is important to fix the objective and point out the way of Salvation.

CHAPTER II

(1)

The transition from one era to another is plunging the world into a critical situation. Analysing this situation, we have come to the conclusion that the *immediate* cause of the troubled period of history that humanity is now passing through is *material* in nature. It has to do with the industrial, or more exactly, the *energy* revolution which has successively substituted steam, electricity, and nuclear energy for the simple human and animal power that were until then the only sources of energy other than the wind. This revolution means that man now has almost unlimited sources of energy at his disposal.

It is difficult to judge their magnitude, but the considerable repercussions of this revolution are forcing us into a direction which is, in principle, that which should be taken by the new humanity.

(2)

First, we must analyse the *material* consequences of the present crisis, which is a result of advances in technology that have transformed the world's structure. Then we will study the deeper meaning of this crisis which, as we have already shown, is of a *moral* order.

What will the new humanity be like, or what can it become? This is what we will try to outline in the present volume. We can already point out some major consequences of this transformation, though these constatations are in no way limiting.

First constatation — The new means of transport and communications have changed our *sense of distance*. No inaccessible places exist today: the world has narrowed down; the antipodes have become neighbours, and distances are no longer calculated in miles or kilometres, but in the units of time required to reach such and such point. Here are a few distances expressed in terms of *time* taken before the coming of the railways:

	(days)
Paris — Saint Petersburg (express mail)	17
Rome — London (express mail)	13
Rome — Saint Petersburg	30
Berlin — Northern Italy	10
Vienna — Berlin	5
Berlin — Spanish frontier	15

In comparison, the air trip from London to New York now takes four hours.

The smaller the world becomes, the more our contacts become obligatory, frequent and close. This is the first consequence of the technical revolution: it requires a complete reassessment of the problems that arise from relationships between States and between individuals.

Second constatation — The perfecting of machinery requires the use of *raw materials* from all over the world: the automobile industry alone uses more than two hundred different types of material. Because of this ever-larger economic community of interest, we have lost our independence.

Third constatation — Mechanization leads to mass production, which, by modifying the law of supply and demand, gives rise to the problem of marketing, then that of overproduction.

Fourth constatation — Thus, as manufacturing becomes the norm, this leads to the unification of civilization: films, tape-recorders, gramophones, radio and television, the architecture of buildings, etc. In its turn, this obvious tendency toward a homogeneous civilization leads to standardization of academic teaching. This is inevitable, because the same or similar problems arise everywhere, and demand similar solutions.

Fifth constatation — Today, man has the use of means that could not even be imagined a century ago. Mass-production, which seems so natural to him with modern equipment, is a result of the ever faster growth of possibilities. The result is that problems such as the abolition of suffering could be resolved today in a practical way. But there are two sides to every coin: this technical power, which could be a blessing for humanity, can also lead to frightful catastrophes.

(3)

The development of international co-operation, which was desirable earlier, has now become indispensable. For the reasons just stated, States are now obliged to solve their problems on the international plane. They can no longer simply act within a national framework. In turn, this interdependence logically calls for collaboration between peoples.

However, although the world is progressing rapidly towards unity on the *technical* plane, it is still formed of States, and on the *political* plane these regard themselves as *sovereign personalities*. This is not a question of something artificial: every nation is a solid reality that is deeply rooted, but this fact is obviously in opposition to the consequences of the technical revolution.

Today, we see nationalities establishing themselves in an increasingly passionate way, and this phenomenon is developing on two planes:

a) *on the surface*, as a result of decolonization;
b) *in depth*, because of its acute and dynamic character all over the world.

In the final analysis, this contradiction leads to two different processes: while the technical revolution urgently calls for the establishment of an international order which, if not a single unit, is at least unified. Opposed to this in many peoples we can constate the rapid and powerful development of a national consciousness which sometimes escalates into xenophobia. These opposed processes threaten to tear our human society apart. We previously pointed this out in the second volume of this work,[1] where we suggested a theoretical solution to the problem. We have repeated this again in the first chapter of the present volume: the question is to find out how to move from theory to practice.

The underlying cause of these difficulties lies in the fact that the two processes are unfolding on different planes of human consciousness. The technical process is of interest on the plane of *civilization*, while the second is taking place on the *cultural* plane, according to the definitions we have given of these two terms.[2] We will repeat them here so that the reader may follow our explanation more easily.

By *culture*, we mean everything on the spiritual plane and the plane of the psyche, which properly, and in an original way, belongs to the whole of a civilizing type. It must be understood, of course, that within this whole, each of the associated peoples is the bearer of a *specific* culture that is a component of the cultural content of the *given historical civilizing type*.

By recognizing the irreplaceable cultural genius of a people, this manner of seeing things assigns their true historical worth to all peoples, big or small. It follows that moral progress necessarily depends on the *cultural* evolution of humanity.

By *civilization*, we mean all the results obtained by technical progress, in the widest sense of this term.

It follows that the specific element of culture always springs from the *national* consciousness, in the broadest sense of the term; whereas civilization, during its development, naturally tends to become *international*, and ends by embracing the whole world.

(4)

These definitions explain the double process in which the universal internationalization, which is the logical result of the technical revolution, is opposed by an ever-growing assertion of national consciousness in all peoples, big or small, free, colonial or semi-colonial.

---

1. Cf. Vol. II, ch. XIV, *passim*.
2. Cf. Vol. II, pp. 148–9.

(5)

It is now easy to understand that the essential cause of the present crisis lies in prolonged neglect of the *cultural* element. This neglect led to the formation of a chimerical idea of the difference between *civilized* people and '*savages*', a word with which we sometimes describe peoples who have attained a very high degree of culture — although different from ours — but whose civilization did not develop at the same pace as in the West.

With time, this error has come to be regarded as a truth in the minds of most Westerners. By accepting Voltaire's *deism*, and by introducing the deification of the Personality established by the French Revolution into our psyche, we have ended by attributing to '*civilization*' the meaning and value of '*culture*', and, as we have seen, culture always belongs to a particular nation, and can only develop within the framework of national liberty and independence. However paradoxical it may seem, it is actually the development of the Western civilization, and its propagation throughout the world, which has created the necessary conditions for the establishment of this *national independence* all over the globe.

II

(1)

We must now study the growth of *culture* in all its varied national aspects. As we have seen, these aspects are specific, and all have equal value. We will add that this equivalence is the best expression of the *Fraternity* of humankind, which is no more than a fact of Nature, although it has been neglected or violated in the course of millennia. This crisis, in which humanity finds itself as a result of its ignorance or negligence, can be resolved only if all peoples become conscious of this fact.

The cultural source of every nation is *traditional*. It is the *spirit of the people* that is the depository of the cultural treasure which is expressed in the national language and *literature*. We can observe that the structure of the language is always original up to the phonetic alphabet, but is always changed a little when it comes to the written alphabet.

The seventy-two original tongues which appear in the myth of the Tower of Babel, with their subdivisions, form between them the great receptacle of the *universal culture* of which each is only a specific aspect. Above these seventy-two original tongues, there is a *Universal Language* on which all of them are based, the language of *Numbers*: this is the divine tongue, the instrument of expression of the *Word*, of the *Logos*, the source of the absolute Truth from which the seventy-two draw their vitality, so that each separately may form a *national Individuality* by bringing to it its own originality.

Here, we are touching on the esoteric plane.

Further on, we will see that, in this sense, the Era of the Holy Spirit will be characterized by the return of different peoples to their traditional sources in order to finally form a Unity. United in all its *legitimate* variety, each national Individuality will be an integral part of the *harmonious* Whole which will then be re-established.

Symbolically, this will be a return to the Tower of Babel, but in the opposite direction: an integral renaissance of all the historical civilizing types in a return toward mutual comprehension based on a revealed and assimilated *Gnosis*. This would be the blossoming of national cultures in the framework of a unified world civilization — an expression of the great principle of human Fraternity.

CHAPTER III

(1)

We cannot compare any other turning-point in history with the present one. Since the Flood, the only one as important as this was the one for which Saint John the Baptist prepared, which Jesus and His Apostles helped humanity to face. However, other less important changes can serve as historical precedents, and even if they are not exact models, they can provide us with valuable clues, revealing factors which were decisive in the accomplishment of certain works — some of which go beyond the limits of what is generally acknowledged as humanly possible. And it is precisely this transcending of the human norm which is of interest to us.

We include in these works those of Alexander the Great and Peter the Great. In each case, the legends of these personalities and their heroic actions have not totally eclipsed the true image. If we cannot penetrate into the depths of their souls, we can closely observe the impulses that drove them and guess the esoteric source of their clairvoyance and superhuman energy. Taking known facts as a basis in this way, we can develop an idea of how superhuman forces intervene in the routine course of human history.

Historical science is hardly concerned with this epic side of Alexander or Peter, as this question is not within the objective of its studies. The question is not raised by history, but by psychology, philosophy, and especially esoteric philosophy.

(2)

It is curious to note that once their work was achieved in broad outline, both Peter and Alexander were suddenly removed by illness at the height of their triumph, when they had been exposed all through their lives to the greatest dangers when they were involved in military operations. Although Alexander had been wounded a few times, Peter had always come out without a scratch.

The aim of the present chapter is to give to the reader who has already assimilated the contents of first two volumes of 'Gnosis', a clear picture of these two great builders of civilization whose iron will, guided by a higher consciousness, changed the course of History to advance the world, in both cases for three centuries, toward the great turning points that mark the passages between Cycles.

We did not choose our heroes at random.

(3)

Let us begin with Alexander III, the Great, King of Macedonia. We refer to Ulrich Wilcken's work, which has a preface by Professor Victor Martin, formerly rector of Geneva University.[1] This preface ends with the passage that we are about to reproduce here, as it will give the reader an idea of a work that was remarkable from every point of view, and especially from the esoteric point of view which interests us most. Of the author of this work on the genius who inaugurated a very important phase of world history, the *Hellenistic* civilization, Victor Martin writes:

'He has accomplished this task, not only as a great historian, but still more as a man for whom the contemplation of the past orients and nourishes the meditation of the present. When we consider the way in which he reveals certain aspects of his hero's career, we feel that he is establishing a comparison with certain circumstance in our most recent history. These discreetly indicated parallels and their conclusions — suggested instead of formulated — always lead to reflections, and these are sometimes contradictory: the dialogue this creates between the author and the reader will not be the smallest profit that the latter will draw from his interchange with this scholarly biographer of Alexander the Great.'[2]

(4)

Let us now see what Professor Ulrich Wilcken says of Alexander and his work. In the *Introduction* to his book, he sketches the following portrait of his hero:

'Alexander the Great belongs to the small minority of men who have inaugurated a new period in universal history. He is perhaps the only one who imprinted the mark of his personal will on the world with such force that the evolution of humanity remained under his influence for several centuries — a phenomenon which is even more astonishing because Alexander died before the age of thirty-three ... His passage on this earth left ... something more durable than the empire he conquered by the sword and by blood: *the blossoming of the Greek civilization into a world civilization*[3] of which he was the founder ... But it was undoubtedly necessary to create the empire first, for here, as always in world history, it was the decision on the battlefields which oriented the development of the civilization.

---

1. Ulrich Wilcken, *Alexandre le Grand*, published in German (Berlin, 1924), French translation by Robert Bouvier, preface by Victor Martin, Paris, Payot, 1933.

2. Op. cit., p. 10.

3. The italics are the author's.

'We are discussing this to discover which forces dominate history: Alexander is an emphatic proof of the decisive importance of the *personality*. We cannot study a genius like Alexander apart from his 'milieu', nor can he be considered as simply a product of his time and his country. Certainly, like all men, he was subject to the conditions of time and place, but his genius followed its own ways which, without him, the natural development of his century and of his country would never have followed. Without a doubt, like all great leaders, he also followed the currents that ruled his epoch; but he did not always let himself be carried away by their waves; when they were contrary to his own ideal, he struggled against them with all his strength.

'Before him, in the fourth century, we may already notice certain phenomena and movements that may be considered as precursors of the *Hellenistic* age — that transformation of classical Hellenism of which he was the initiator—but these, to be precise, were only harbingers; it was he who made them blossom, yet they show that, from many points of view, Alexander was the man that his era awaited.'[4]

(5)

Let us now study the conclusions drawn by the author of this remarkable work. In chapter IX: 'A retrospective glance at Alexander's work', Ulrich Wilcken expresses himself thus:

'Alexander was not even thirty-three years old when he died. He was cut down in his prime like his ancestor and model Achilles. His reign had not lasted thirteen years. A glance at his gigantic work puts us in the presence of a unique genius, a marvellous mixture of vehement passion and clear, cold reflection. Endowed with an iron will, this man of action, whose policy was most realistic, also possessed certain irrational tendencies, such as that 'nostalgic attraction' toward the unexplored and the mysterious which, along with his will to conquer and his taste for scientific discovery, finally led him to the farthest limits of the inhabited world. His conviction that he was a descendant of Heracles and Achilles also belonged to the order of irrational imponderables. It was this living faith that gave him so much mettle, and so much strength. Religious, not given to philosophical criticism, he was firmly persuaded that the gods had taken him under their personal protection, and so he believed in his mission. Recently, in an important conference on *Ancient Strategy*,[5] the following aphorism was voiced: "It is characteristic of the great men of antiquity that they considered all their acts to be inspired by divinity." This applies to Alexander

---

4. Op. cit., pp. 15–16.
5. General Hans von Seeckt, *Antikes Feldherrntum*, Weidm, 1929, p. 11.

more than anybody. When the prophet hailed him as Ammon's son, he took it as a simple statement of fact, an affirmation of the divine force that lived in him.

'This was also why he could later ask the Greeks to recognize the sacred element in him, and demand that they accord him the honours due to a divinity. This unshakeable faith in his mission inspired him with the absolute certainty that he would conquer. Without recognising this we could never understand his actions. The supernatural power with which he was endowed enabled him to dominate men.

'The general and the *Statesman* are closely linked in Alexander, for, as Commander-in-Chief, he executed his own political will. The general in him is more understandable, for he completed this part of his work, while at the time of his death the political tasks were still unfinished. Alexander was the type of *king-commander* who had unlimited power over his people and over the resources of his country, and who was responsible to no one but himself. He did not have to fear those 'trials of generals' that the Attic democracy loved to stage in order to acquit itself of all guilt. As the head of the Corinthian League, he was shielded from all military criticism, even by the synedrion. Besides this, Alexander was fortunate enough to inherit from his father the best army in the world. A great general himself, he initiated his son in the art of war, and left him a company of well-trained officers. These favourable circumstances helped Alexander develop his military genius to the maximum, but the main point was that he had genius ... among his great military qualities, one must not forget ... the *tenacious perseverance* with which he completed whatever he judged to be necessary. He stayed seven months at the gates of Tyr before he conquered it. This small example should be sufficient to prevent us from drawing a parallel between Alexander and Pyrrhus as so many have already done, in antiquity as today; for Pyrrhus was always vacillating: he abandoned the siege of Lilybee after only two months, and his whole Sicilian expedition came to naught as a result.

'Alexander proved himself to be a great *leader*. He knew how to draw his troops after him by participating with them in work and in danger. In battle, he gave them the example of great personal courage. On the long marches, he shared their fatigue. During the sieges, if there were boats to build or other tasks of this nature, he always put his hand to the work. He encouraged the good workers and punished the lazy. When a great victory was won, he took pleasure in rewarding his troops by organizing games, competitions and other festivities. He paid his army handsomely in money as compensation for the rule which forbade them to pillage a conquered country ...

'Alexander is more difficult to know and judge in his role as *Statesman*, since his political ideas were still in development when he died ... Not one of his political creations took a definite form, and new projects were forever springing from his indefatigable mind. It is impossible to conceive how the face of the world would have changed had he lived ten or twenty years more. We would then have quite a different judgement of his work in his youth — of all that he accomplished before the year 323! We must, therefore, never forget that we are dealing only with beginnings. The last word was never said.'[6]

(6)

This quotation from Wilcken's book gives us a fair idea of the greatness of Alexander and of his work, as well as of the impossibility of explaining this in terms of what we generally recognize as *humanly possible*, that is, in *exoteric* terms. The same characteristic marks the work of Peter the Great.

Peter and Alexander had the same kind of mentality even in the smallest details. For example, both these men showed a hostility toward convention, visible, for example, in their unwillingness to wear a beard, considered in those times to be a sign of virility and masculine elegance.

Before considering Peter's work, let us return to that of Alexander. We will look at it from the esoteric point of view which Ulrich Wilcken has neglected. It is interesting to note that an appreciation of this kind was given tacitly during Alexander's lifetime, since his superhuman nature was generally recognized: he was given the title of son of Ammon, and divine honours were attributed to him, as they sometimes were to heroes of the Hellenic world. We are so distant from that epoch, and we live in such a different civilization, that we cannot imagine the value of these honours, but we know that the centuries immediately afterwards recognized them. Certain primitive Christian Churches looked upon Alexander as a saint. For what precise reason, and in consideration of which part of his work, did they raise him to this rank?

On reflection, the reply to this question seems quite clear: it is because, three centuries before Christ's Advent, Alexander was responsible for the creation of the *Hellenistic* world that was to become the cradle of Christianity.

Jesus said to the Jews:

Did ye never read in the scriptures, The stone which the builders rejected, the same is become the head of the corner: this is the Lord's doing, and it is marvellous in our eyes?

Therefore say I unto you, The Kingdom of God shall be taken from you, and given to a nation bringing forth the fruits thereof.[7]

---

6. Op. cit., pp. 242–7.
7. Matthew xxi: 42–43; Psalms cxvii: 22–23.

Which, then, was this *nation*? Unquestionably, it was the Hellenistic world. Is it not clear that the timely appearance of this world of considerable vastness, and its development at the time of the advent of Jesus and of his failure due to the denial by the chosen people, was the *marvellous thing* of which the Prophet spoke? The *Sacrifice* was only a *substitution formula* in case of failure: the Hellenistic world, established by Alexander, was the *receptacle* which received this *Sacrifice*, the *propitious soil* on which the seed, sown by the Son of God appearing as the Son of Man, would be fruitful. This is indeed 'the Lord's doing'.[8]

It would not be too daring to affirm that Alexander was Christ's forerunner on the political and cultural planes, as was John the Baptist on the spiritual plane.

That is as far as his work is concerned. As for the man, if we interpret the word saint in the way it was interpreted at the time of the early Churches, the fact that he was recognized as a *saint* by the early Churches, and later, by Islam, shows that he belonged to the esoteric plane: in other words, Alexander came into the world *charged with a mission*. For this, he had to be an *Individuality*, and not simply a Personality.

From the esoteric point of view, this was equally true of Peter the Great. It is not our intention to outline Peter's characteristic traits, as we have done for Alexander, for in this sense there are parallels between the two heroes, and a comparative study of the two *Individualities*, all proportions retained, reveals striking resemblances. Although in the end both had the same significance, their respective tasks were undertaken in opposite directions, so to speak.

Alexander introduced the Hellenic culture to a vast portion of the world, which included the Orient and the Occident, and this world became *Hellenistic*. Peter, on his side, cultivated Science on Russian soil — the same Science that came from ancient Greece at a time when Russia was piously imbibing the esoteric Tradition and putting it safely aside in the crypts of traditional Orthodoxy — an Orthodoxy that was jealously defended and preserved through the centuries, in spite of storms, political catastrophes, invasions, and the Mongol yoke which lasted two hundred and fifty years.

It is easy to see that the two heroes worked in opposite directions: a disciple of Aristotle, and the bearer of the most developed culture and most brilliant civilization of that time, Alexander spread both civilization and culture by force of arms. He was also himself a *source* of cultural values. The best proof of this is the famous *Prayer of Opis*, in which, after his victory, Alexander expressed the wish that beside general prosperity,

---

8. Without this 'receptacle' *prepared* in advance in case of failure, the *Sacrifice* would have been rendered useless, and would not have led to its 'fruition'.

the Macedonians and Persians would enjoy '*harmony in the community of power.*'[9]

It is in these words that a leader of high esoteric culture proclaimed the principle of federalism in a multinational empire created by the sword. This work met needs that arose only three centuries after his death, although they had been prophesied through a 'miracle of the Lord' seven centuries earlier ...

Though their characters greatly resembled one another, Peter, unlike Alexander, was self-made. He had to rely entirely on himself to accomplish his work. To meet the urgent needs of national defence, he had to modernize the army, and create the navy and the whole arsenal of war.

When he came to the throne, Russia was at a high level, *culturally* speaking — especially its spiritual culture. If this had not been the case, the Russian people could never have preserved their national consciousness or that of the State, from which flowed the decisive force that enabled it to triumph against all invasions and maintain itself as an entity. But this culture was leading toward a sort of '*kitaism*',[10] as they used to say in those days. The best minds realized this and knew that Russia lacked the element of *civilization*. Peter's task was to re-establish this equilibrium. The intellectual development and technical progress that had been realized in Europe since the Renaissance, as well as the military experience built up during the whole of the Thirty Year's War, had placed Russia in a state of material inferiority. This situation was becoming dangerous, and there was a danger that centuries of effort on the spiritual plane might be annihilated by a show of strength from the West. Aware of this gulf even in his early youth, Peter found himself faced by a problem that was humanly insoluble: to learn first, and afterwards to teach others, each according to his inclination. His will, like Alexander's, knew neither insurmountable barriers nor crises of discouragement like those Justinian the Great experienced.

It was necessary to act in stages. The first problem was to educate himself, and to create the embryo of a modern army. Peter set out to do this *at the age of fourteen*. The motto engraved on his seal as Tsar gives us an idea of the work he undertook at that time of his life: *I class myself as one of the students and I call for teachers.*

Yet, above all, Peter was a self-made man. His insatiable desire to know and to obtain savoir-faire made him a great Statesman, organizer and diplomat in the grand style as well as a great general and admiral. Perceptive and realistic, he was a clever politician and originated the principle of 'politics of interest'. This strategist was also a mathematician, a civil and military engineer, and figured among those who for the first time outlined a theory of naval construction. He proved to be a great artillery specialist,

---

9. Ulrich Wilcken, op. cit., pp. 223–4.

10. *Kitaism*: isolationism, like ancient China behind its Great Wall.

as well-versed in the production of these materials as in their use; he was also an economist, financier, physician and surgeon. He was a legislator who was also a historian, philosopher, and man of letters. As an artist and an artisan he knew nineteen handicrafts perfectly.[11]

(7)

From whom did Peter inherit all these talents? His father, Czar Alexis I, called the *Very Kind*, was a highly respected monarch, intelligent and devoted to his Country, but nobody could compare him with Alexander's father, of whom Theopompe said, 'all things considered, Europe has never produced a man like Philip, son of Amintas.' Peter's mother, the Czarina Natalie, was far from being Olympias' equal. According to a historian of the time,[12] she was 'incapable of ruling'. From where, then, did he get these extraordinary qualities?

The question remains, for attempts to answer it by rational means always lack certain details. This is why all attempts to explain this phenomenon in a logical way are incomplete and do not hold up. As Klioutchevsky said, to judge Peter's work clearly, one must admit that he was born with the plans for his Reform 'ready-made in his head.'

Voltaire gives us the best portrait of the Reformer. He was Peter's contemporary and outlived him by fifty years. This enabled him to follow the Emperor's work from its beginnings and to judge its effects half a century after Peter's death, when he published its history.

Voltaire's work has a special value, for the author was as great as his hero. A philosopher himself, Voltaire was the first to acknowledge Peter, not only as a hero, a legislator, and a diplomat, but also as a great philosopher. Voltaire's qualities — particularly the greatness of his mind — give his analysis a quality of impartiality inaccessible to historians with a political background.[13] Without resolving the enigma of Peter the Great, Voltaire presented him in an impressive way. 'What is most astonishing,' he said, 'is the small hope that mankind must have had to see a man like Czar Peter born in Moscow. There was one chance in a million, nay,

---

11. In *Peter the Great's Cottage* (his first dacha in St Petersburg), several specimens of his handiwork were on exhibition. Amongst them one could admire his ivory sculptures. It is hard to understand how Peter found the time to execute such minute handicrafts with a craftsmanship that may be compared with that of the artists of antiquity.

12. Prince B. I. Kourakine.

13. With time the accuracy of Voltaire's judgements, which appeared for the first time in 1727 in his *History of Charles XII* and for the second time in 1775 in *The History of Russia under Peter the Great*, proved to be more and more obvious. This phenomenon is due on one hand to the fact that Peter conceived his Reform in relation to the distant future. Today, after two and a half centuries, it still lies ahead of us. On another hand, Voltaire's genius, which outstripped his century, could appreciate Peter's work not only in the framework of his period but in the misty future that the farsightedness of the two men enabled them to pierce.

one against the entire number of Russians that ever lived, that this genius, that was so contrary to their national genius, should be given to any Russian. And there was only one chance in sixteen million, the number of Russians that were alive then, that nature's lot should fall on the Czar. Yet it happened.'[14] Further on, Voltaire wrote:

'Today this Empire is counted among the most flourishing States, and Peter is among the ranks of the greatest legislators. Although his enterprises did not have to meet with success in the eyes of the wise, his successes have forever reinforced his glory. We think today that Charles XII deserved to be Peter the Great's first soldier. Yet one left only ruin behind him, the other is a builder in every field. Thirty years ago, when I wrote Charles' history, I dared to make nearly this very same judgement. The memoirs from Russia which I have today, enable me to make known this empire, whose peoples are so old, but whose laws, customs and art are a new creation. Charles XII's story was amusing, but Peter's is instructive.'[15]

(8)

What escaped Voltaire, who was not Russian — and what sometimes escapes even Russian historians — is precisely the fact that Peter's genius was in no way 'contrary to the genius of his people.' In reality, Peter was the bearer of the *integral consciousness* of the people who gave birth to him, and this in two forms: historical and dynamic, the second being organically linked with the first. He was the focal point of the tendencies and historical aspirations of the Russian people, of the traditions of the Slavonic race and the whole Orthodox-Hellenistic world.

With the spirit of synthesis and fusion of the latter, Peter *incarnated* Russia through his genius, which was simultaneously abstract and yet practical, as well as through a latent energy that he transformed into a dynamism that knew no insurmountable obstacles. Even physically, over six foot tall and with Herculean strength, he symbolized this immense empire of peoples of which he was elected Czar, and of which he became father and emperor.

(9)

We do not wish to extend the bounds of this chapter, so we will not go into Peter's Reform in detail. It is, however, necessary to comment

---

14. Voltaire, *Anecdotes sur le tsar Pierre le Grand*, Paris, Librairie Firmin-Didot Frères, 1846, pp. 542–3.
15. Op. cit., p. 261.

on the esoteric aspect of his work and of its artisan, which is what we are about to do here.

When we consider the Reform superficially, we often overlook the fact that it was *rigorously systematic*. Peter adapted his plans to circumstances: sometimes he modified them in the light of experience; at other times, he demanded that they be altered to fit in with his requirements. In keeping with his role, he demolished everything whenever he judged it more practical to begin a new order than to renovate the old. We have often said that the Reform was, above all, conditioned by the needs and circumstances of war; it is remarkable that, although carried out in the midst of crises and dangers, and though Peter was always on the move, wielding the sword in one hand and the pen in the other, it does not appear improvised or makeshift in any way. We can always see the whole rising above the immediate circumstances, so that each part of the work fits in perfectly with the whole, as much in space as in time. This is because, being an *Individuality* like Alexander, Peter was *always logical and true to himself*. Guided by the Reform he had undertaken, in his own words, '*for the common good, so that the people may be relieved,*'[16] he consecrated his whole life to this cause. This explains the extraordinary fact that his Reform contains no contradiction in itself; that its different parts, realized at different periods and in different sectors of the life of the State, and often in haste under the pressure of urgent needs, appear, in the end, like the members of a living and harmonious body. It was like this for thirty-eight years, beginning with the first measures he took at the age of fourteen. How can one come to any other conclusion than that the general plan of the Reform had already been conceived and developed *before* the young Czar began to execute it? This is a logical conclusion, though it may seem absurd, humanly speaking: as with Alexander, the work that Peter accomplished in Russia appears as the fulfilment of a mission.

(10)

From the *esoteric* point of view, it would be interesting to know what the Emperor himself thought about his Reform. Unfortunately, he expressed practically no opinion about it. However, when he heard the news that his plenipotentiaries had signed the peace of Nystad, he was filled with joy and cried out: '*This ends the education of the Russian people in a school of three stages!*' He came back to this formula several times, even in writing, but only explained it once, during a 'reception', when his aides asked him to enlighten them on this point. He took up a pencil and wrote:

$$3 \times 7 = 21$$

---

16. Complete collection of the laws of the Russian Empire, Series I, no. 3840.

underlining that the Reform had been carried out in three stages, each lasting seven years:

1. The accumulation of strength (1700–1707).
2. The growth of Russia's glory (1707–1714).
3. The establishment of the 'good order' (1714–1721).

This brought to light the fact that the Reform was accomplished in *three seven-year plans*, with successive displacements of the centre of gravity. It is still impossible to say *how* and *when* these plans were conceived and elaborated, or where the Czar found his ideas. All Peter's historians agree that he easily broke with routine in any domain to establish a new order. But if one keeps in mind the circumstances in which Peter worked, the introduction of such changes seems impossible without the existence of a complete and pre-established plan. Once again, then, we have to recognize that, *positively*, we face an enigma.

We will repeat that, in the case of Peter as well as Alexander, we can only find the solution on the *esoteric* plane.

(11)

Peter the Great's Reform called forth a great deal of criticism and many pessimistic forecasts. Many people in Europe affirmed that the Reformer's work held only because of his iron will, and that after his death the country would inevitably fall back into its previous state. Events proved the contrary. This appears even more remarkable when we note that, among the thirteen sovereigns who succeeded the Emperor on the Russian throne, from the time of his death in 1725 until the Revolution of 1917, only his daughter, Elizabeth I, continued his work. Aided by her father's collaborators, she saved the Reform.[17] Her successors proved to be weak and without understanding: the foreign dynasty that reigned over Russia during the one hundred and fifty-five years after Elizabeth's death methodically put a brake to the application of the Reformer's precepts and mutilated his work.[18]

How then can we understand the success of the Reform? This success was conditioned by the following factors:

1. The beauty of the cause and its appropriateness to the time, both immediate and in the long term;
2. The utility and viability of the enterprises;
3. The well-defined goals and the 'open door' policies which let new talent in: the first serious attempt to establish *equality of opportunity* (Peter never stopped repeating 'merit before ancestry');

17. Boris Mouravieff, *La Monarchie russe*, Paris, Payot, 1962, *passim*.
18. Ibid.

4. The fervour with which the author of this Reform served the national cause, without sparing himself, as he was always present at the most critical moments, and in the most dangerous places; it was a fervour that he knew how to communicate to Russian youth, who were with him body and soul;

5. The strength of Peter's personal example;

6. The almost supernatural quality he had of recognizing talented people at a glance, and the art with which he knew how to make use of them.

(12)

A very interesting document exists, which enlightens us on the Emperor's estimation of the road covered during thirty years of war; this is his hand-written programme for the festivities celebrating the peace of Nystad. This document is dated the 27th April 1724, so Peter wrote it six months before his death.

The following appears in his notes:

'Commemorate the victories first. Afterwards, during the festivities, enlarge on the following:

1. Our *artlessness*[19] in all affairs, especially at the beginning of the war, which we undertook like blind men, in complete ignorance of the enemy's forces;

2. Our former enemies used to say, not only verbally but in writing, in treaties and conventions, that it was necessary to avoid prolonging wars against us, as in this way we would not have time to learn the art of war.

3. Mention all the internal difficulties, including those with my son. Also show how the Turks were turned against us;

4. All other peoples have always pursued a political plan aimed at maintaining the balance of power, especially to prevent us from benefiting from the light of reason in all affairs, and, above all, in the art of war. Now, they have ceased to follow this rule, as if it had been suddenly hidden from them. This is, in truth a divine wonder, which leads one to believe that all human conspiracy is powerless against God's will.

It will be necessary to develop the last point extensively, as it is so full of meaning.'[20]

---

19. Translated literally, in order to preserve the spirit of the Russian expression.

20. Quoted by S. M. Soloviev, *Histoire de Russie depuis les temps les plus reculés*, in 29 volumes, St Petersburg, Ed. Ob. Polsa, Vol. XVIII, Ch. III, col. 860.

(13)

Let us add a few touches to the portrait of Peter the philosopher. We have seen that Voltaire was the first to discover the philosopher in the Emperor. Since then, no one has risked writing on this subject.

On the personal, social and political planes, Peter's philosophical basis was *Faith*, *Hope* and *Knowledge*, upheld in *sincerity* by the boundless *Love* he had for his people, in whom he had an unshakeable faith.

Among the Emperor's papers, a manuscript was found which had probably been prepared for his personal use in his hours of meditation. It was dated 1722, and contained a brief résumé of the *Decalogue* compared with the doctrine of the *Gospel*. It was conceived as a two-column table: in the left-hand column, the Ten Commandments of Moses appear, one after the other, and on the right hand are brief notes about each, listing the corresponding sins. The following text came next:

'After having enumerated all the sins for each commandment, I find that there is one missing, namely, hypocrisy. Why? Because though only one category of sins corresponds to each commandment, hypocrisy encompasses them all together.'

Then, after having shown that hypocrisy is the basis of each of the ten categories of sins, Peter concludes by showing the importance of hypocrisy in relation to all the other sins, as well as its own place. For this, he takes the New Testament as a basis and ends on an original note:

'After all, Christ our Saviour commanded his disciples to fear nothing except hypocrisy when he said: '*Beware of the leaven of the Pharisees, which is hypocrisy.*'[21 & 22]

This note lays bare Peter's heart. There is no question here of a merely 'intellectual point of view': never, in all his life, did Peter stoop to hypocrisy.

(14)

To close this chapter, we will relate the circumstances in which the Reformer died. It is known that Peter suffered from nephritis; yet, confident in his robust constitution, he neglected his health and, as he grew older, the crises became more and more frequent and painful. On the 10th of October 1724, after one of the worst attacks he had ever suffered, while present at the launching ceremony of a new ship, he turned to the Dutch minister and simply said that he felt a little weak. A few days later, against the advice of his doctors, he went to inspect the Ladoga canal, and from

---

21. Luke xii: 1
22. Cabinet, Libre 31; Soloviov, op. cit., Vol. XVIII, Ch. III, col. 808–9.

there, went on to the ironworks at Olonetz, where he forged a 100 lb. iron bar with his own hands. From Olonetz, he continued his journey to Staraya-Russa to visit the salt-lakes there, and, toward the middle of November, he boarded his yacht and headed towards St Petersburg. On arriving at Lakhta in the Neva estuary, he saw a lugger from Kronstadt that had just run aground. The Emperor rushed to its aid, for the sea was rough. He jumped into the water and saved two unconscious men by carrying them to land on his back. Then, waist-high in the icy water, he worked at setting the ship afloat. This exploit proved fatal for him. He caught a cold and was immediately plunged into another crisis. He returned to St Petersburg, no longer having the strength to overcome it. The attack took a particularly acute turn on the 28th of January, causing him great pain. On February 2nd, the Emperor took communion and received the extreme unction, but he did not stop working until his last breath; he issued four ukases and, as death approached, proclaimed an amnesty for all those (civil or military) who had been sentenced to capital punishment.

(15)

In principle, the Russian monarchy was elective, but, as in Rome and Byzantium, the reigning sovereign sometimes designated his successor. Peter the Great established this custom as a right. However, he died without being able to name a successor. On the afternoon of the 7th of February 1725 AD, when he was already at death's door, he asked for a slate and a piece of chalk, and began to write when, suddenly, the chalk fell from his hand, which had become paralysed. He then called for his daughter Anne, who was his secretary, to dictate his last wishes. As the princess approached his bedside, the emperor lost his power of speech as well. From what he had written on the slate, one could only decipher the words: '*Leave everything to ...*'

The Emperor died at eight o'clock on the morning of the 8th of February 1725.

The throne was vacant. The death of this extraordinary man faced Russia with an alternative: to return to the old regime of the boyars, as the enemies of the Reform wished, or to follow the path traced out by the Reformer for centuries to come.

For sixteen years, the country marked time under a regime of 'favourites'. Nothing short of a palace revolution could remedy the situation, and this was led by Elizabeth, the Reformer's daughter. The new Empress called all her father's faithful followers to power, and during the twenty years of her reign she resolutely put Russia on the path traced out by Peter the Great.

The first part of the Reformer's esoteric work was thus saved. It then met with a tragic fate. One and a half centuries after Elizabeth's death, it passed through a *Trial by Fire*.[23] The Russian Revolution stirred the national consciousness to its foundations, and shook the social structure of the whole of humanity.

Today, the second part of Peter's work is being carried out.

In the following chapter, we will try to show its relation to the Era of the Holy Spirit. For that *is near, even at the doors*.[24]

---

23. Cf. *La Monarchie russe*, op. cit., *passim*.
24. Matthew xxiv: 33.

CHAPTER IV

(1)

Without a doubt, the major problem in the political sphere today is that of world peace.

Can it be solved? In theory, yes, for everything necessary to organize a life of paradise on Earth is now available. In practice, however, the under-development of the human Personality may give us serious doubts about the chances of finding a happy solution to this problem. Even when gifted with the faculty of reason, and when, at least in potential, it possesses good faith, this underdeveloped Personality too often acts illogically, not only against its own interests, but against common sense. This is why, against the will of peoples and responsible Statesmen, war sometimes breaks out.

But our aim, in the present chapter and the next, is not to analyse the risks of a new world war; we are only trying to outline, in the general international situation as it has developed in history and as it now appears, the probable destiny of the geopolitical group, mostly made up of Ortho-dox and Muslim peoples, who today occupy the extended territory of the old Hellenistic world.

The cradle of Christianity, and later of Islam, this geopolitical ensemble — as we have already pointed out — is called on, unless it fails, to be the matrix from which the Era of the Holy Spirit will emerge. With regard to this, let us remember the famous but often forgotten words of Peter the Great:

'We place the ancient seat of the sciences in Greece. They were then established in Italy, from where they spread to all parts of Europe. It is now our turn, if you are willing to support my plans by uniting study to obedience.

' ... The arts circulate in the world like blood in a human body; perhaps they will establish their empire among us before going back to their ancient country, Greece.'[1]

As we will see further on, the prophetic meaning of this appears more and more clearly.

(2)

The Empress Elizabeth saved Peter the Great's Reform and vigorously pursued her father's policies.

The regime of the favourites — German adventurers for the most part — lasted sixteen years after the Reformer's death. It made Russia the toy of

---

1. A fragment of the speech delivered in the Senate on the 14th of May 1714 before State dignitaries, Naval squadrons and Regiments of the Guard. Boris Mouravieff, *La Monarchie russe*, Paris, Payot, 1962, pp. 21–2.

European political powers, pushing the Empire towards a precipice and the Reform towards chaos.

The Emperor's daughter was conscious of this situation and, on the night of the 25th of November 1741, led three hundred grenadiers of her father's Guard, arrested the Regent, who was the Duchess of Braunschweig-Lüneburg, and mounted the throne amid popular rejoicing. She was the last national Empress in Russian history.[2]

The Empress put up a fierce resistance against the Germanic *Drang nach Osten*,[3] at the same time consolidating the ties between Russia and the Ottoman Empire. The two oriental empires then had almost the entire territory of the old Hellenistic world under their sway.

II

(1)

We must understand that it is not possible to grasp the deeper meaning of great historical movements without placing them in the wider context of esoteric evolution, which occurs in Cycles. Indeed, it is necessary to learn to encompass vast totalities of time which, because of their amplitude, generally escape the vision of the human mind. But the underdeveloped human Personality deifies itself ridiculously and considers that it has reached the summit of all that is possible. From there, it imposes a ban on men who dare to see things beyond the boundaries of the *Ignorabimus*. Did not the Apostle St Peter say: ' ... *one day is with the Lord as a thousand years, and a thousand years as one day.*'[4] So, if we wish to grasp the real meaning of historical evolution — which is always esoteric, because it is determined by the Lord's will — we must learn to consider it on His scale, and no longer on our own: that is, to hold it in mind in sections whose duration covers several *days of the Lord*. In the second volume of 'Gnosis', the reader may have already recognized such a historical projection, simultaneously covering the past and the future. Divided into stages, this projection covered sixteen thousand years in all, starting with the fall of Adam and ending at the last Judgement.[5]

What interests us particularly is to follow the general evolution of the history of those peoples who live within the perimeter of the Hellenistic world — this world, which after becoming the cradle of Christianity, and then that of Islam, has been chosen to see the first-fruits of the Era of the Holy Spirit ripen on her soil.

---

2. Ibid., pp. 31–41.
3. This phrase describes Germany's 'hunger for the East'. (Ed.)
4. 2 Peter iii: 8.
5. Vol. II, fig. 2, p. 48.

(2)

With the little information that science has placed at our disposal, we must try to show, that, from the esoteric point of view, the 'Hellenistic perimeter' really marked the boundaries of a geopolitical body.

After this, we must outline and try to understand the play of the political and cultural forces for which this region was the theatre, and sometimes the stakes as well — as it continues to be.

An attentive study, covering a period of about four thousand years up to the present day, will help us discern the limits of a vast area whose perimeter corresponds with what we described earlier. We will continue to call this geopolitical area 'Hellenistic', because this is convenient on the one hand — though we go back much farther than Alexander the Great — and on another hand because in the intended study this term becomes increasingly appropriate.

(3)

Now we find ourselves within the *Hellenistic Perimeter* as we have just defined it, which, *grosso modo*, includes the whole of the Orthodox and Muslim worlds so often labelled the 'East'.

The line from Stettin to Trieste marks the approximate boundary between what has always been defined as the 'Orient', and the 'Occident'. Extended in the north by the Baltic — the Gulf of Bothnia — up to Tornio, and beyond, up to Murmansk and on to the North Pole, this is the demarcation line between the zones of Eastern and Western influences in contemporary history.

The Duke of Richelieu created a political system known as the *Eastern Barrier*, which we find again as the 'Cordon Sanitaire' after the First World War, and as the 'Iron Curtain' after the Second. Louis XV found a clearer expression for this, as we learn from a memorandum presented by the Count de Broglie, former director of the monarch's occult ministry, to Louis XVI. Regarding the reversal of the alliances which took place in 1756, after which France entered the Seven Years' War and fought at Russia's side, de Broglie noted:

'... This monarch (Louis XV) ... had only very regretfully abandoned the old ideas of forming and maintaining an impenetrable barrier between Russia and the rest of Europe, starting from the pole (North) to the Archipelago.'[6]

---

6. Boutaric, *La Correspondence secrète inédite de Louis XV*, 2 volumes, Paris, Plon, 1866, vol. II, p. 682.

We could quote hundreds of opinions of this kind, expressed by Western Statesmen over the centuries, about Russia and the particularly touchy[7] problem presented by the Straits of the Black Sea. The chief motive for this political approach lay in a fear of Russia: it was a question of creating a zone of protection that could be used if necessary as a depot for arms and ammunition to launch attacks against that country. We know that, since the time of Cardinal Richelieu and King Gustavus-Adolphus, Russia has been invaded four times by the West—that is, regularly every century. The last and most terrible invasion was launched by the armies of the Third Reich, flanked by those of Finland and Rumania; as in Napoleon's campaign in 1812, divisions from many other western nations took part, notably from Austria, Spain, France, Hungary, Italy and Slovakia.

(4)

Towards the South, the Stettin-Trieste line is extended by the waters of the Adriatic, then, on the other side of the Mediterranean, it touches the Arab or Islamic world, which in its expansion towards the west since the *Hegira*, has reached the Atlantic, although remaining faithful to its Oriental origins in its racial character and its specific culture and beliefs.[8]

(5)

To the west of the European Occident, beyond the Atlantic, the New World that we will call the *Far West*, which is a world in formation, is characterized by a simultaneous process of integration and differentiation that can give birth to new *civilizing historical types*.

(6)

To the east of the classical Orient, the ethnic Chinese world, a very ancient original culture, is surrounded by peoples of different races, pure or mixed, who are all subject to a marked Chinese influence. This is the world which is the *Far East*.

---

7. The French has here *névralgique*.

8. In this marking of frontiers, we have left contemporary Italy outside the limits of the Hellenistic Perimeter. One must not however forget that since the fifth Century BC, there were many Greek colonies in the Southern Peninsula and Sicily, and that this region was known as *Greater Greece*. On another hand, the North of Italy was strongly influenced by Byzantium from which the Italian Renaissance was born. Besides, it is not superfluous to mention the present movement, which seems strange and even paradoxical at first sight, of the spontaneous return to Orthodoxy that one may observe in the rural population of the Peninsula; this movement is certainly still insignificant quantitatively, but qualitatively it is significant precisely because of this spontaneity.

(7)

Whereas the East and West are divided by the Stettin-Trieste line, the Far East and the Far West meet and merge in the waters of the Pacific.

Besides Australia and New Zealand which, like South Africa, were colonies peopled by the Occident, so that they lean toward the West because of their ethnic and cultural ties, we still have to locate two more vast worlds; that of the black Continent, and that of the Indian Ocean.

(8)

It is still too early to make any predictions concerning the black race which, as we have pointed out, is at the beginning of its renaissance[9] and finds itself between concurrent influences: Christian, Islamic, Communist and pan-African.

We locate the Indian world with its northern limits stretching to the Pamir and the Himalayan chain, to the Straits of Bab-el-Mendeb in the West, to the Malay Straits in the East, and to the Indonesian Archipelago which it surrounds in the South.

This group, which is well-defined by natural limits in the North, West, and East is separated from the populations of Australia and New Zealand in the South by a frontier of a moral nature — an ethnic and cultural difference. As for its political orientation, although it is a world that lies between the East and the Far East, it seems that its sympathies lean toward the former.

The depository of the ancient Aryan culture, and containing two Islamic groups, it seems that its different links with the Arab and Russian worlds will be developed and consolidated with time, especially if modern socialist ideas develop within the traditional Hindu consciousness of the *Aryan Dharma*.

---

9. Vol. II, p. 148.

CHAPTER V

(1)

Humanity has now reached the great historical crossroads. Here each of the geopolitical groups we have defined must make a choice and trace out its political and cultural path for the coming centuries. Several factors, some of them common to all the groups and others different, must be regarded as *components*, whose *resultant* will determine the character of each of these groups as well as its fate for the duration of the Era of the Holy Spirit.

Without trying to play the prophet, we can easily foresee that, in its renaissance, the Black World will take its place between the West and the Far West. Its special influence, which is already very strong in America, is spreading from there to take root in old Europe where, in spite of some resistance, it is constantly gaining ground. Mainly through the rhythms of its music and dance it is penetrating ever further into the vast and almost uncontrollable domain of human subconsciousness, so that in future it will manifest spectacularly in that sector of Western life that relates to the passions.

Regarding the World of the Far East, the palace revolution in Japan in 1868 marked an awakening and movement in the peoples of this region. The Japanese renaissance became really intense after the Chinese revolution of 1911. Since the Second World War, a unified China has pursued an active political line and is trying to dominate this region, if not to establish its hegemony. Everything leads us to believe that the dynamism with which it follows this direction has not yet reached its peak.

Proud of their ancient original culture, and conscious of the great strength that resides in their numbers, the Chinese hardly worry about the rest of the human race, whom they consider — apart from a few exceptions — as more or less civilized barbarians who cannot hide their inferiority.

As Russia's neighbour, China borders on the *Hellenistic perimeter*, but is of interest to us, along with the other peoples of the Far East, chiefly because of its geopolitical attitude. Today, this group is mainly dominated by its demographic situation. As we see it, the Far East now has a population of over one billion, with a density that is often more than two hundred inhabitants to the square kilometre.

History teaches us that this state of things creates a demographic pressure which first shows up on the psychological plane, then in action: unless a sufficiently large safety valve opens in time, this pressure creates a spirit of expansion which too often degenerates into a spirit of aggression. Conscious of this phenomenon of the psyche, certain Western observers and diplomats think that this pressure will be fatally resolved by an invasion, and to be more precise, by an invasion of Russia. From this point of view, the 'fraternal' quarrels between Chinese and Russian Communists confirm the probability of a Chinese expansion toward Siberia.

Those who think this way — and who, perhaps, hope that a conflict between China and Russia will neutralize the power of the two communist colossi in an epic struggle — overlook certain historical factors that are nevertheless obvious. This is why the Russians and Chinese, who have a common frontier of thousands of kilometres, have never bothered to fortify it. This frontier remained open throughout Russia's worst trials, which included the First World War, the Revolution, the *Intervention* and the civil war which followed it, and finally, the invasion by the Third Reich. A Chinese attack was unthinkable in the past and, in our opinion, in spite of everything, it will remain so in the future.

Other observers seem to think that the Chinese invasion will be directed toward India. Nobody noticed any sign of this in the recent attack, although it was in that locality. We make a big fuss over China's anxiety to establish her prestige, and her desire to eliminate any rival that may prevent her from gaining hegemony over all Asia ... but to what end? We must not forget that the Indian world is a world apart, and does not belong to the world of the Far East. Besides, the idea of leaving one overpopulated and undernourished human reservoir to invade another where the same conditions prevail seems against common sense.

(2)

The multi-millennial history of China proves that her people do not really suffer from an imperialist complex: this is so true that, until the last century, the Chinese regarded the military career with disdain. On the contrary, it is China that has been the victim of many aggressions: by the Tartars, the Manchus, the Mongols and lastly the Europeans and the Japanese. The Great Wall that Emperor Tsin-Chi-Hoang-Ti constructed in 247 BC, after having repulsed one of the Mongol invasions, was a magnificent expression of the ardent desire of the Chinese people to live in peace and keep working.

However, the Old World seems even more afraid of China than of the progress made by Russia. The combination of 'demographic pressure' and Communism, and the fact that China is trying very hard to become a great nuclear power, are all nightmarish subjects for Western observers and Statesmen. They keep trying to guess in which direction the inevitable

Chinese expansion will take place. The *Yellow Peril*, evoked by the famous view which Emperor William II of Germany suggested to Czar Nicholas II of Russia, still continues to haunt Western minds in different ways ...

(3)

History teaches us that imaginary dangers sometimes provoke real catastrophes. The present armaments race may find its origin in such dangers, reinforced by the desire to forestall an eventual Russian invasion of Europe. Yet, we must not forget that Russian armies have never appeared in Western Europe except in two situations: either at the request of European powers, or in pursuit of European armies driven from the Russian plain. A Russian invasion of Europe would be mad — and is therefore unthinkable. However, in the West, and then in the East, this unjustified and purely chimerical fear has already provoked the creation of enormous weapons, all in the hope of preserving peace. This is a real danger, given the explosive psychological and material elements it brings together.

II

(1)

While we consider the problem of the internal demographic pressure from which China now suffers, it would not be superfluous to give our idea of the probable form that Chinese expansion could take if it takes dynamic form as armed aggression, as some think it may.

To imagine the direction of a massive Chinese military expansion, we must keep in mind the direction of their Pacific expansion, which has been going on for several centuries. The Chinese are clever merchants and financiers, besides being patient and persevering colonizers. Intrepid sailors, they have never considered the seas to be an obstacle. On the contrary, for centuries they have mainly gone toward the Levant: they can now be found everywhere east of Singapore.

We must not forget too that the Chinese mentality is dominated by a consciousness of their great numbers. We can see this fact in many speeches and political writings, and it is this attitude which causes them to consider an eventual war or nuclear conflict in an entirely different light from how Westerners would view it.

If, one day, a Chinese Moses, capable of creating a mystique of the Promised Land, comes to power, it is not improbable to imagine an onrush of these masses across the islands and archipelagos of the Pacific toward the United States and Canada. There is a great difference between China and the United States. It would be quite conceivable today to paralyse the US by atomic bombardment of its cities; but to stop the onrush of hundreds of millions of Chinese attacking in many different ways, from the most advanced, like the atomic bomb, to the most primitive, like junks, would be a more difficult task. One might annihilate half of them—and the Chinese know how to smile at death!—but this would not prevent the other half from reaching the shores of the Promised Land. What then would be the attitude of the Chinese, the Japanese, and the American Blacks, who, together, now represent fifteen or even twenty per cent of the population of the United States? Nobody knows. And who would raise not his voice but his sword to save the Americans? It is difficult to foresee this.

So there seems little doubt that, for the Chinese, the conquest of the United States of America, or of Canada, which are highly prosperous countries, is an infinitely more tempting perspective than an invasion of an undernourished India or of a Russia that, they know, will put up a massive and united resistance, as she did against the armies of the Third Reich and its allies.

III

(1)

It is now necessary to study present and future historical aspects of the relationship between the two Worlds which are at the centre of the problem: the Orient and the Occident from the esoteric point of view.

We have said that to separate out the *constants* in the geopolitical attitude of human groups, it is necessary to go back much farther than the limits of contemporary, modern, or even medieval history. The motives that impel the masses to act often remain in a latent state in the national or racial subconsciousness for centuries or even millennia. The elements of these motives can accumulate there as dim memories of resounding victories, or of aspirations for revenge after defeat or uprisings after oppression or slavery. Though effaced from the immediate memory of peoples, the memory-consciousness of these passionate aspirations remains in the corridors of the subconsciousness, and it makes up part of what we call, in the largest sense of the term, the *spirit of these peoples*.

When a leader appears who incarnates this part of the subconsciousness of the masses, he communicates a dynamic character to the latent forces that it contains; and if the masses follow him 'blindly', it is because each one really answers a call from the depths of his own subconsciousness.

If the leader incarnates this collective feeling more or less consciously, (Charles XII, Hitler), or after deep reflection and study (Napoleon), if he obeys an inner voice, if he is conscious of a mission (Alexander, Peter), or if he is awakened by a shock (Moses), we find in every case that, behind the Personality of the hero—whether he is a builder or a destroyer—there is a categorical imperative which he cannot disobey even if he wished. In fact, either consciously or unconsciously, they all act as bearers of a mandate.

This mandate comes from the esoteric plane. Its content and raison d'être are generally unseen by the very limited waking consciousness of human beings — even highly developed or cultured Personalities who give the impression of being awake. Napoleon, who considered himself wide awake[1] — and who was indeed so, in human terms — built his career by firmly believing in his 'star' ...

(2)

When we study the relationship between the group of Germano-Roman peoples rooted in the West and the Slavo-Hellenistic peoples of the East over the largest possible timescale, we can easily discover a *constant*: strongly anchored in the subconsciousness of the Romans, and then of the Germans and Germano-Romans, this constant first took the form of an instinctive movement which, every now and again, became active and pushed them toward the conquest of the East. In 147 BC, ancient Hellas ceased to exist on the political plane. It was conquered by the Romans, who reduced it to the status of a province known as Achaea. During the Crusades, when the Eastern Empire already showed signs of weakening, the movement from the West became even more marked: in 1080, Robert Guiscard led the first Norman expedition into Greece and subdued Epirus, as well as a part of Thessaly; in 1146, Roger, King of Sicily, ravaged Etolia and Acarnania, penetrated into the Gulf of Corinth, took Corinth and Thebes and captured a horde of Boeotians; lastly, during the 4th crusade (1204) Enrico Dandolo, the octogenarian Doge of Venice, took Constantinople. Though refusing the Imperial crown offered him by the Crusaders, he proclaimed himself despot of Roumania and obtained, for the republic of St Mark, a ward in New Rome, as well as the Isles of the Archipelago and Candia (the Isle of Crete). Although the reconquest of Constantinople by Michael Palaeologus in 1261, tolled the knell of the Roman Empire, ancient Hellas was finally liberated from the Westerners only when the latter were pushed

---

1. Cf. Marquis Louis de Caulaincourt, *Mémoires du Général de Caulaincourt, duc de Vicence*, first equerry of the Emperor. Introduction and notes by Jean Hanoteau, 3 vol., Plon, Paris, 1933, *passim*.

back by the successive Turkish victories. The action of the West against Greece was thus stemmed.

(3)

When the IVth Crusade, preached by Foulque de Neuilly during the pontificate of Innocent III, triumphed at Constantinople, the Roman Clergy at the instigation of Pope Gregory IX launched a Crusade against Russia. It was led by the Teutonic Knights, Swedes, Norwegians and Danes, under the command of Birger de Bielbo, future regent of Sweden. This crusade was crushed by 22-year-old Prince Alexander of Novgorod on the 15th of July 1240, soon after the Crusaders had landed on the southern bank of the Neva. Attacking the invaders with his cavalry, he managed to reach Birger and wound him in the face with a stroke of his sword, forcing him to retreat. While reembarking, many of the crusaders were killed or thrown into the river.

Two years later, the crusade was resumed. The Teutonic Knights and the Sword Bearers, reinforced by German and Livonian Militia, attacked and took Pskov, then marched on Novgorod crying: 'Humiliation to the Slavs.' Then Alexander Nevsky put himself and his guards at the head of the regiments of Novgorod and marched against the Knights. The decisive battle took place on April 5th 1242, and the shock was produced on the ice of Lake Peipous. Alexander inflicted a crushing defeat on the Orders and their militia. The ice on the lake, thinner than in winter, would not support the weight of all the mass of fugitives, who were swallowed in the depths of the waters.

(4)

The Tartar Invasion of Russia began in 1223 with the Battle of Kalka— named after a small river that flows into the sea of Azov. Coming from conquered Persia, a strong Tartar army suddenly appeared in the Russian steppes and overcame a hastily assembled army of princes. After their victory, however, the Tartars disappeared as suddenly as they had come, and so this battle had no political consequences.

Fourteen years later, in 1237, after having devastated the Bulgarian kingdom of Kama, the Golden Horde commanded by Batu-Khan crossed the icebound Volga and undertook the methodical conquest of Russian principalities over a period of three years.

The Tartar invasion was at its peak in the summer of 1240, when Prince Alexander Nevsky was combating Birger's crusade. On the 6th of December of the same year, Kiev was taken by assault and devastated: this was the beginning of the Mongol yoke, which lasted two and a half centuries.

Like Greece, Russia was hemmed in by a huge pincer made up of the Tartars coming from the East and Germans coming from the West. With extraordinary foresight — and despite the horrible sufferings that the Russians endured at the hands of the Tartars — when he became ruler of Russia in 1252, Alexander's political policy was based on his loudly proclaimed principle that the real danger did not come from the Tartar conquerors, but from the West, from the *Romans*, as the Russians then called the Occidental peoples who owed obedience to the Pope.

The great prince was right: the Tartar conquest of Russia — like the Turkish conquest of the Oriental Empire—did not overcome the national and cultural entity of the Russians or the Greeks: in both cases, the conquerors proved themselves incapable of absorbing the vanquished and did not even leave any perceptible traces of their original culture. These invasions brought suffering and the loss of a considerable amount of material and men, but nothing more. On the other hand, if it had been successful, the German or Germano-Roman invasion would have profoundly changed the spiritual and psychological identity of the Russians and Greeks. The best proof of this is the fact that the Western steppes of the Slavo-Hellenistic world became Catholic, and were thus westernized for centuries.

From the esoteric point of view from which we must study the deeper meaning of the great currents of history whose axis is found within the *Hellenistic perimeter*, the appearance of the Turks in Europe is more significant. A paradoxical fact which science overlooks, but which is nevertheless real, is that their overwhelming attack, which reached right into the heart of Europe, neutralized the Western action against the East and thus saved the Russians and the Greeks from a serious blow to their psyche.

At the same time as the Turks, came the sermons of John Hus (1369–1415), which ignited the religious wars. Powerfully backed against the imperialists by John Zizha (1370–1424), this preaching heralded the Reformation, which was recognized the following century with the peace of Augsburg (1555), from which the West emerged disunited, weakened, and therefore momentarily less dangerous to the East.

IV

(1)

However, the real danger for the Hellenistic perimeter came, as it still comes, from the West. During the Second World War, the armies of the Third Reich and its allies penetrated into Russia as far as the Crimea and the Caucasus, and even reached the Volga. The situation inside the *perimeter* then became critical: until the defeat and surrender of Marshal von Paulus and his army, the risk of slavery was very real for the people concerned. It was only in 1943, after the Battle of Stalingrad decided the fate of this epic struggle between Germans and Slavs, that one could be sure that the Slavo-Hellenistic world and its centre, Greece, were saved.[2]

The reader should understand that the attack on Russia in 1941 by the Third Reich was not merely an 'accident of history' due to the 'hypnotic hold' that Hitler had over the German people. We must not forget that the Fuhrer became Chancellor of the Reich by constitutional means, and that he was invested with power by Marshal von Hindenburg, President of the Reich. This attack was simply the expression of a strong subconscious tendency that had been nurtured for more than fifteen centuries. The desire to 'humiliate the Slavs' had been proclaimed more than once in history, notably in the famous formula of *Drang nach Osten*: an instinctive, subconscious call acting against all reason.

Suffering from an immense superiority complex, the Germans considered themselves a *master race* who were called upon to dominate the others by force. Obeying this 'mystic' call, they often engaged in wars of conquest, sometimes against all common sense. The two World Wars are examples of this. But we insist that in fact these aggressions were not the personal acts of William II or of Hitler. We can detect the same spirit and motives in the Germans as far back as the beginning of our era. Here, it would be useful to recall the testimony of Josephus Flavius:

'When Vespasian was still in Alexandria, and Titus was still busy with the siege of Jerusalem, many Germans revolted: their neighbours, the Gauls, followed suit. Both peoples nursed the hope of together overthrowing the Roman yoke. In their emancipation, the Germans were guided, above all, by their national character, on the strength of which they thoughtlessly and blindly hurl themselves into danger with only the minimum chance of success.'[3]

When we deal with the subject of the *Hellenistic Perimeter*, and through it, of the *Time of Transition*, in considering the boundaries of this region which is called on to become the cradle of the Era of the Holy Spirit, we must not neglect the danger already hinted at. Instead, we must keep in mind that this danger will always exist, however great the sincerity and cultural level of Germany's leaders. Instincts of this kind slumber in a subconsciousness whose imperatives too often win over reason, even in highly civilized people.

---

2. Note that American aid began to arrive in the USSR *after* the victory of Stalingrad (Kravtchenko, *J'ai choisi la liberté*, *passim*).

3. Josephus Flavius, *The Judean War*, Book VII, ch. III–L (translated from the Russian text).

The double defeat inflicted on the Germans in the two World Wars could contribute to a fresh outbreak of this complex, this dark 'messianic' mystique of domination by force, raising the hope that next time they will prove *worthy* of their god *Wotan's* confidence. Let us not forget, either, that the apogee of *German culture*, marvellous in its essence, coincided with a feudal division of the *Germanic body* which, until a short while ago, was divided into three hundred States, kingdoms, and principalities, that were only nominally united into an elective empire.

(2)

B y initiating the Russian renaissance and so giving the signal to the whole of the East, Peter the Great had wide vision. In the speech quoted at the beginning of the preceding chapter, he foretold that a new Greek renaissance would bring the Cycle to a close. Greece, which has already inspired two great civilizations, is now called upon to take its place at the heart of the third and to be the core of the culture inspiring the new Cycle, that of the Holy Spirit.

Peter the Great's prophecy is now being fulfilled before our eyes: on the 25th October, 1962, on the Isle of Kos, Hippocrates' native land, King Constantine II, then Crown prince, laid the foundation stone of the *International Hippocratic House* or Palace of Medicine, where medical Olympiads will take place, and where the *Hippocratic prize* for medical research will be awarded.[4]

Important in the history of human culture, this event gives us an opportunity to grasp the deeper meaning of History, which is profoundly logical if we try to view it on the scale of the Lord, Master of evolution, for Whom one day is as a thousand years, and a thousand years are as one day. This perspective can be grasped by the minds of superior beings like Alexander, Peter, and by others as well.

---

4. International Hippocratic Foundation of Kos, ratified by Royal Decree No. 731, 29th October 1960.

CHAPTER VI

(1)

In previous chapters we have examined several elements which, from the esoteric point of view, provide data about the problem of the advent of the Era of the Holy Spirit on our planet. We have emphasized the fact that the beginning of the twentieth century coincided with the beginning of the *Time of Transition* between the Cycle of the Son, which is now coming to an end, and that of the Holy Spirit, which is just beginning. We drew the reader's attention to the grave responsibility which falls on contemporary man for the outcome of this period. In case of failure, we cannot hope that the world will return to the *status quo ante*. The Era of the Holy Spirit has two faces — one of Paradise regained and the other a Deluge of Fire. We must not forget that God is also a *Devouring Fire*;[1] in case of failure, the situation will rapidly lead to an eschatological cataclysm.

The advent of the Era of the Holy Spirit is imminent, and it would be an illusion to think that once the hour has struck we can go on living in the same way as before. One cannot settle down as a bourgeois in the Kingdom of God.

The way this alternative described by St Peter[2] will be resolved will depend on the attitude taken by contemporary man. The preparations that will decide the outcome should have been made by now by the elite of human society, especially the ruling elite. Today, just as two thousand years ago, it is not enough to repeat, '*Lord! Lord!*' to enter the Kingdom of Heaven,[3] which is once more near, but this time in the new conditions that correspond to the Era of the Holy Spirit.

Everything will therefore depend on man's work; on conscious efforts during the remainder of the *Time of Transition*. However, we will easily understand that this is not a question of efforts applied in just any direction, but only of action that is aimed directly at a positive solution of the problems of the Transition seen in all its fullness and complexity.

(2)

In fact, this has to do with the creation of what Jesus called the *leaven*: a living leaven like that represented by the numerically small, even infinitesimal group of the Apostles and their disciples, lost to sight in a

---

1. Hebrews xii: 29.
2. 2 Peter iii: 10.
3. Matthew vii: 21.

rebellious province of the Roman Empire, but whose influence has reached the farthest corners of the world.

Jesus said: '*The Kingdom of heaven is like unto leaven, which a woman took, and hid in three measures of meal, till the whole was leavened.*'[4]

These words lead us straight to the heart of the matter. The parable, whose meaning is clear, applies precisely to our problem, so we will try to analyse its content.

It is certain that the leaven was fresh and good, otherwise in three measures of flour it would not have been sufficient to make the dough rise. However, leaven may be good, as it was here, or it may be bad, and this is why Jesus said to His disciples: '*Take heed and beware of the leaven of the Pharisees and the Sadducees.*'[5]

There is no possible doubt about the leaven of the Pharisees: it is hypocrisy.[6] The Gospel says nothing about the leaven of the Sadducees that allows such a clear interpretation, except a passage where it is said that the Sadducees did not believe in the resurrection.[7] The Acts of the Apostles throws more light on the question in the following phrase: '*For the Sadducees say that there is no resurrection, neither angel, nor spirit.*'[8] To have a larger view of their doctrine, and to grasp the real meaning of the divergences that separated them from the Pharisees, we must glean our information elsewhere. The most authoritative source in this matter is, without a doubt, Josephus Flavius, who, as he mentions in his autobiography, himself became a Pharisee. He gives us quite a detailed description of the three Jewish schools of philosophy. The first two were the Pharisees and Sadducees, and the third — which visibly pursued a very particular virtue — were the Essenes.[9]

According to Flavius, the Sadducees belonged to a sect that was formed in the third century BC. Numbered among them were military leaders, especially the commanders of forts, town and State notables, and the landed aristocracy. They taught that the Mosaic Law was of divine origin and that nobody had power to alter it. They believed that God was the foundation of the Universe but that the human soul perished with the body. Lastly, they said that God did not interfere in human affairs, so that men were free to fashion their own destiny. They denied the existence

4. Matthew xiii: 33.

5. Ibid. xvi: 6; Mark viii: 15.

6. Luke xii: 1.

7. Matthew xxii: 23; Mark xii: 18; Luke xx: 27.

8. Acts xxiii: 8.

9. Josephus Flavius: *The Jewish Wars*, II, 8, 14. From the Russian translation. Joseph described these schools in this work as well as in his *Judaic Antiquities*, XIII, 5, 9; XVII, 2, 4; XVIII, 1, 2–4. The teachings given in the *Mishna* were almost entirely concerned with these divergences which separated the Sadducees from the Pharisees. As for the doctrines of the *Gemara*, these have a mythical character.

of angels and demons, and rejected the theory of predestination, or even of existence after death; from this they deduced that the idea of a reward for virtuous acts, or punishment for faults, was inadmissible. They were also in favour of a compromise between the Mosaic Law and Greek philosophy.

The Pharisees, on the other hand, were sworn enemies of Greek philosophy and culture. Adapting the prescriptions of the *Torah* to suit the demands of the period, they taught that the Pentateuch contained all of philosophy, law, science and even art, and that it was the source of all wisdom. Based on this conception, they elaborated a series of rules and directives (Galah) to which the life of every Jew was supposed to be rigorously subjected. Jesus pointed out the strong tendency toward proselytism there, as well as an anxiety for preserving the Jewish people from non-Judaic conceptions and culture.

'*Woe unto you, scribes and Pharisees, hypocrites,*' said Jesus, '*for ye compass sea and land to make one proselyte, and when he is made, ye make him twofold more the child of hell than yourselves.*'[10]

(3)

This brief account from Flavius, which gives us an idea of the two major currents of Jewish thought which flourished at the time of Christ's ministry, also shows us several points in common between them and what we can observe in the cultured layers of our contemporary civilization. Today, like the Sadducees, we willingly profess a sort of Voltairian deism which does not commit us to anything. Instead, it enables us to enjoy the wealth and pleasures of this world without taking responsibility for our actions, other than those punishable by human law. This attitude of the Sadducees, ancient and modern, fits in very well with what the *General Law* tolerates, as well as with the demands of the Absolute III. If any scruples arise, as they inevitably do from time to time, we turn for aid to that magical instrument the auto-tranquillizer, which suggests to us dogmas behind which we hide. If these scruples begin to bother us, we get rid of them like a *scrupulus*, which originally referred to a small stone which, by damaging the foot, would force someone to lag behind. Do not universally acknowledged authorities say that 'women, young people and *the feebleminded* are more prone to scruples and superstitions ...'[11]

This Sadducean mentality has become very widespread, especially since the Renaissance, and today we find it amongst the youth of both sexes.

---

10. Matthew xxiii: 15.
11. Nicholas de Malebranche, *Recherche de la Vérité*, book IV, Ch. XII. Italics are the author's.

Admit that God exists? Why not? Outside unsubstantiated hypotheses it is obvious that if He does exist, He does not intervene in human affairs ... From this point on, there is only one more step to take to worship the *Golden Calf* in all its modern forms. Some of the Reformed Churches which enter into the vicious circle of rationalism applied to religion teach their followers that to accumulate money and wealth in general, by legal — that is, unpunishable — means, is an obvious sign of divine approval.

In our civilization, many layers of the population have this mentality. Even if we do not mention the extremists, the profiteers and cheats, we find it in the ranks of those who are called 'honest citizens', the positive elements in all sectors of social and public life, where they act within the limits allowed by the *General Law*.

From the esoteric point of view, these elements are generally passive. This means that their contribution to our progress through the *Time of Transition* only acts indirectly, and their participation in this great work is purely unconscious. On the other hand it is largely due to the efforts of these contemporary Sadducees that we have made the great technical progress that, in spite of the danger it holds, is an indispensable element in the coming of the Era of the Holy Spirit, for which it forms the material foundation.

Although they are passive on the esoteric plane, the Sadducees are very active on the material plane. This is as true of the 'white' Sadducees as for their 'red' counterparts. Further on, we will come back to this distinction when we define the characteristic traits of each in relation to the desired esoteric evolution of human society during the *Time of Transition*.

(4)

It is more difficult to speak of the Pharisees of our civilization and of our time. Ever since the Renaissance, the Reformation, and then the 1789 Revolution, followed by the triple industrial revolution, the 'Sadducee' philosophy — often incorrectly called 'Cartesian' — has won acceptance. This contemporary Saducean *creed* has become a kind of sacred tradition. Mistaken for bourgeois liberalism, and based on the tacit deification of the human Personality in its incomplete condition, it has become the code of the free world. This is why the analogy we made cannot and does not shock anybody.

The question of the Pharisees is quite different. Let us first note what Josephus Flavius states about the relative positions of the Sadducees and Pharisees in Jewish society. About the former, he says that their doctrine 'had few adherents, though they belonged to high society. Their influence over the masses was insignificant. When they were in public office they were forced to side with the Pharisees, otherwise the people would not accept them.'[12]

(5)

The term 'Pharisee' has developed such an odious connotation that it is difficult to make comparisons as we have with the Sadducees. Though they were somewhat degenerate by the advent of Christ, the Pharisees were originally considered as the bearers, defenders and authorized commentators of the Mosaic Law and tradition. They were supposed to be incorruptible, and austere in their habits. Searching for an analogy in the Hellenic world, Flavius compared them with the Stoics. At one time the Roman Catholic Church also adopted this stand. In both cases, we can note analogous factors favouring the prestige of the Pharisees.

The latter, however, being part of an orderly and over-disciplined organization, attributed the strength of dogma to their traditions, and so, being prisoners of their intransigence, they proved incapable of an inner evolution. This is why, in time, they became a major political party. They subordinated their originally purely philosophical and religious doctrine to the requirements of their struggle. Gradually, this doctrine became the instrument that enabled them to take control of public affairs and the consciousness of the masses. This mixture of spiritual and temporal affairs, which was normal during the Cycle of the Father when religious law governed civil life, became a dangerous anachronism with the approach of the Cycle of the Son ...

Now that the Roman Catholic Church is revising its historical position on spiritual and temporal matters, it is hardly timely to start another controversy. It is anyway true that, throughout past centuries, nothing positive has ever emerged from polemics of this kind. However, as our studies are a search for Truth, we cannot entirely overlook this question.

We only wish with all our heart—and this for the sake of the Transition—that the Roman Catholic Church, conscious of its great mission, will find the courage at this irrevocable hour, when preparation must be made for the future, to abandon the temporal to the temporal powers and concentrate all its efforts on the spiritual. This task is great, and is bound by an eschatological responsibility. Said in other words, this is to leave to Cæsar what is Cæsar's and to be dedicated to the things of God; we are not afraid of repeating that 'the Kingdom of Heaven is at hand.'

---

12. *Antiquités*, op. cit., XVIII, 1, 2–4.

(6)

W e can also find Sadducees and Pharisees on the 'red' side. As on the 'white' side, the Sadducees form the technocracy. In this domain, they accomplish remarkable feats which, according to Peter the Great's prophetic speech, 'put to shame[13] the most civilized nations.'[14]

Yet many of these Sadducees would be surprised to learn that the work they accomplish in their domain meets the urgent needs of the *Time of Transition* that will lead human society into the Era of the Holy Spirit. Everyone generally agrees that a new Era is approaching, but whether this era will be that of the Holy Spirit is another question. However, these two ideas are drawing closer every day, and in the future they will naturally come together.

Though there are some common points between the 'red' Sadducees and the 'white' Sadducees, a fundamental difference separates them. In the blaze of technical progress, the latter are visibly obsessed by speed. Dominated by the past, they are more and more prisoners of a conservative spirit and a defensive mentality, whereas the dynamism of the 'red' Sadducees never stops growing. The difference in ideologies is at the root of this. Western technocracy is based only on *interest*, and generally on *private* interest, whereas the 'red' technocracy forges ahead, driven by *faith* and *self-denial* in favour of the masses. Contrary to what happens in the West, the 'red' Sadducees in this field present a common front with their Pharisees, and even with their Essenes,[15] for faith, in many varieties, lights the hearts of the masses who are divided into these three categories of philosophical or religious faith, with only minor differences between them.

It is undeniable that the hearts of the red Pharisees burn with faith, otherwise, they would never have been able to make their revolution yield results that seemed unthinkable even yesterday. It is this faith that makes their strength in the midst of a decadent civilization and a blasé society. Nevertheless, they are not immune to a common error similar to that committed by the Roman Catholic Church throughout the course of history ... to mix the temporal with the spiritual beyond measure. This error, in their case, would be to crystallize into dogmatism.

---

13. The French word here is *'rougir'*, a possible play on words. (Ed.)

14. Cf. *La Monarchie russe*, op. cit., pp. 21–2.

15. That is to say, believers, principally Orthodox and Muslims. Flavius regarded the historical Essenes as Jewish Pythagoreans. (*Antiquités*, op. cit., XVIII, 1, 4.)

(7)

At the beginning of the second volume of this work we mentioned that divine Revelation is not static, and that it is an error to take antiquity as an infallible sign of Truth, as certain seekers do in the esoteric domain. In this domain, the ill is not incurable, as the example of St Paul bears witness: he used to call himself the 'Pharisee of Pharisees'.[16] When we progress on the cosmic scale of consciousness, we automatically leave behind all that is outdated or crystallized. Did not St Paul say: *'When I was a child, I spake as a child, I understood as a child, I thought as a child: but when I became a man, I put away childish things.'*[17] It is quite different in the case of a dogmatic materialist: although esoteric evolution is a gradual progress of human consciousness toward the very source of Life, materialistic evolution does not go beyond the evolution of *means*. Thus the possibilities that technical progress now offers us have changed the data concerning the problem that Karl Marx posed a century ago. The world of today has very little in common with that of his day, or even with the world as Lenin knew it. As positive science progressed, the materialism of that day lost its substance. Since then, we have discovered that matter is only one aspect of energy, while the notion of energy itself evolves toward higher and higher planes — an evolution that brings it near to the origin of all power.

It is time to abandon this materialistic dogmatism, which is too rigid and so becomes more and more reactionary. It has been outdated by the rapid evolution of positive science — the very science in whose name the Marxist dogma was created. This demands courage and conscious efforts, for the obsession with the past always weighs on the weak human mentality and sometimes provokes gigantic errors just when people think they are following the right path.

Marxists should understand — and all modern science bears witness to the fact — that coarseness is always an *effect*, while refinement is a *cause*. In its laboratories, contemporary science looks as though it will very soon attain the summit of the scale of finer and finer elements, and one can now believe that it will soon reach the point where it will cross the path of esoteric spiritual research. We sincerely hope that the 'red' Pharisees will abandon their old attitude that is outdated today and has become truly reactionary.

In one of our recent historical works, we asked the following question, putting it as a conclusion:

'Russian man is not made to live with a cold heart. As long as the struggle for the required standard of living continues, and since the danger of a third world war weighs on him, he burns and makes superhuman

---

16. Acts xxiii: 6.
17. 1 Corinthians xiii: 11.

efforts to find a positive solution for the problems of his life. Let us imagine for a moment that we have solved these problems: what then will the Russian heart burn for, since, as we have said, it cannot live without burning?

'Here again in its history, Russia shows its Sphinx-like face.'[18]

18. *La Monarchie russe*, op. cit., p. 203.

CHAPTER VII

(1)

THE WAY is the theme of this first part of the third volume of 'Gnosis'. As we have seen, it is an attempt at the practical application of the *Gnosis* described in the first two volumes of this work.

The time has now come to formulate certain considerations that will help to place things in the whole frame of the problems whose solution is a necessary condition for a happy outcome to the *Time of Transition*.

Before starting our synthesis, let us study certain points which, although they may appear isolated, are, in fact, organically linked to this whole and exercise a direct influence over it.

To be precise: in the esoteric domain the time for private research and for the pursuit of individual salvation has come to an end. Imperceptibly, esotericism has become a public affair, and from now on it is only by keeping this new fact in mind that we can conceive and conduct practical esoteric studies.

The author is quite aware that what he is advancing may appear surprising and perhaps even disagreeable to certain readers, but these are the facts.

(2)

Here, we are not talking about some practical application of *Gnosis* in a direction chosen by the seeker and aimed at a definite result. Naturally, a detailed and attentive study of the Doctrine revealed in 'Gnosis' will enable the student to learn and understand many things about himself, as well as about others and about the Universe in which he lives. It will also enable him gradually to discover a hidden meaning in the Holy Scriptures, one that is generally beyond the reach of those who approach these texts solely with their underdeveloped Personalities, even when their intellectual faculties are great and refined. Yet, whether or not we are conscious of the fact, all times — and ours especially — give rise to specific unprecedented problems for human society. We can easily understand this, since historical evolution is a perpetual movement toward the *new*, and therefore toward the *unknown*.

Every era is accompanied by an appropriate ambience, which can provide a satisfactory solution to the problems it causes. But man is also allowed freedom of choice and, in each case, chooses according to the level of his understanding, and thus of his level of being. And, as we may constate, the ambience that reigns at the end of an epoch opens up new possibilities for man on all planes, while it eliminates those that belong to the preceding era.

This is a fact that we may constate quite often in external life, yet it generally escapes our notice in the inner life, especially on the esoteric plane. The reason for this is that, in the domain that interests us, the forms of the new direction are always connected with man's inner life, which does not have the spectacular quality of life on the exterior plane. Besides, these forms do not impose themselves on the individual's attention as the forms of civilization do. Although there is something new in their orientation, they remain subtle, intimate, and almost imperceptible.

This means that new data for the human problem are already available: it is up to man to grasp them, to appreciate their significance, and to get down to work with application. He must also understand that he cannot do this usefully except by working on the esoteric plane, and by channelling his efforts in the new direction that has been revealed. It is the same in this domain as in technology: for example, it is obvious that, when we have created ultra-rapid means of communication we do not think of installing relays for post-horses along the roads.

II

(1)

If, in the technical domain, the facts direct man toward more and more daring research and experiments, signposts also exist in the esoteric domain, even though by their nature they are less visible.

In particular there are two points we would like to call to the reader's attention.

First, experience shows that if, as in days gone by, the seeker undertakes esoteric studies with the intention of choosing his own aims or gaining his own individual salvation, a curious phenomenon takes place: he does not make much progress.

We may ask, is not this goal praiseworthy, and is not our salvation consistent with Divine Will? Certainly, but the conditions are no longer those that applied in the past, as these do not correspond to the esoteric needs of the present. Naturally, this does not alter the fact that, from the time of the great Doctors of the œcumenical Church right down through the centuries, the light of holiness has been attained—except for a few rare exceptions — by seekers who, in deserts or cells, practised individual exercises of concentration and contemplation with the will to reach the light of Christ by means of ecstasy.

The technique of esoteric work is the same today as it was in the past. But the conditions in which it will be applied, as well as the orientation of the efforts, have changed. Someone who undertakes esoteric work without keeping these changes in mind moves in a circle with the impression of continuing to move forward.

Secondly, it is always in periods of history when one can observe an esoteric effervescence — as in our era — that seekers are offered real possibilities of advancing on the straight path not only in words, but in actions, and without any risk of falling back into the Wilderness. This is because workers capable of esoteric evolution are sought at such times, while they are not so much needed when the world is in a 'dead calm,' esoterically speaking, under the rule of the Absolute III. In the same way a doctor would be little use in a society of people in a robust state of health. The law is precise: deprived of a point of application, every force, moral or physical, is condemned to disintegrate.

(2)

Today, the demand for esoterically formed workers is great in all branches of human activity, on the scientific plane as well as the moral. Each in their own way, positive science and esoteric science are reaching the point in their respective developments where they must join together. As with a demand for workers in external life, those who aspire to spiritual progress will be given the means for this training. The seeker is told precisely the goal, and the reward that will be his if he succeeds. For it is written: '*The labourer is worthy of his hire.*'[1]

III

(1)

Let us now try to learn the place that Eastern Orthodoxy occupies within the framework of our study of THE WAY. This is very necessary, especially as its meaning and mission are generally little known in the West, although it has always played a primary role within the *Hellenistic Perimeter.*

First, let us consider some characteristics of the organization of the Eastern Church. Where the Roman Church is based on the principle of ecclesiastical *unity*, and subjected to an aristocratic and monarchic regime under the supreme authority of the Sovereign Pontiff, the Orthodox Church is based on the democratic principle of *union*. It is a federal union of autocephalous Churches, that is to say, each is administratively

---

1. Luke x: 7.

autonomous, and as far as possible they reflect the autocephalous early Churches.

Normally, all the autocephalous Churches are *national*, in the sense that the jurisdiction of each covers every diocese within the boundaries of the State in which it exercises ecclesiastical authority. This makes for a better relationship between Church and State. Thus, the creation of new autocephalous Churches is always possible. This happened with the reconstitution of the Polish State after the First World War. Besides the territorial factor, another characteristic of these autocephalous Churches is the linguistic factor. Unlike the Roman Catholic Church, there is no special liturgical language in Orthodoxy. Instead of Latin, they hold services in the languages in common use. The territorial factor, however, ranks before the linguistic factor: this is how three autocephalous Orthodox Churches, those of Constantinople, Greece and Cyprus, can all use the same language.

(2)

The autocephalous Churches recognize each other as such. Yet from the canonical point of view, Orthodoxy is one and indivisible. This unity is ensured by a major principle in the Orthodox Church, which, unlike its Roman counterpart, does not allow dogmatic evolution. On this point it remains consistent to the decisions of the seven early *œcumenical* Councils. It does not recognize the thirteen others that were summoned by Rome.

The profound meaning of this stand is contained in the principle, tacitly admitted throughout Orthodoxy, that prayer, and spiritual work in general, including efforts aimed at Redemption, are more important than disciplinary questions. In practice this excludes the very need for dogmatic innovation. What explains this is a very important fact that often goes unobserved, namely, that for the Orthodox, as for the Muslim, prayer is essentially a *need*, not a *duty*.

(3)

This explains the past and present history of the Eastern Church. Contrary to what happens in the West, the Orthodox Church does not interfere in outward life. During the reign of Constantine the Great it was a victim of State abuses, but it accepted them as *tests*, and refused to lower itself by struggling against the temporal on the temporal plane. Strictly holding to the spiritual plane, it always triumphed over persecutions and the severest attacks, without ever losing its purity.

This attitude was possible because, on principle, the Orthodox Church has very few links with the temporal life of human society. In this way it offers a real contrast to the Roman Church. In the first place, it is poor. It has no financial backing, does not control any press, does not concern itself with formal teaching, nor organize 'Orthodox' colleges and universities. One cannot find any 'Orthodox' political parties or professional syndicates. It is only rarely that Orthodox prelates assume public office, and they have never accepted any military posts. Neither individually nor jointly do the autocephalous Churches maintain diplomatic representatives in foreign States, nor have they ever maintained religious orders of chivalry such as the Knights Templar, the Teutonic Knights, or the Sword-bearers. The Orthodox Church has never given birth to monastic orders like those found in the Catholic Church: Benedictines, Jesuits, Dominicans, Franciscans and others. Every Orthodox monastery is directed by a *hegumen* (superior) who himself belongs to the autocephalous Church in whose jurisdiction the community is located, and the same principle applies to the faithful; an Orthodox member automatically falls under the jurisdiction of the autocephalous Church within whose territory he finds himself. This is how the spiritual *union* of administratively autocephalous Churches[2] is expressed.

In the second place, the Orthodox Church never knew the Inquisition, begun by St Dominic, which set funeral pyres alight in Europe for six centuries, and caused 'crusades' of Christians against Christians. Neither has it known the Catholic theory of *Merit*, by which *Indulgences* were sold or granted.

(4)

It is important for the reader of this work to have an idea, however brief, of the meaning and mission of Eastern Orthodoxy, since this represents the heart of the Hellenistic Perimeter, the area in which the struggle has already begun and in which it is hoped that the Era of the Holy Spirit will first triumph.

---

2. There are a few exceptions which, however, do not encroach upon this principle. In this way, the great Orthodox sanctuary of Mount Athos which, under the Ottoman Empire and before it under the Byzantine Empire, was dependent on the patriarch of Constantinople, continued to be so even though the peninsula was incorporated with Greece. Before the First World War, in non-Orthodox countries, one found churches placed under the jurisdiction of their autocephalous Churches. For example, in France, there were six Russian churches, (Paris, Cannes, Nice, Villefranche, Biarritz, Pau), which depended on the Holy Synod of St Petersburg, and in London there was an Exarch of the Patriarch of Constantinople for the whole of Western Europe.

The waves of Orthodox refugees who have arrived in countries all over the world has now necessitated the creation of national exarchates under the different jurisdictions. But this is only a temporary state of affairs; it will naturally end with the repatriation, assimilation or death of the members of this massive emigration that was due to upheavals that everyone knows about.

We must not believe that the author, himself Orthodox, was driven simply by a desire to launch into polemics. Far from it. As an historian, he shares the opinion of those who maintain that if, after the fall of the Roman Empire, Western Europe had been left to itself, without the guidance of the Catholic Church, the difficulties it would have had to surmount to get out of the chaos and permanent state of war caused by rival fealties would have been much worse: we only need to think of the wars of religion to be convinced of this fact ...

The Orthodox Church is against proselytism. It does not send missions anywhere, except when asked to do so. This attitude may be approved or not, but it is a historical fact. The West has the merit of having spread Christ's word to corners of the world that were unknown at the time the Apostles lived. The East has the merit of having preserved the *Gnosis* revealed by our Lord. Divulged now in systematic form, it enables us to have an idea of the efforts made by sincere seekers during centuries and millennia in their quest for the Truth. This is what we are about to study.

IV

(1)

In order of succession, the *Gnosis* that Jesus revealed to John, James and Peter after His resurrection reached Clement of Alexandria (about 160– 215) and his direct disciples. Due to the persecutions of the third century, and the troubles that arose in the heart of Christianity after it became the State religion, it became imperative to make it 'hermetic' if it were to survive. Hidden like a treasure buried in the earth, it silently made its way and, like a subterranean stream, flowed from master to disciple and from generation to generation until the present, when it rose to the surface again. Stripped of its occult character, it reappears with its original significance as an esoteric projection into the future taking the form of a *New Covenant*, or, in other words, a *Third Testament*.

The Law of the Old Testament, dictated to Moses on Mount Sinai amid thunder and lightning, took the form of a command. On the other hand, the New Testament was not imposed on human beings, it came to them as *Good News*, and each was free to welcome or reject it. Though of great significance, this difference goes unnoticed. We will try to understand this different attitude of the divine Will in the two cases. This will enable us to penetrate more deeply the true meaning of the *Third Testament*, as well as its message.

(2)

Considered from the angle that interests us, the *Decalogue* that was dictated to Moses appears as the instrument which was to cause a first selection, to distinguish the tares from the good seed among the chosen people, who were a mixture.

This first Decalogue commanded man to restrain his bestial instincts, those which we indulgently describe today as 'only human'. The Decalogue implies that man, an animal by nature, is quick to kill, to steal, to commit adultery, to bear false witness, to covet his neighbour's wife and goods, so that he does not do the Will of God but of the idols to which he abandons himself. This postulate throws light on the *negative* nature of the commandments, which we could not otherwise explain. In fact, one does not say: '*Honour thy father and thy mother*,' to someone who respects his parents, but to someone who, in word or in thought, treats them ill. This attitude is quite widespread. If it is demanded that the seventh day be consecrated to God, this is because, without this obligation, God would be rapidly relegated to the background of the subconscious by outer and inner anxieties as a result of the circumstances in which human beings live ...

From this point of view, the Decalogue appears as a touchstone. The history of the Jewish people under Moses' leadership gives us a picture of man's rebellion against the Divine Will!

The first Decalogue, the text given in the twentiethth chapter of the Book of *Exodus*, met with fierce resistance from the ranks of the people. The account that appears in the thirty-second chapter, verse 19, informs us that, when he was faced with the persistent idolatry of the people, Moses was seized with rage, broke the tablets on which the Commandments were written, and threw them down the mountainside. Then, in Chapter 34 (verse 1) of the same book, we read that *Jehovah* commanded him to carve two new tablets like the old ones, and told him: '*I will write upon these tablets the words that were in the first tablets which thou brakest.*' But the contents of this Second Decalogue are not at all the same as those of the First: while the first, which is used in the catechism of the Christian Churches, is a moral code of eternal value, the second repeats none of the standards that appear in it.

First Decalogue	Second Decalogue
1. I am the Lord thy God ... Thou shalt have no other gods before me;	1. Thou shalt worship no other god: ... Thou shalt make thee no molten gods;
2. Thou shalt not make unto thee any graven image, or any likeness of anything that is in heaven above, or that is in the earth beneath, or that is in the water under the earth: Thou shalt not bow down thyself to them, nor serve them;	2. The feast of unleavened bread shalt thou keep. Seven days thou shalt eat unleavened bread;
3. Thou shalt not take the name of the Lord thy God in vain;	3. All that openeth the womb is mine; and every firstling among thy cattle, whether ox or sheep, that is male;
4. Remember the sabbath day, to keep it holy. Six days shalt thou labour, and do all thy work: but the seventh day is the sabbath of the Lord thy God;	4. Six days thou shalt work, but on the seventh day thou shalt rest;
5. Honour thy father and thy mother; that thy days may be long upon the land which the Lord thy God giveth thee;	5. And thou shalt observe the feast of weeks of the first-fruits of wheat harvest, and the feast of ingathering at the year's end;
6. Thou shalt not kill;	6. Thrice in the year shall all your menchildren appear before the Lord God, the God of Israel;
7. Thou shalt not commit adultery;	7. Thou shalt not offer the blood of my sacrifice with leaven;
8. Thou shalt not steal;	8. Neither shall the sacrifice of the feast of the Passover be left unto the morning.
9. Thou shalt not bear false witness against thy neighbour;	9. The first of the first fruits of thy land thou shalt bring unto the house of the Lord thy God;
10. Thou shalt not covet thy neighbour's house, thou shalt not covet thy neighbour's wife, nor his manservant, nor his maidservant, nor his ox, nor his ass, nor anything that is thy neighbour's.[3]	10. Thou shalt not seethe a kid in his mother's milk.[4]

---

3. Exodus xx: 2–17.

4. Ibid. xxxiv: 14–26.

We know that the texts of the two Decalogues are not absolutely uniform in all the different languages, nor even in the same language. In the present case, this is of no importance. We have presented the two Decalogues together so that the reader may realize the basic difference between the two versions. The texts here are from the *Revised Version of the English Bible* (AD 1611); British and Foreign Bible Society, 146 Queen Victoria Street, London.

To underline the fundamental difference between them, we have presented these two versions side by side. If we find a moral Code in the first, the second contains a ritual Code, not one that deals with man's relationship with his fellow men. As such, it was naturally not included in the catechism of the Christian Churches.

(3)

Moses' anger, which drove him to break the tablets on which the first Ten Commandments were written, betrays the disappointment he experienced on seeing that the mass of his people were incapable of beginning the work of 'debestialization'.[5] The latter was the preliminary but necessary condition for the esoteric evolution of the chosen people according to the timetable established by God. His anger was in fact due to the realization that he had overestimated the moral stature of his people, and that they were not going to stand up to this test. After this failure, they no longer formed a single unit, and their common psyche was divided into two unequal parts. A minority were capable of following the prescriptions of the First Decalogue, but the majority were obedient to the purely ritual Second.

Already a minority in Moses' time, the first part dwindled during the years that followed. By the time of John the Baptist's and Christ's ministries, they formed only a numerically feeble group. Over the centuries, after a dramatic history of dissensions and calamities, the chosen people had become a mere shadow of itself. It was politically and religiously divided between Israel and Judah, between Samaria and Jerusalem, and even within Judaea it was divided by the same struggles.

In spite of the broken Tablets, for every *Catechumen* who aspires to cross the First Threshold and to progress on the Staircase as one of the *Faithful*, animated by the will to reach Love and, with it, the second Birth, the First Decalogue still remains a Code of obligatory esoteric standards.

V

(1)

The traditional dualism made tangible by the two Decalogues was maintained throughout the history of the chosen people, during which the two branches crossed and crossed again so that sometimes

---

5. A modern parallel exists in the disappointment of philosopher P. D. Ouspensky on his return to London after the Second World War. (Ed.)

one and sometimes the other exercised a dominant influence on the ideas and acts which, at each turning-point, determined the fate of Israel.

In current language, we can say that the Second Decalogue represents human law, while the first, which is esoterically meaningful, is an expression of the divine Will exhorting man to master the demands of the instincts in his impulsive nature.

We may easily recognize that this inspiration comes from the Absolute II, whereas the Second Decalogue interprets the will of the Absolute III.

The current of 'B' influences from the Absolute II was received by Moses, who transmitted them to his people. It was this that made Israel different from the other nations, who lived immersed in 'A' influences under the religious domination of tribal gods. Having thus become the chosen people, depositories of the higher revelation, they received the Promise of the Advent of the Christ-Redeemer, of their own Redemption and that of the other nations through their ministry. Now the Jewish conception of Jehovah was originally the tribal god of Judah, but was later recognized by the other tribes, although with reservations. It was thus elevated to the rank of God of Israel, yet in the religious imagination of the Jews it was never raised above the attributes of the Absolute III, even when, much later, the monotheist conception of the one God came to light. This was a question of a *relative monotheism*, placing at the height of the celestial pyramid a sort of Demiurge, ('craftsman' in Greek), Jehovah, who was precisely established in the consciousness of the Jewish people as the *God of Israel*.

This deviation is important. It even penetrated into Christianity. In the catechisms we find that Jehovah, (the God of Israel or the image of the Absolute III), is confused with God the Father, the Creator of the Universe.

We have already had occasion to call the reader's attention to the fact that Jesus never identified God the Father, the Heavenly Father, with the God of Israel,[6] of whom he never spoke.

---

6. The authors of the canonical Old Testament easily attributed the adjective *Eternal* to the God of Israel. Throughout the text, one may find this mentioned two hundred times. Now, the readers of 'Gnosis' know that eternity is only a cycle of time, and therefore, limited. In this sense, the Absolute III, who was the first creature and whose characteristic is the number FOUR, is really eternal. If the adjective *Eternal* was applied to Jehovah in the esoteric sense, one would have to admit his identification with the Absolute III.

We will notice that the idea of the eternal in a substantive form never appears in the canonical books of the New Testament; it only figures in the form of an adjective, qualifying facts and conditions, but never God — the Holy Trinity being, in essence, above eternity.

(2)

Since it emanated from the Absolute II, the first Mosaic Decalogue was of Christian inspiration and, in spite of everything, it was never completely eclipsed in the consciousness of the chosen people by the Second Decalogue. The Second was of pagan inspiration, in the sense that it emanated from the Absolute III. In the consciousness of the spiritual elite of the Jewish people, the monotheism relative to Jehovah never managed to replace the *true monotheism* of the consubstantial and indivisible Holy Trinity that was openly proclaimed in historical Christian history.

This esoteric tradition was revealed from the time of Moses through the line of the prophets, and found its highest possible expression in the Old Testament period in the person of the prophet-king David. It is true that, as a man, King David was not unblemished—the Bathsheba-Uriah affair is a flagrant proof of this—but the nobility of his soul and the greatness of his work brought him not only absolution but the sublime promise that the Messiah would be born of his line.[7] Psalm CXVIII, which summarizes the esoteric doctrine, designates him as a prophet, and the creation of the unified State of Israel crowns his work as a king.

As long as Solomon continued his father's work, Israel, which was a political and economic power, was also a worthy focus for the Promise. But in spite of the revelations he was given at the start, and in spite of his *human* wisdom, King Solomon did not manage to prevent himself from falling '... *and women corrupted the heart of King Solomon ... and Solomon went after Ashtoreth, the goddess of the Zidonians, and after Milcom, the abomination of the Ammonites.*'[8] In these sad and memorable words the chronicler summarized the moral catastrophe of the King's life, a catastrophe that, through a chain reaction, provoked the one that was to sweep down upon Israel. Abandoned to its fate, torn asunder by fratricidal struggles, a prey to invaders, Israel was never again a political power.

This drama of a famous King's abandonment of the spiritual for the temporal has marked Israel's history up to our day, and we are not at all sure that it has ended.

It is necessary to understand that this is not, as some think, the result of a revolt of the forces under heaven. This conception is contrary to the facts.

---

7. We know that the genealogies of Jesus given by Matthew and Luke do not coincide completely. They are, however, identical in the branch that goes from Abraham to David inclusive. After this point, they bifurcate. According to Matthew, Joseph was born of David's line through Solomon, and according to Luke, through Nathan, another of the king's sons. The genealogy indicated by Luke also starts from Joseph and goes back. A legend exists in Orthodoxy, according to which the latter genealogy is that of Mary, Jesus' Mother. This would explain the bifurcation and its profound meaning.

8. 1 Kings xi: 4, 5 (from the Slavonic text).

Israel's privilege — and the great danger that it ran because of this very privilege — was precisely to become the depository of the revelation of the Absolute II in the midst of a world drowned body and soul in the 'A' influences emanating from the Absolute III; a world not having passed the stage of tribal gods in permanent rivalry one with the other, with the different types of phenomenalistic magic associated with each. Only unconditional fidelity to the revelation from Christ could have ensured the accomplishment of the esoteric mission of the chosen people, and its preservation from the calamities that were bound to fall upon them like a terrible boomerang, and which did indeed strike them. So it was not an imaginary struggle under heaven which determined the fate of the Jewish people, but the attitude of the latter to this traditional dualism, which pursued them right down the centuries from the time of Solomon, and which still follows them, requiring of them a conscious and free choice. The successive misfortunes that they have experienced are due to the weakness of their heart, which compels them to succumb to the temptations of the General Law.

This is a delicate difference: we must not confuse causes with effects. More than a choice, the traditional dualism demanded a firm stand. But Israel wavered; sometimes it leaned toward the Absolute II, and sometimes it fell back under the empire of the Absolute III, as one can affirm by analysing its history in the light of the system of the three Cosmic Octaves. This provides us with an esoterically penetrating and historically verifiable explanation of the prolonged drama of the Jewish people, with the great alternations that are so much in keeping with their passionate nature.

(3)

The repeated misfortunes of Israel were to progressively orient the mind and heart of some of its sons toward the idea of revenge. This was natural, since the spirit of sacred vengeance is a characteristic of peoples organized in tribes. In this psychological climate, the memory of the greatness of the State under David and Solomon exercised a double hypnotic influence: it anaesthetized the people on the esoteric plane, and gave rise to the unjustified hope of a magnificent revenge on the political plane. Of course, it is natural for men who have been enslaved, plundered and buffeted by the blows of fate to project into the future the splendours of the past. Sometimes this is even necessary for their recovery, as history shows. We can easily understand that at the time, in the midst of its misfortunes, its common psyche torn asunder, Israel imperceptibly transformed the image of the Messiah who was to introduce the new spiritual Era, making him into its future king — blessed, even anointed, endowed with supernatural strength, and able to defeat his enemies, (of whom the Romans were the latest), and so ensure a final triumph in the resplendent glory of the new Jerusalem — no longer descended from Heaven, but essentially of this earth.

In time, these ideas became deeply rooted in the overexcited imagination of the people, which was the result of this chain of uninterrupted calamities, so that after the conquest of Palestine by Pompey in 63 BC, the eschatological aspirations of the Jews were led to a double failure a century later. This was a failure of the attempt by the Jewish rulers to force the Messiah to play a political and military role, and a failure of Jesus' mission, which was to accomplish the transition from the Cycle of the Father to the Cycle of the Son in joyous unanimity.

The taking of the Temple and the entry of the Romans into the Holy of Holies produced an extraordinary impression on the Jewish people, who considered this an unpardonable offence against God. It is therefore understandable that, in that state of stupor, they implored God to send them a Messiah who would be an Avenger-King in his heavenly might. An extract from one of the *Psalms of Solomon*, written at that time, shows that the spirit of this people was obsessed by the idea of a just vengeance:

Look, Lord, and raise them their King, son of David, at the time that thou knowest, thou, O God, so that he reign over Israel, thy servant.
And Gird him with thy strength, so that he may destroy the unjust rulers;
Purge Jerusalem of the pagans that oppress her, by ruining them so that the sinners against the heritage may be driven away by wisdom, by justice, so that the pride of the sinners may be broken like the potter's vases, so that all their substance may be broken with a rod of iron;
So that the unholy pagans may be destroyed by a word of his mouth, so that, before his threat, the pagans may flee far from his face, finally, so that sinners may be recovered by the utterance of their hearts.
Then he will assemble the holy people whom he will lead with justice, he will govern the tribes of the people sanctified by the Lord his God;
He will not let iniquity tarry in their midst, and no man knowing evil will live with them;
For he will know them as being all children of God; he will spread them in their tribes all over the land;
The immigrant and the stranger will no longer dwell with them.
He will judge peoples and nations with wisdom and justice,
And the pagan peoples will serve under his yoke; he will glorify the Lord before all the earth;
He will purify Jerusalem through sanctification, as of old,
So that nations will come from the ends of the earth to contemplate his glory, bringing their sons as an offering, bereft of all their strength,
And to contemplate the glory of the Lord, with which God has glorified him. For he is a just King, instructed by God, placed over them;

And there is no iniquity in the midst of them during these days; for all are holy, and their King is Christ the Lord.[9]

All the traditional dualism is expressed in these lines. We can see that — whatever the 'assurances' and 'reassurances' on the side of the Absolute II — the accent was on the terrestrial, purely national task of the incarnated Christ, from whom they expected a great deal. In the first place, they expected him to liberate the Jews from the Roman yoke and make them a race of overlords to whom all nations would be subject.

Among other writings of the period, we can quote a passage from the *Sibylline Oracle*, where we find allusions to the Second Triumvirate, as well as to Anthony and Cleopatra. These *Oracles* were composed in the last quarter of the first century BC. The text is as follows:

'And when Rome will rule over Egypt ... the all-powerful Kingdom of the immortal King will be revealed to man. The Holy Lord will come then, whose sceptre will hold sway over all the earth for all the centuries of time, and will pour down upon the Latins an implacable anger. Through the Three, Rome's fate will be miserable, and all its inhabitants will be buried in their dwellings under the fiery torrent raining down from the heavens.'[10]

(4)

After the views exposed in the preceding lines, the reader will understand why the chosen people oscillated between the wonder of the Promise and the marvels of the terrestrial glory offered by the Absolute III in the domain of the 'A' influences. At the same time, he will realize the imperceptible transformation that took place in the aspirations of the Jews under the double influence of the misfortunes they suffered and this representation they made of the Messiah — Lord of the Kingdom of Heaven — who would appear as a marvellous King sent to triumph over their invaders and to subjugate them.

---

9. Quoted from the *Psalms of Solomon*, introduction, Greek text and translation by J. Viteau, with the principal variants of the Syriac version by François Martin, Paris, Letouzey and Ané, 1911, Psalm xvii: 23–36, pp. 351–361 (literal translation from the French).

10. Translated from the Russian. The 'Three' is an allusion to the Second Triumvirate that then ruled Rome.

VI

(1)

K ing Solomon's fall consolidated the traditional dualism that, until then, had been intermittent, clearly giving it the meaning and form of an esoteric split. David's *Christian* tradition, neglected, deformed and largely forgotten by the ruling elite of the chosen people, who were preoccupied with political problems, was received and kept chiefly by the simple people — rarely by intellectuals — and continued to make its way silently through the centuries. After the split, the psychic and non-spiritual branch of the Tradition developed its own esotericism, second-class (if one may say so), since it was limited within the boundaries of the Absolute III's authority. In its turn, this ritualistic esotericism gave birth to a whole science, equally traditional and hermetic, with Solomon as its head — Solomon, who is sometimes taken for God himself.

Connected with the Temple, this Solomonist tradition of initiation was saved after the destruction of the temple by Titus in 70. This was the last calamity, and gave the signal for the dispersal of Israel. Having become occult, it continued to exist, carefully protected from local Christian persecutions, until the Arab conquest of Palestine gave it a refuge. The ruins of the Temple served as a rallying point and as a sacred symbol for its adepts. Thanks to the Crusades, contacts were established when European knights came to the Holy Land and settled there. The legend of the Knights Templar finding Solomon's treasure in the Temple ruins and making it an object of their special initiations, even though allowed by the Pope, surrounded the White-Coats with the mystical halo of a higher occult science as a complement to their Catholic confession, which remained effective. Parallel to this the Jews, dispersed all over the world, brought their mysticism, which was of Solomonist origin, into Western Europe, where it flourished in their ghettos during the Middle Ages.

By the time it reached us, this Judaeo-Christian or purely Jewish tradition consisted of a large number of treatises, legends and rituals, accompanied by an over-abundant literature. Spread across Western Europe and America, it has become the object of study in the 'lodges' of different secret societies and the Commanderies of different Orders, as well as for Christians working in isolation. Let us remind the reader that the Muslim and Orthodox Orient have never had such secret and *initiatory* societies within their perimeters.

It is surprising to constate how easily Christian seekers, (or at any rate, those of Christian origin), brush aside the purely Christian Tradition of Moses-Elias-David which Jesus enriched with the New Testament, along with its projection into the future contained in the *Gnosis* revealed by our Lord after His Resurrection. Too often, seekers of perfectly good faith omit the Gospel and the Epistles, and delve into the Old Testament and the Solomonist *psychic* tradition. Theoretically, this research is not harmful. But if we take into account Jesus' principle by which the disciple cannot be greater than the master, the work of these seekers cannot lead them any higher than a narrow psychic esotericism, limited to the domain of the Absolute III.

But our period, which is right in the midst of the *Time of Transition*, needs esoteric workers who are enlightened with the revealed Orthodox *Gnosis*, which forms the Second *Promise*: that of the Advent of the Kingdom of Heaven in the approaching Era of the Holy Spirit.

Today, as in olden times, the situation can be described by the following words of Jesus: *'The harvest is great, but the labourers are few; Pray ye therefore the Lord of the harvest, that he will send forth labourers into his harvest.'*[11]

Instead of turning aside; it is high time for capable seekers who are currently absorbed in the divided tradition of the Old Testament to answer the Master's call and begin to work in the Lord's field ... *'to reap that which they have not sown.'*[12] So that, in case of success, once again ... *'he that soweth and he that reapeth may rejoice together.'*[13]

---

11. Matthew ix: 37; Luke x: 2.
12. John iv: 38.
13. John iv: 36.

SECOND PART
THE TRUTH

CHAPTER VIII

(1)

Traditional Knowledge in its different forms recognizes the *Circle* as the *Symbol of Eternity*. It is important to know why.

Readers of 'Gnosis' know the meaning given by the Doctrine to the ideas of the *eternal* and of *eternity*. We touched on them briefly in the previous chapter.

In traditional philosophy, which is cyclic and not linear, Eternity is not regarded as Infinity. The idea of Infinity goes beyond the limits of Manifestation, since that which has no end naturally has no beginning. So, in our theorizing, we only apply the term *infinite* to that which is beyond the whole *Macrocosmos*.

Great Eternity therefore appears as the Great Cycle of Manifestation, encompassing the whole scale of subordinate Cycles and *relative* Eternities, as well as all Times, which are also *relative*. Thus it contains the Beginning — the first creative impulse that begins from the Absolute 0 — and goes all the way to the End, that is, to the general and absolute Accomplishment. In this it passes down the whole length of the scale of the Macrocosmos, which contains all relative Accomplishments.

The Love from the Absolute 0 fills all Manifestation to its uttermost limits, in all directions and all its specificities, under the aegis of the Absolute I and through the person of the Absolute II, after which, enriched by all the experience gained from one end of the scale to the other, including the kingdom of the Absolute III, it returns to its source in a primitive, unmanifest state at the heart of the *Inexpressible*.

Certain teachings consider this End of ends as a *General Annihilation*. This is an aberration caused by the psychological structure of our intellect, which is incapable of conceiving ideas outside time and space, although, in scientific speculation and with the aid of mathematical ideas, we can reach a generally accepted conclusion of the relativity of both. It is a question of an abstraction which, pushed to the limit, is out of reach of the imagination to which human beings can claim to have access solely by means of their Personality in its so-called 'normal' state, which is an underdeveloped condition.

What we have described above refers to the very Source of Manifestation. At the next degree, which is the first degree of Manifestation, forming the Great Cycle which is also described as the Cycle of Great Eternity, the human mind halts. It lacks the necessary capacity to encompass this in its entirety, or to retain an image of it that will make it understandable.

The same phenomenon takes place when we try to imagine Life or Manifestation in all its diverse forms, which range from the fine to the coarse, from the dynamic to the inert and vice versa. We do not live among things and phenomena as they are in themselves. Instead we live with representations of them that we make for ourselves using the limited means available to our psyches. Thus the phenomenal world accessible to us is only part of the whole. The remainder is hidden from us because of our total incapacity to imagine it.

Yet we seek solutions to great questions that touch each of us most deeply, such as: are there any permanent values in this Life, and if they exist, how can we discern them? When devotion to an ideal is taken right up to the supreme sacrifice, is this a mark of heroism or of absurdity? What is the real meaning of death? Etc.

Answers to these questions can be found only in the ideas and circumstances of the invisible world, and they are not perceived by the waking consciousness of the exterior man, however gifted or cultured he may be. Theophan the Recluse says that *'Here, neither erudition, nor ecclesiastical dignity are of any use.'*

It is only after the Second Threshold that the awe-struck Faithful begin to progressively discover this world through the medium of their higher centres. About the working of these centres we have already quoted the following words of St Isaac the Syrian: *'The soul, like the body, has two eyes: but while the eyes of the body both see things in the same way, those of the soul see them differently; one contemplates the Truth in symbols and images; the other contemplates it face to face.'*

Readers of 'Gnosis' will understand that he was referring to the higher emotional Centre and the higher intellectual Centre respectively.

(2)

W e said earlier that from time immemorial the *Circle* has been considered a *Symbol for Eternity*, and we pointed out in what sense we should understand this term *Eternity*. Now, to understand this phrase in its entirety, we have to determine the esoteric meaning of the words *Symbol*, and *Symbolism*.

(3)

I f we go back to the origin of the term we will find that by *symbol*, σύνβομον, the Greeks meant the words and signs by which those initiated into the mysteries of Ceres, Cybele and Mithra,[1] recognized each

---

1. *Littré*, Gallimard et Hachette, Paris, 1959, p. 2194.

other. It was in this spirit that Christianity applied the term Symbol to the *Creed* of the Faithful, of which there are three versions: the *Apostles' Creed*[2] (second century), the *Nicene Creed* (325), which establishes the consubstantial nature of the Father and of the Son, and a third that, in the year 380, completed the latter by defining the nature of the Holy Spirit.

Beginning with the last century, the word *symbol* began to assume a wider significance and to lose its original Hellenistic or Christian meaning. For example, in modern literature, *Symbolism* appeared as a reaction to the totally representative art of the *Parnassians*. Here the symbol is conceived as the expression of the intimate relationship existing between two objects, in which the one that belongs to the physical world is supposed to evoke that which belongs to the moral world and so reach the deepest layers of the human soul. This is how people compared the poetry of the *Symbolists* to music, in which the rhythm and tones generate feelings and emotions that escape analysis.

It is clear that in this idea the *symbol* is understood as a sign created by man to help the communication of his ideas, impressions and messages — in short, everything, however refined, that is situated on the *human plane*. This conception leaves a great deal of freedom for the creation and interpretation of individual symbols.

In short, such a creation is wholly the product of the underdeveloped and unbalanced human Personality, and consequently symbols of this kind, along with the symbolism to which they give birth, have only relative value. The fact that they are accepted by large sections of humanity, all belonging to the same civilization, is due to a certain uniformity in the deformation of their Personality — a uniformity that is a reflection of their education and upbringing. It also often happens that this deformation is voluntary due to the hypnotic effect of *Fashion* — especially in weak natures that wish to appear strong. This usually originates in a fear of being 'outmoded'. This fear can become an obsession that leads to 'avant garde' activities of every sort — in Art, as elsewhere.

In the esoteric sense, *Symbols* are always *revealed*, and their deeper meaning is precise and cannot be subject to free interpretation, since, whether expressed in human words, diagrams, or works of Art, they express *objective truths* that have been reached in a higher state of consciousness. Therefore a symbol that is of value esoterically speaking could be partly or completely understood, depending on the level of consciousness reached by the one who tries to understand its meaning. But the measure to which it is understood will not change its general meaning, which will remain the same whatever the level of comprehension. It cannot be otherwise, since, as we have said, revealed symbols give access to a world that is situated

2. In French, and in Greek, the term *symbol* is more commonly used to describe what in English we commonly call the *creed*. (Ed.)

beyond simple subjectivism. It is ruled by objectively valid ideas, of which they are the expression.

In other words, these symbols are messages intended for those in search of the Truth. They are transmitted from a higher world to the world here below, and not from man to man, as in the symbolist schools of the nineteenth and twentieth centuries. Every symbol which has some esoteric validity therefore contains in itself a sum of real knowledge — of *Gnosis*—touching on certain aspects, facts, or laws of the noumenal world that is beyond our senses. Simultaneously, it offers a *key* that helps us to decipher its deepest integral meaning.

In esoteric teaching, the practical value of symbols goes even further: they allow the seeker who by conscious efforts develops new faculties in himself to control his progress in the wider understanding of facts which each symbol interprets, and which belong to the noumenal world. This is the case of the *Apocalypse* that was *revealed* to St John on the Isle of Patmos, when he was 'in the Spirit.'[3] Though the apostle translated it into human language, this symbol can only be completely grasped by those who have access to the consciousness of the higher emotional centre, which was the state in which St John himself received the revelation. Even the most refined human intellect — available to the Personality in its normal state — is unable to *understand* the Book of Revelation, because human intelligence, left to its own resources and without the help of a methodical esoteric formation, comes to a halt before the uncrossable wall of the *Unknown*: Virchow's *Ignorabimus*.

II

(1)

We have already underlined how important for esoteric philosophy as well as for mathematics was the discovery of *Zero*. The modern decimal system, and all that flows from it, would have been unthinkable without the revelation of this symbol. Instead of figures, the numerical system of the Ancients used the letters of their alphabet. Compared to this procedure, the Roman system represented a great step forward, as much because of its simplicity as its universality. In all these systems, instead of *Zero*, we find a gap: a void. Now, we have already said that *Zero* is not a void; on the contrary, it is an *Integral of the Numbers*, a centre from which come two series: one positive and the other negative, which are perfectly balanced and go on the one side up to $+\infty$, and on the other, down to $-\infty$.

---

3. Revelation i: 10.

The formula of this, which has already been shown:

$$- \infty \ldots\ldots -4, -3, -2, -1, 0, +1, +2, +3, +4, \ldots\ldots + \infty$$

represents the symbol and its Manifestation from the esoteric point of view. This series may be represented in cyclic form in the following way:

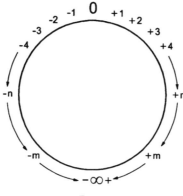

FIG. 1

One may recall that the Arabs, who discovered—or rather, rediscovered — Zero, drew their whole system of numbers from it, and that the word *cipher* that has come across into certain European languages is only a deformation of the Arab word *Sifr*, which means precisely *Zero*, since it was starting from *Zero* that the Arab decimal system was created. The following schema represents the geometric design from which the Arabic system of numbers was drawn:

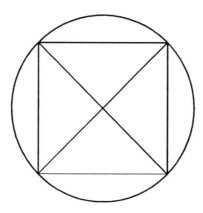

FIG. 2

81

We can now understand better why, in traditional knowledge of every nuance, the *Circle* has always symbolized *Eternity*. Revealed as such, it then evoked all Manifestation from Alpha to Omega, from the Beginning to the End, that is, to the Fulfilment.[4]

The symbolism of the bare *Circle* stops at this. It points out the fact, but it does not explain how *Manifestation*, with all its cosmic systems, was conceived and realized. This will be the theme of the following chapters. However, we must remember that the system of Arabic numbers gave us access to Algebra (*Al-jabr*), the science of calculating the sizes represented by abstract ideas. This enables the human mind to make definite progress, with innumerable consequences. For instance, it is because of this that we can pass harmoniously from geometric ideas, which are stable and fixed by nature, to the dynamism of higher calculations.

---

4. On Mount Athos the monks refer to this by pointing out the domes of their churches, which, they say, represent Christ as a sphere whose centre is everywhere and its circumference nowhere. (Ed.)

CHAPTER IX

(1)

Though the revelation of the Circle as a symbol for Eternity goes back to times immemorial, it took millennia for the human mind to abandon its immobility, and so become able to receive a new revelation, one that led it to recognize the Circle as the symbol for *Zero*, from which it later drew a system of numbers that encompasses the Whole.

It is true that, even before the Arabs discovered the Zero, ancient initiates knew that the Circle contained in it a whole system of secondary symbols from which the sacred alphabets were drawn. However, without applying the system of decimal fractions to this, the Circle remained a petrified figure. It expressed the static form of the Cosmos well, but could not reflect the pulsation of life, which is in perpetual movement. To reveal this pulsation, it was necessary to progress from static, 'geometric' conceptions, to dynamic, 'algebraic' ones.[1]

The diagram above (fig. 2) represents this great progress of the human mind: it was precisely by letting his pen wander at random — and so giving it movement — that the Arab managed to build up his system of numbers and figures starting from Zero. Without abandoning thought in the form of *representations*, which also exist in animals, it was also possible from then on to cultivate thought based on *ideas*, which only occur in man. This was how man could in time improve his means of investigation, passing progressively from concrete speculation to abstractions — in other words, forcing himself to reach out to the sources of the phenomenal world by returning, degree by degree, up the scale of associations from effects to causes.

From then on, the increasing power of human thought did not cease to manifest itself. We know how much the application of algebra enriched Euclidean geometry. New horizons opened up: from plane and spherical trigonometry and analytical geometry with Descartes, to the analysis of infinitesimals with Leibnitz, non-Euclidean geometry with Lobatchevsky, and, finally, to all the pure and applied mathematical sciences that today form the prodigious modern scientific arsenal.

---

1. There is a simple relation of number to time expressed in this paragraph. Whole numbers express duration, or the number of repetitions, while decimal fractions represent the principle of division which allows the division of units of duration to more easily express tone or frequency. (Ed.)

(2)

The traditional division of the circumference into 360° remained uncontested until the nineteenth century, during which, under the influence of the metric system, someone advanced the idea of dividing the right angle into 100 degrees instead of 90. This idea was seriously debated, but was virtually abandoned due to the material impossibility of replacing at one stroke the engraved graduations on every precision instrument then in use. This was an impossibility which would in practice have led to the coexistence of the two systems, which would have caused innumerable complications in scientific relationships. Apart from this argument, the defenders of the classical method of graduation did not bring up any other powerful fundamental reason in favour of the 360 degree system. They simply emphasized the point that the number 400 for the entire circumference was less convenient than 360 because it could only be divided by two, four and five, whereas 360 can also be divided by three. If we take the series of divisors from 1 to 10, we obtain:

for 400 : 1, 2, 4, 5, 8, 10.
and for 360 : 1, 2, 3, 4, 5, 6, 8, 9, 10.

In the first example, four divisors: 3, 6, 7 and 9, are missing, while in the second, only 7 is missing.

This was how the idea of the 400 degree circle was set aside ... reluctantly, it seems, for even today, for example, slopes are measured in percentages,[2] not in degrees.

(3)

The reason for and the meaning of the division of the circumference into 360 degrees goes back farther than the above argument, which is comparatively modern. Normally, when making a comparative study of the two numbers, we only consider the practical aspect without concerning ourselves about the philosophical meaning, and we are even less concerned about the esoteric significance of the division of the circumference into 360 degrees. Yet this division was made by the priests of Ancient Egypt long before the discovery of the zero, and probably well before Euclid. We will see later why this was so.

---

2. This is Continental European practice, now applied also in Britain. (Ed.)

(4)

We know that a *geometric consciousness* is innate in man. A part of the subconsciousness, it is cellular, or in other words instinctive. It also exists in animals and in due proportion in plants. We can quote many examples, especially beavers, which cut down young trees to strengthen the dams they build across streams. They construct real villages of mud huts, and divert the course of streams by series of sluices. Bees are another example. Their hives are hexagonal geometric constructions. The habitations of ants are shaped as regular cones. These sometimes reach two meters in height. These are just a few examples among thousands of others that point out the geometrical consciousness that exists in animals of every kind. The instinct of plants for geometric equilibrium becomes evident if we stop to think of it. And let us not forget that primitive man knew how to build huts better than beavers: ignorant and illiterate, he nevertheless learned how to build houses that did not fall apart.

The core of this geometrical consciousness is common — in different degrees — to all the species that form organic Life on Earth. Geometrical consciousness is not found in the lower intellectual centre, since this centre does not exist in animals and certainly not in plants, but it is located in the intellectual sectors of the motor centre, which can be found in all living creatures, even single cells. With the progressive development of the intellect in *homo sapiens recens*, the instinctive geometric consciousness has *partially* risen into the motor sectors of the intellectual centre, where it then plays a part in waking consciousness. This is how man could progressively make use of it as he pleased, so that this intellectualized geometric faculty has governed his activities since the Stone Age. Cultivated, it later produced the extraordinary progress in architecture and in the plastic and figurative arts. In the art of war, it manifested itself in the oblique front tactics inaugurated by Epaminondas, adopted by Philip, and then developed and perfected by Alexander the Great.

(5)

We know that, apart from the Circle, the first of the basic geometric figures is the triangle—especially the equilateral triangle. In esoteric symbolism, this figure plays a primary role as the symbol of the principle of *To Be* (verb) and of *Being* (state, existence, quality of what is). It marks the upper and lower limits of esotericism. This was the sign attributed to the disciples of the esoteric *Didascalia*, and it appears at the summit of the scale of esoteric values as the *Delta*. Even today, when completed by an 'all-seeing', radiant eye, it is the symbol of the Holy Trinity proceeding from the Unmanifest and limited by Its own Manifestation. Inscribed in the circle, the equilateral triangle divides the circumference into three parts of 120 degrees each.

The second basic figure of esoteric Christian symbolism is the inscribed square, which divides the circumference into four parts of 90 degrees each.

Among all the inscribed equilateral polygons, these are the only two figures within whose lines no other closed geometric figures can be drawn. We should keep this in mind.

The *Circle* with the *Triangle* and the *Square* inscribed in it forms a symbol of great esoteric importance, with multiple meanings. Here is the first of them:

CIRCLE   — SPIRIT   — (Pneuma)
TRIANGLE — SOUL   — (Psyche)
SQUARE   — BODY   — (Hyle)

This schema is presented in the following way in esoteric Christian teaching:

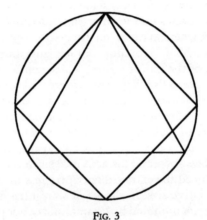

FIG. 3

86

CHAPTER X

(1)

In a geometric study of this symbol, the persevering seeker will find many generally unknown ideas on the nature of the interdependence of the three fundamental elements of the human being who, in fact and in potential, possesses the most complete and most perfect organism of all those belonging to organic Life on Earth.

For this, it is necessary to complete the above diagram (fig. 3). We will next draw a second equilateral triangle in it, with the apex downwards. The reader will then notice that the vertical diameter of the circle, which passes through the centre of the triangle, is divided into four equal parts. Then, if we draw a radius which passes through the point of intersection of the base of the first triangle and one side of the first square, we will see that it divides this side, as well as the arc of which it is a chord, into two equal parts. Repeated in the four possible directions, the operation allows us to find the corners of the second inscribed square. This is no longer diamond shaped, but placed upright.

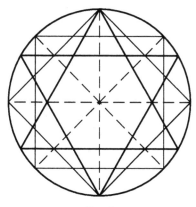

Fig. 4

This geometric figure is full of symbolic meaning. It is a valuable subject for research into the framework of the esoteric cycle in teaching the Doctrine. In the reciprocal positioning of these figures, and the intersection of the lines which result from these positions, judiciously chosen and placed, the interdependence of the geometric figures in the system of inscribed equilateral polygons faithfully reflects the interdependence of those elements of nature—in this case, human nature—that it symbolically represents.

St John says: '*Here is wisdom. Let him that hath understanding count the number of the beast: for it is the number of a man: and his number is Six hundred threescore and six.*'[1]

This is one aspect of this symbol, an aspect concerning the common run of man, known as the *Man-Beast*.

We repeat: this is only one aspect, there are others. This is the first, the bottom of the ladder of *Gnosis* that the untiring seeker will climb, step by step, until *finally* he reaches the integral meaning of this whole complex of symbols.

(2)

The practice of this work of research is marvellous. As we progress in this direction, alongside the *geometric* discoveries that we make are discoveries about our own nature. In the past, nobody has published the teaching about those symbols, not even in the closed circles of the Didascalia. Starting from the first key (fig. 3), the teaching was continued by a method in which successive discoveries were made by the student himself. It is still the same today; the only difference is that a second key (fig. 4) and others after that are now given to the seeker.

It is important to add that the student reached these discoveries only after an accumulation of tension arising from his desire to learn, accompanied by a concentration which is both willed and necessary. This concentration must be focused on the point of research chosen, while *simultaneously* being directed toward the student's own depths. This demands the application of double attention.

With success in this, the student passes successively from one *partial* revelation to another, until he finally attains an *integral* revelation of the symbol, which then appears to him full of meaning, Beauty and Life.

It would be vain to ask for explanations. All that can be communicated in substance to the yet underdeveloped Personality of the seeker is already in the symbol. Work on this symbol, as on those that follow, demands progressive and real development of the Personality. Without this development, the student cannot go beyond the level of speculation; he may find it interesting, but it will be purely intellectual, and that cannot take him very far in his researches.

Thousands and thousands of books on symbols and symbolism are now on the market. They are written by erudite and sincere men, but all attempts to 'decode' and explain a true esoteric symbol by purely intellectual means, however great and however refined they may be, are insufficient and cannot lead to the desired goal.

---

1. Revelation xiii: 18.

This is an objective fact, and it is the real reason, the *natural reason*, (that is to say, the reason arising from the nature of things) for the secrecy of the mysteries of true Initiation.

II

(1)

We have already said that the circle whose circumference is divided into 360 degrees allows the inscription of several different equilateral polygons, each of which, (as well as certain of their combinations), is contained in the complete system of esoteric graphic symbols. These polygons are limited in number: there are TWENTY-TWO in all, starting with the equilateral triangle.[2]

In the following list, the two Arabic numbers that appear alongside each of the Roman numerals indicate: first, the number of sides of the polygon, and second, the degrees of the arc of which each side forms a chord.

I	—	3 — 120°		XII	—	24 — 15°
II	—	4 — 90°		XIII	—	30 — 12°
III	—	5 — 72°		XIV	—	36 — 10°
IV	—	6 — 60°		XV	—	40 — 9°
V	—	8 — 45°		XVI	—	45 — 8°
VI	—	9 — 40°		XVII	—	60 — 6°
VII	—	10 — 36°		XVIII	—	72 — 5°
VIII	—	12 — 30°		XIX	—	90 — 4°
IX	—	15 — 24°		XX	—	120 — 3°
X	—	18 — 20°		XXI	—	180 — 2°
XI	—	20 — 18°		XXII	—	360 — 1°

In this system of twenty-two inscribed polygons we may recognize, without any difficulty, sacred alphabets such as the Egyptian and its derivatives, the Phoenician and the Hebrew, and we will also now understand that the division of the circumference into 360 degrees was not made by chance, nor simply for 'convenience in calculation'.

(2)

The diagrams below represent three of the twenty-two symbols, notably the *pentagon*, with the triple five-sided star, the *hexagon* with the triple six-sided star, and the *octagon*, with the triple eight-sided star. By adding the triangle and the square to these, we complete the system of five

---

2. Among contemporary authors one can find indications on this phenomenon in the works of Raymond Abellio.

geometric symbols which forms one of the cycles of what may truly be called *esoteric* studies, dedicated to the *structure* of the whole Universe as well as of all living beings. This extends from the micro-microcosmic cell right up to the Macrocosmos seen as a whole.

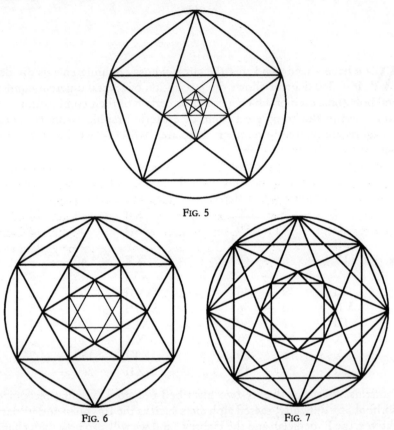

FIG. 5

FIG. 6   FIG. 7

CHAPTER XI

(1)

The symbols reproduced in the preceding chapter reflect the *structure* of the Universe, whose triple principle reappears uniformly as the basis of the whole Macrocosmos, as well as of its subordinate organisms from the most primitive to the most complex. Among those belonging to organic Life on Earth, the human organism is clearly the most complete and the most perfected.

In the same way that, in the study of medicine, anatomy precedes physiology, in the study of esoteric science it is important to learn the structure of Man before studying his functioning. We have already given an outline of the functioning of the Universe in the two previous volumes. The description of the three cosmic octaves in the second volume of this work contains a precise schema[1] of this that can be applied to any cosmos,[2] and is all that is needed for the assiduous reader involved in true esoteric work to progress in this part of the *Gnosis*. To succeed, he should fit each problem that interests him into the place it should occupy in the framework of this system, which should be visualized as in *movement*.

We know that the system of three cosmic octaves embraces the whole Universe with all its parts: the physical, psychological and spiritual organs that form its *Body*, its *Soul* and its *Spirit*.

We will not get involved in definitions here. For the moment let us simply keep in mind the traditional statement that the Universe is a living Organism and that Man has been created in its image and likeness.[3] Now let us begin our study of Man, who is also made up of these same three elements: *Body*, *Soul* and *Spirit*. Let us try to do this by placing him among the corresponding three elements of the Universe, under whose direct influence he evolves. We will make use of the symbols mentioned above (figs. 5, 6, and 7) not only simply by examining them in their static aspect, but also by communicating movement to them. This will give us a dynamic, 'physiological' view of them.

---

1. In the earlier part of this book, including the whole of volumes I and II, we have translated the word *schema* used in the French by *diagram*. Here, the meaning develops from the earlier static concept of a diagram to an active, moving structure and in this usage — which of course was implicit in the earlier uses as well — we will retain the word *schema* from the French, as the English language has no simple way of rendering this expanded meaning. Students of Cabbala are recommended to note possible parallels. (Ed.)

2. Vol. II, Ch. VIII, fig. 5.

3. Genesis i: 26–7.

(2)

As they are derived from the Zero, the three symbols are shown drawn inside the Circle. For each of them, this symbolizes the Universe. But to simplify our study, we will separate the Circle from the polygons. In their turn, the polygons symbolize, in each case, the plane to which the symbol belongs, as well as the sphere in which the forces that it expresses find their point of application, i.e., their field of action.

When we analyse each symbol and comment on it, it is essential not to isolate each from the whole, as the totality forms a closed system which faithfully reflects the structure of the three cosmic octaves, especially:

> The *Octogram* — the First cosmic octave.
> The *Hexagram* — the Second cosmic octave.
> The *Pentagram* — the Third cosmic octave.

Let us now explain what we mean by the study of a schema in *movement*. We already pointed this out when we evoked the image of the Arab with his pen following the lines he had drawn (fig. 2). The conception of the Zero and the system of Arabic numbers flowed from the movement of the thoughts and attention of the one who wielded this pen — the movement was made concrete by thought, and through it the schema came to life. The student should continue in the same way when he studies the symbols, shown as geometric figures, in more detail. However, he must have some means of approaching this study.

The fact that this method of approach has been lost in the course of time explains why these symbols, which were once known to everybody, at least in elementary form, no longer speak to us. They are simply reproduced because it is a tradition, in the same way that we reproduce the signs assigned to the four evangelists without recognizing that they are keys that make possible esoteric study of the related Gospels.[4] This is how we regard the Pentagram on the portico of the Church of the Holy Sepulchre, and also on the shrines of certain saints; how the Hexagram continues to be the symbol of Christmas or the incarnation of the Word in the Christian world; how it appears in the Old Testament as the Seal or Shield of King David;[5] how, in the Hindu Tradition, we often find it circled by a serpent which bites its own tail; and lastly, how Orthodox priests have an Octogram embroidered in gold thread on the back of their chasubles. Yet people who can explain the profound meaning of these symbols or who can give the reason for their use are very rare.

---

4. Cf. Vol. I, pp. 180.
5. Sometimes known in English as the 'Star of David'. (Ed.)

(3)

The method of approach that we have just mentioned has two elements. It is a question first of the indication (one that the student would find for himself only with difficulty, because it demands training in epicyclic thought in a contemplative state of mind) of the order in which the study of the symbol should be conducted. This indication will be given further on by the sequence in which the numbers are placed in the schemata. The student will later learn that these figures not only represent the line that his thought and attention should follow, but that each of these numbers that corresponds to this — and this is essential — also contains a group of ideas on which he should meditate in correlation with the global meaning of each of the three cosmic symbols, and then in relation to what they have in common. Of course this is not easy, but the main thing is to begin. He should then continue to work with courage and perseverance, and what is lacking will come as a series of successive partial revelations that will be accorded by divine grace to persevering seekers.

There is, however, one stumbling-block. This is impatience, the wish to get results immediately. If we give way to this desire, we fall into the error which is typical in this kind of research — that is — we will tackle the problem by purely intellectual means. But in this domain, nothing can be acquired by the Cartesian spirit acting alone. This is no longer purely a question of *intelligence*, but also of *wisdom*, and a simultaneous and sufficient *emotional* participation is necessary. Neither the head alone nor the heart alone can lead the student far. We would not know how to pick up an object with only one finger: we could touch it or push it, but to hold it, the simultaneous action of two fingers is necessary. If he does not wish to fail, the student who tackles the elements of *Gnosis* or higher Knowledge must realize from the beginning that work on these symbols requires a simultaneous effort of head and heart.

(4)

The second element of the method of approach is the *Table of Major Numbers*. These are the ordinal numbers of the system of twenty-two inscribed polygons whose numbering we have given above. These numbers are called *Major* because each of them reflects one specific aspect of all the others. The nature of things is such that this property, in its *integral* form, disappears above the number XXII.

TABLE OF MAJOR NUMBERS

    I. LOVE (coming from the Absolute I) AFFIRMATION, IMPERCEPTIBLE LIGHT.

    II. LOVE (coming from the Absolute II), VERB, LOGOS.

    III. LOVE (coming from the feminine principle), QUEEN OF THE HEAVENS.

    IV. LOVE (coming from the Absolute III) PRINCE OF THIS WORLD.

    V. NUTRITION (from the coarsest food right up to supreme Knowledge (*Connaissance*).

    VI. REBIRTH, RENEWAL.

    VII. LIVING MATTER.

    VIII. WORD.

    IX. LETTER.

    X. LIFE, perpetual vibration.

    XI. THE SEARCH, PROGRESS.

    XII. ATTENTION.

    XIII. FALL, DECOMPOSITION, DEATH.

    XIV. TIME.

    XV. THOUGHT, CALCULATION, LIE, ILLUSION.

    XVI. RECOVERY, RECTIFICATION, RECONSTITUTION, RECOMPOSITION.

    XVII. APPEAL.

    XVIII. FIXATION (from immobility to ecstasy), WAITING.

    XIX. REINTEGRATION (Into the bosom of the Lord).

    XX. REALIZATION.

    XXI. THE POINT. THE PAUSE. THE FINAL POINT.

    XXII. THE WHOLE, in Space and Time as well as out of Space and Time, comprising the perceptible and the imperceptible, the imaginable and the unimaginable. The integral Love belonging to the Androgyne.

This has been known since time immemorial, which is proved by the fact that each of these numbers gave birth to a letter of the sacred alphabets: in the Egypto-Judaic tradition these letters had as prototypes the twenty-two images from which they had been derived.

Represented by the letters of the Hebraic alphabet, the twenty-two Major Numbers are known in the Christian Tradition, where they are not associated with images but are systematically revealed in King David's Psalm CXVIII,[6] which forms twenty-two verses. (Each begins

---

6. CXIX in the Revised Version of the English Bible.

with a Hebrew letter, in alphabetical order, and is composed of eight lines which form twenty-two octaves).

It is difficult to find a single term that can give the significance for each of the twenty-two Numbers, or for each of the twenty-two letters of the sacred alphabets. This difficulty is because, as a symbol, each of these Numbers in its turn contains a whole bundle of ideas, bound together by a general idea that often escapes the mind that is still untrained in this contemplative research. For example, the number FIVE, in its ultimate generalization, signifies NUTRITION. Now, we have seen how complex is the process of nutrition.[7] The idea of nutrition is inseparable from that of food, and food, being physical, psychological and spiritual, can have either a sensory or an extrasensory nature. From this point of view, we can find all kinds of indications about Knowledge (*Savoir*), and Savoir-faire, in the study of the Number FIVE.

Clearly a mind that has not been accustomed to speculation of this kind will run a risk of getting lost in a labyrinth where no Ariadne's thread exists. This is why we give the above *Table of Major Numbers*, which views them from a *particular angle*: that of the study of Man in the midst of organic Life on Earth, and within the system of the three cosmic octaves.

When using this *Table*, the student should observe and take care not to forget that the Major Numbers, from I to XXI, form three octaves of seven notes. These three octaves, which form the *Major Triangle*, are in one sense included in a Whole represented by the Number XXII, which, in turn, is formed by the last inscribed polygon, which has 360 sides. Making allowances for the *principle of Imperfection*,[8] this polygon is almost identical to the Circle: almost, but not completely, otherwise we would find that the *Protocosmos* was completely stable. Then the *principle of Imperfection* would no longer apply, and Life as we can conceive it would cease.

When working with the aid of this Table the student must also not forget that the significance of the Major Numbers is given here in connection with the problems that are discussed in the Second Part of this volume. This means that it is only an *indication*. It is not *definitive*.

---

7. Vol. II, Chapter XI.
8. Vol. I, pp. 126–127, 130–131, 195, 242, 243, 245 and 246.

CHAPTER XII

(1)

Once again, we call the reader's attention to the essential difference between the usual meaning and the esoteric meaning of the idea of a symbol.

In general we can say that, in the first case, symbols are conventional signs. Anyone who has learned their meaning can decipher them. They are created by intellectual means, and anyone who knows the necessary code can decipher them by the same means. The meaning of symbols of this kind can be—and often is—hidden behind a *secret* figure like those used in diplomatic and military communications.

The meaning of even the finest and most subtle of these symbols does not go beyond the intellectual level, so that the student can grasp it without the need to undergo a profound transformation of his being. In addition, such a transformation in him would require more than the simple fact of this kind of *initiation*.

The same goes for someone who dedicates himself to scientific studies. However far he advances, he will find nothing changed in himself. He will remain as he was, good or bad, upright or deceitful, generous or avaricious, however important his discoveries or inventions in the scientific domain.

On the other hand, the understanding of esoteric symbols is the result of *revelations* given by divine grace, and this demands a progressive opening out, in quality and in strength, of adequate faculties latent in the student. One arrives at this through a tension of the will toward the goal of the search. When it is strong enough and properly oriented, this tension resolves itself in a series of partial revelations that are *acquired*, and which lead by stages toward those that are *given*.

These partial revelations can only be obtained through a *double* work which, on the one hand, calls for an ardent desire to discover — through this maximum tension of the will — the significance of the symbol being considered. On the other hand, it also demands a simultaneous and equal concentration of the seeker's mind in his inmost being, turned toward his 'I'. For this latter aspect of the work, the student who knows how to pray will fervently solicit the Light of Christ.

To be fruitful, these efforts must be founded on *Faith*, and they must be pursued in the attitude of *confident waiting* which is characteristic of *true will*. The support of Faith is absolutely indispensable to lead the pupil to achievement. A sceptical attitude, or even a Cartesian spirit, will close the door that was half-opened to the student through the *given revelation*.

This explains a maxim that seems paradoxical at first sight, but to which the Faithful in the early centuries frequently had recourse in their discussions with the Gentiles: '*If you do not believe, neither will you understand!*'

It is understood that every *acquired* revelation, even though partial, marks progress realized by the student in his search and, by this very fact, transforms his being in equal measure.

(2)

We can easily see now that, in the first case, there is a *secret initiation* giving access to conventional signs, and that this can form a scale with a whole series of degrees. In the second case there is no secret transmitted from one man to another through purely intellectual channels—nor one that can be kept or betrayed. It is an *initiation into a mystery*: a mystery that by its very nature is open to all, yet is accessible only to those who manage, through effective and generally difficult esoteric work, to raise the level of their being or, in other words, to augment their capacity to *contain* it.

Among other things, this is how we should interpret the following words of Jesus: '*All men cannot contain[1] this saying, save they to whom it is given.*' And further on: '*He that is able to contain it, let him contain it!*'[2]

II
(1)

As we have already indicated, the first of the three symbols that can be obtained from the Circle and the polygons is the *Pentagram*, or five-branched triple star. The study of this symbol-in-movement requires precise indication of the order in which the student's attention and his pen-point should pass from one to the other of the branch-points of the three stars through the intersections of the lines that form them. This is how our numbered Pentagram is drawn (fig. 8):

---

1. This word '*contain*' appears to be derived from the Slavonic Bible. In the King James Bible, all three words here translated '*contain*' are given as '*receive*'. (Ed.)

2. Matthew xix: 11, 12. From the Slavonic text.

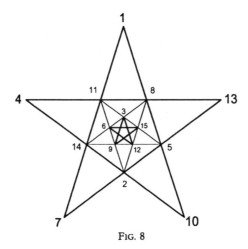

FIG. 8

The Pentagram numbered in this way was revealed by the author during the lectures he gave at the Faculty of Letters in the University of Geneva. It was also published in the *Summary* of these lectures.[3]

We have already said that this symbol, taken as a whole, reflects the real positions of the elements and forces that form the Third Cosmic Octave. The student should apply the meanings of the *Major Numbers* to the corresponding figures and study them from this point of view.

Here, he will come across the first difficulty: that of interpreting the terms characterizing each of the *Major Numbers*. In order to interpret them, he must specially train himself to think 'in harmony' and not 'in melody', if we may put it this way. In other words, instead of a chain of reasoning he should form a *bundle of ideas*, of which each section should present a harmonious chord.[4]

Then, and only then — keeping the meaning of the whole continually present in his mind — the succession of the figures as it is shown will enable him to make his thought and attention progress according to a precise order and so reach the desired goal.

Except in a few rare cases, as long as the student's mind has not attained the degree of training needed to enable him to pursue his research in an independent manner, this will require outside help. This is one reason why esoteric teaching has always included an oral Tradition that vivifies the Letter of the written Doctrine.

---

3. Boris Mouravieff, *Initiation à la Philosophie ésotérique*, according to the Oriental Orthodox Tradition. Summary of the lectures delivered at the Faculty of Letters of Geneva University during the period 1955–1958, Geneva, 1958–1959.

4. Fr. *accord*.

(2)

Here are the other two great cosmic symbols: the *Hexagram* and the *Octogram*:

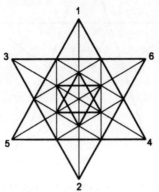

FIG. 9

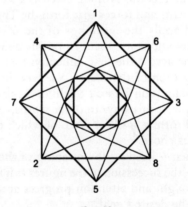

FIG. 10

III

(1)

In esoteric science, what are the meaning and practical usefulness of the three *cosmic Symbols*? The reply to this question may be contained in a few words: these symbols are the three great keys of the universal *Gnosis*, or *absolute Knowledge*.

This calls for a commentary.

The problem of absolute Knowledge is raised from time to time in writings dealing with esoteric questions or concerned with man's possibilities of attaining it. Apart from the Gospel, which attributes this Knowledge to Jesus and through Him to His Disciples, we may find a few careful allusions here and there in the *Philokalia* and in certain other early writings. Yet the specialized literature does not tackle the problem directly, but only gives vague hints about a few people belonging to the ancient world who are supposed to have possessed this kind of Knowledge. *Hermes Trismegistus, Pythagoras, Plato* and certain others are named in this context, but the student is not offered any practical means that could lead him to a solution of the problem.[5] Hardly any mention is made of King David or his 118th Psalm, which contains a concise yet precise exposé of the question; to our knowledge, only one authorized commentary exists on this Psalm: it is by Theophan the Recluse, whose writings we have quoted more than once.[6]

Let us now try to explain how the problem of *Gnosis*, in its integral expression, appears in the esoteric teaching of the Eastern Tradition.

(2)

It would be too naïve to think that the term *absolute Gnosis* refers to a simultaneous knowledge of the whole *Macrocosmos* on all its planes and in all its aspects, from the summit of the Holy Trinity right down to the last grain of sand on a dead planet, or to the faculty of keeping this Knowledge ever-present in one's mind. There is a very old formula describing *absolute Gnosis* that sometimes appears even in contemporary literature, with attributions to varying sources. It is as follows: '*Try to grasp what, when you learn something, will teach you all.*'[7] How should we interpret this maxim?

Let us make an analogy: a navigator knows how to steer his ship toward any point on the seas or oceans without having been there before. To learn how to do this, he studied the science of navigation, which combines several subjects, such as nautical astronomy; in addition, he learned the use of certain instruments, such as the compass, the sextant, the chronometer, the log, the lead, etc., which enable him to find his position. What is more, he has marine charts at his disposal, and a whole library where he

---

5. The reader who is familiar with the classical sources of Hinduism may remember Patanjali's treatise concerning the third great system of an orthodox nature, that of Yoga. In his *Sutras*, Patanjali tackles the problem directly and indicates the method, based on discipline of the psyche, for acquiring this absolute Knowledge. Cf. the *Sutras*, IV, 7, 8.

6. Psalm *One Hundred and Eighteen*, commented by Theophan the Recluse (in Russian) Moscow, University Press, 1880, 458 pp.

7. *The Golden Book*, cf. Vol. I, p. 253.

can find a detailed description of every corner of the seas, oceans, islands, of the coasts of continents, of the routes of access to all the gulfs, bays, roadsteads, ports, etc.

All these elements form the method of approaching the solution to each problem he encounters in his work. Strong in his knowledge and savoir-faire, this navigator, when he receives his captain's order, can make his plans and steer his ship to its destination by the shortest way, although he has never been there before.

The problem of *absolute Gnosis* is in some way analogous to the problem of navigation. In each case, it boils down to a method of approach that enables one to find a natural and absolute solution to the question posed.

The three Great cosmic Symbols, taken together, form a general library of maps that allow the objective classification of ideas, and give the references required to answer every question. For, as with navigation, it would be impossible and useless to collect and keep ever-present in the mind all the innumerable elements of the *absolute Gnosis*. It is sufficient to know how to tackle each particular problem by quickly finding an objective indication to its solution. In addition to the precise 'marine chart', the three Great cosmic Symbols provide us with a way of thinking 'gnostically', in an orderly manner, sheltered from deviations that would otherwise happen under the influence of the Law of Seven.

In the next chapter we will describe a general method — taken from the high tradition — for studying the properties of Numbers. This is a graphic method which makes it possible to find appropriate references for any situation in the different aspects of the three Great cosmic Symbols. Then, using this method, we will bring out whatever will make possible the practical study of the problems that concern us more closely, that is, those of adamic Man and pre-adamic or anthropoid Man, both of these being in the midst of organic Life on Earth and, with this, in the whole Universe in which we live.

CHAPTER XIII

(1)

E ver since ancient Egypt, scholars have pored over the properties of
numbers, especially the *Major Numbers*. From the study of these on
the banks of the Nile, a science developed which spread throughout
Greece with the mysteries of Orpheus and the teachings of Pythagoras
and Plato, and was introduced as part of the complete traditional Christian
Gnosis simultaneously with the Hellenic initiatory wisdom. This science
was confirmed by Jesus several times during his lifetime, and it was
enriched after the Resurrection by revelations made to the *Taborites*,
Peter, James and John. Transmitted orally from generation to generation, it is partly revealed today — in a measure appropriate to, and sufficient to fulfill, needs that have come to light simultaneously both on the
esoteric plane and on the public plane. These needs appear in the midst of
the Time of transition where humanity finds itself at present, which must
lead it either toward a happy outcome and the Era of the Holy Spirit, or
toward failure and the Deluge of Fire.

(2)

W e know that a knowledge of the properties of numbers is also an
objective of positive science, and that studies based on this subject
form an important and highly instructive branch of mathematics. However, these studies, interesting in themselves, are too abstract because they
are never viewed in a cosmic context.

Again, we remind the reader that in every scientific study, to achieve
concrete results, it is essential *to follow a plan that corresponds to the structure of
the object studied*. Considered from this angle, the contents of the preceding
chapters bring into relief a remarkable effort of the human mind, one that
has made possible the interception of divine revelations and their trans-
mission to posterity.

To conceive an idea of the system that is briefly described in the second
part of this volume, it is necessary to grasp and accept the fundamental idea
that the structure of all Creation, as a whole and in the smallest detail, is
based on Numbers. Linked with the principle just stated, this idea,
(whether revealed or acquired) has made it possible to take the study
of the properties of Numbers out of the domain of abstract speculation.

The system of the twenty-two equilateral inscribed polygons, from
which the XXII *Major Numbers* and the sacred alphabets were derived,

completed by the three Great Symbols (corresponding to the Three Cosmic Octaves), contains a summarized version of all the revelations and of all the results of the conscious efforts made by the ancient Sages, by the Apostles, and by their spiritual descendants.

The present description forms a whole, which *organically* corresponds to the cosmic structure seen from this angle: however succinct it may be, the elements it contains should be sufficient to allow valuable research to be carried out on any particular problem related to it.

This is not all: we still have to show the method that was employed in ancient times, which was first Hellenized, then Christianized, and was finally modernized by the application of the system of decimal fractions that was the result of the discovery of the Zero and of Arabic numbers.

(3)

In ancient times, to make a systematic study of the properties of Numbers, scholars had to resort to a geometric method, since algebraic ideas did not then exist.

This method is based on three fundamental elements: the *Circle*, symbol of Eternity, the *Law of Three* (of creation) and the *Law of Seven* (of functioning), and it requires a compass and a ruler as working instruments.

The reader of this work knows that all living creation begins from the *Law of Three* and is subject to the *Law of Seven*. He also knows that because of the application of the latter law to Creation by the will of the Absolute, the great Octave is completed by two elements intended to fill the intervals between the notes DO, SI, FA and MI respectively. However, he will now understand this divine artifice better. We have already given an explanation of it in the first two volumes of 'Gnosis' but we will repeat it here to emphasize the marvellous plan that enables everyone and everything to exist in space and in time:

a) to curve Time by means of the Law of Seven, giving it a cyclic nature to prevent 'Chronos from devouring his children,' at least, not immediately;

b) then to fill the intervals separating the notes DO and SI, FA and MI respectively by using the system of the Three Cosmic Octaves.

Thus completed, the Great Octave comprises *nine autonomous elements*: its seven notes and the two intervals, now filled. If, to close the cycle and reflect the natural cyclic process in the schema, we add the final DO, we arrive at *ten autonomous elements*.[1]

---

1. The decimal system was derived from this reasoning, which Pythagoras brought from Egypt to Greece.

Starting from there, the Ancients divided the circumference of the circle into nine equal parts. To each of these they attributed corresponding numbers from one to nine. Placed at the top of the circle, the Zero was covered by the number IX, as in the schema below:

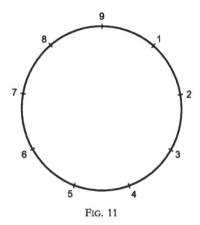

FIG. 11

It would be superfluous here to describe the way in which they reasoned in ancient times, when letters took the place of numbers.[2] The road they had to follow was much longer and less practical. Now, we will go on to explain the method in its modernized form.

(4)

Hidden behind the number IX in the schema above, the Zero represents the beginning and end of the cycle, the whole of which is characterized by the Major Number X, which signifies LIFE and VIBRATION, that is, movement that is itself cyclic.

At first it may be a little difficult to admit that every number represents a living being, but we could accept this idea easily if, instead, we regarded it as a *living symbol*. It is in this sense that we can say that every number, especially every Major Number, is much more that a conventional sign intended for some specific nomenclature or classification of facts and ideas. In addition to filling this role, a number that is correctly interpreted reveals the nature and process of Life, considered from the viewpoint to which it is *organically linked*.

---

2. Before decimal fractions were known, scholars were unable to approach these ideas in an algebraic way. (Tr.)

(5)

We have already had the opportunity to emphasize the well-known fact that the geometric method for expression of mathematical thought is much older than the algebraic method. We have also shown how, in the studies now presented, we follow the method in modernized form, although we have kept the ancient sequence of its logic unchanged. But we must be exact about the fact that — as one can easily understand — this 'modernization' is more than a millennium old.

The modernized geometric method of studying the properties of numbers was conceived and is carried out, for each number given, like a graphic operation that is applied to the basic schema (fig. 11). This is performed by following the figures that form the decimal fractions obtained by successive division of the numbers, starting from 1, 2, 3 ... etc. ... up to the number studied, which obviously closes the cycle, symbolizing the operation achieved by the formula:

$$x : x = 0.999999... = 1$$

For our esoteric research, special importance is attached to the properties of the two following Major Numbers:

XIII — DEATH

and VII — LIVING MATTER

These numbers symbolize the two great problems of Life, on whose solution depend the salvation of our Psyche (the Personality) on the individual plane, and, on the general plane, a happy outcome for the Time of transition and — in consequence — the fate of humanity as a whole.

In the next chapter we will analyse these two Major Numbers, using the method we have already explained.[3]

---

3. When applied to the study of the properties of different numbers, the application of the described method by the divisions indicated sometimes gives series which at first seem too short or far too long. To be of any value, their graphic interpretation must be made according to the very large general meaning of the number studied. This interpretation is not always easy; yet if properly handled it proves to be always correct.

CHAPTER XIV

(1)

Let us begin to study the two Major Numbers we have picked out, XIII and VII, in that order. These numbers characterize two great categories of human beings who coexist on our planet and constitute two *humanities* at the heart of organic Life on Earth.

In the first volume of 'Gnosis', we had already referred several times to this coexistence of two essentially different races: one of *Men*, and another of *Anthropoids*. We must emphasize the fact that from the esoteric point of view the latter term has no derogatory meaning.

First constated very long ago, this fact, although it has been distorted because it is generally seen in a false light, was part of the national, social and judicial consciousness of many ancient and modern peoples. One finds its influence in the Indian idea of the *Untouchable*, the Greek *Helot*, the Jewish *Goy*, the medieval European *white Bones* and *black Bones*, the German Nazi *Untermensch*, etc. ...

Incidentally, the legend of *blue blood* does not belong to the domain of pure fantasy. The error is not in the conception of blue blood as a 'psychosomatic' phenomenon, but in the naïve medieval belief that this so-called aristocratic blood passes automatically from father to son. Readers of 'Gnosis' will easily understand the reasons why this attribute can belong only to twice-born beings.

We must also note that the other extreme, the equalitarian conception of human nature, so dear to the theoreticians of democratic and socialist revolutions, is also erroneous: the only real equality of subjects by inner and international right is *equality of possibilities*, for men are born unequal.

(2)

The Scriptures contain more than one reference to the coexistence on our planet of these two humanities — which are now alike in form but unlike in essence. We can even say that the whole dramatic history of humanity, from the fall of Adam until today, not excluding the prospect of the New Era, is overshadowed by the coexistence of these two human races whose separation will occur only at the Last Judgment. It is to this that Jesus referred in parables when he spoke to the crowds, but described in clear terms for the benefit of his disciples; the most noteworthy description is the parable of the *tares* and the *good seed,*[1] on which he made the following commentary when asked to do so by his disciples:

'*He that soweth the good seed is the Son of man: the field is the world: the good seed are the children of the kingdom: but the tares are the children of the wicked one: the enemy that sowed them is the devil: the harvest is the end of the world.*'[2]

Jesus then added:

'*... every scribe which is instructed unto the kingdom of heaven is like unto a man that is a householder, which bringeth forth out of his treasure things old and new.*'[3]

The coexistence of a race of Anthropoids and a race of Men, confirmed here, is necessary, from the point of view of the General Law, to maintain uninterrupted the *stability in movement* of organic life on Earth.

It is also necessary because of the Principle of Equilibrium. The first race is a counterbalance which allows the race of Men to pursue its esoteric evolution. Jesus confirmed this when He spoke about the End in the following terms:

'*Then, shall two be in the field; the one shall be taken, and the other left. Two women shall be grinding at the mill; the one shall be taken, and the other left.*'[4]

These words call for comment: tares grow without having to be cultivated. Good seed, on the other hand, demands a great deal of care if it is to bear fruit: the land has to be ploughed, fertilized, the seed sown carefully, and the soil harrowed, etc., and even so, if the crops are not harvested but left where they grow, not one sheaf of wheat will be left at the end of a few years, as the tares, which grow naturally from the Earth, stifle the wheat and barley, which are fruits of heavenly cultivation.[5]

(3)

The human tares, the anthropoid race, are the descendants of pre-adamic humanity. The principal difference between contemporary pre-adamic man and adamic man — a difference which is not perceived by the senses — is that the former does not possess the developed higher centres that exist in the latter which, although they have been cut off from his waking consciousness since the fall, offer him a real possibility of esoteric evolution. Apart from this, the two races are similar: they have the same lower centres, the same structure of the Personality and the same physical body, although more often than not this is stronger in pre-adamic

---

1. Matthew xiii: 24–30.

2. Ibid., 37–39.

3. Ibid., 52, according to the Slavonic text.

4. Matthew xxiv: 40, 41.

5. It appears that these cereals do not exist in a natural or wild form. Similarly the eglantine, for example, when cultivated properly, becomes a rose. (In fact, wild barley does exist, but it is true that the cultivated varieties do not survive neglect. Ed.)

man than in the adamic; regarding beauty, we must not forget that pre-adamic man and woman were created by God on the sixth day, in His image and after His likeness,[6] and that the daughters of this race were particularly beautiful.[7]

II

(1)

N ow let us return to the proposed study of the Major Numbers XIII and VII.

By applying the method already described to the first of these two numbers we obtain the following series:

$$1 : 13 = 0.076923...$$
$$2 : 13 = 0.153846...$$
$$3 : 13 = 0.230769...$$
$$4 : 13 = 0.307692...$$
$$5 : 13 = 0.384615...$$
$$6 : 13 = 0.461538...$$
$$7 : 13 = 0.538461...$$
$$8 : 13 = 0.615384...$$
$$9 : 13 = 0.692307...$$
$$10 : 13 = 0.769230...$$
$$11 : 13 = 0.846153...$$
$$12 : 13 = 0.923076...$$
$$13 : 13 = 0.999999...$$

We may notice that the decimal fractions flowing from this series of operations are of two different initial types:

$$1)\ 0.076923...$$
$$\text{and } 2)\ 0.153846...$$

and although they are derived from different numbers, the fractions below contain the same figures, and these follow each other in the same order. This, as we will see in a moment, gives birth to two independent figures within the circle (fig. 12).

If we mark the first series by the letter x and the second by the letter y, we obtain the following perfectly balanced formula for the whole group of the first twelve fractions:

$$x + y + 2x + 4y + 2x + y + x$$

which comprises 6 x and 6 y in all, of which the values are:

$$6x = 2.999999...$$

---

6. Genesis i: 26, 27.
7. Genesis vi: 2.

$$6y = 2.999999\ldots$$

from which:

$$6x + 6y = 5.999999\ldots$$

that is, at the limit, 6.

If we now add the thirteenth fraction of the above series:

$$13 : 13 = 0.999999\ldots = 1$$

we obtain:

$$6 + 1 = 7$$

or, according to the transcription allowed for the Major Numbers:

$$VI + I = VII$$

(2)

T reated in the same way as the number XIII, analysis of the number VII gives the following series:

$$1 : 7 = 0.142857\ldots$$
$$2 : 7 = 0.285714\ldots$$
$$3 : 7 = 0.428571\ldots$$
$$4 : 7 = 0.571428\ldots$$
$$5 : 7 = 0.714285\ldots$$
$$6 : 7 = 0.857142\ldots$$
$$7 : 7 = 0.999999\ldots$$

We may notice that when it is analysed in the same way as the number XIII, a series of six fractions of a single type flows from the number VII, each composed of the same figures. They occur in a different order, yet always in the same sequence. If we mark each fraction with the letter z, their total is found to be:

$$6z = 2.999999\ldots$$

from which:

$$6z = 6x, \text{ just as}$$
$$6z = 6y$$

On the other hand, at the limit, the $6z$ will form the number 3; and if we add the value of the seventh fraction of the series:

$$7 : 7 = 0.999999\ldots = 1$$

we obtain

$$3 + 1 = 4$$

or, according to the transcription allowed for the *Major Numbers*:

$$III + I = IV$$

(3)

Before passing on to interpret the results we have obtained in this way, let us inscribe the twelve first fractions derived from the number 13 and the six first fractions from the number 7 in the circle that was divided earlier (fig. 11):

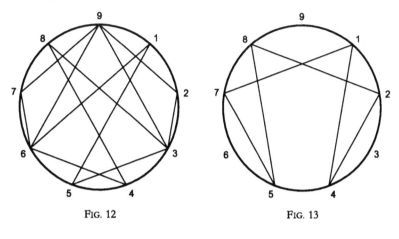

FIG. 12   FIG. 13

III

(1)

The Major Number XIII, which, when analysed, gave us the following equation:

$$VI + I = VII$$

describes the law to which *living Matter* (VII) is subject, created to form the physical and psychological bodies of creatures of every species at the different degrees of the cosmic scale. In the present case, it forms the bodies of those creatures which form organic Life on Earth.

Thus, the existence of bodies of all species (I) is ensured by the law of perpetual renewal (VI), that is, by the interplay of the two extremes: of birth and death. During its ephemeral existence, the principal biological characteristic of living matter is the capacity to absorb and assimilate mineral, vegetable and animal elements through the equally ephemeral process of *Nutrition*, and eject the residue.

Since the different species are nourished on elements as ephemeral as themselves, although on a different scale, we will see that the process of renewal has two aspects: on the one hand, living matter eats in order to exist, on the other it is also eaten in its turn, in some way or other, in the great cycle of *cosmic Nutrition* of which we have already spoken.[8]

This law, in which matter exists in time through the perpetual renewal of species and devours while waiting to be devoured, is common to the three notes LA, SOL and FA of the Second cosmic Octave. Together, these notes make up organic Life on Earth, and in the midst of this pre-adamic man, the creature of the VIth Day, finds the place assigned to him by this law in the note LA, while his psyche derives from the note SI.

But Adam was not created on the VIth Day, at the same time as pre-adamic man and the animals. The Book of Genesis tells us that he was created on the VIIIth Day, after God had consecrated the VIIth to His rest.[9] The process of his creation was not simple, as with the man of the VIth Day. Like the latter, Adam was *created* first, and *conceived* later. As far as his hylic body was concerned, he was *created* in the note LA, but of a light matter — the dust of the ground. His psychological body was also *created* — this was in the note SI. But his pneumatic body was *conceived* in the Ψ, through direct contact with the Absolute II, from which he received the *Breath of Life*, the divine essence that dominates ephemeral life and, according to the Scriptures, turns it into a *living Soul*.[10] This is added to his hylic substance and that of his psyche, both of them of a higher nature, although still *human*. This process, accomplished by means of the higher centres of consciousness through which Adam was linked with the *mind (intelligence) of Christ*,[11] is symbolized by the Major Number VII.[12]

The analysis of the latter Number led to the formula:

$$III + I = IV$$

in this the Major Number IV intervenes as the Love of the Androgyne, which is therefore *integral in its perpetual vibration*. It acts through the *Breath of Life*, the emanation of the Love of the Absolute II that Adam received in the Ψ of the Second cosmic Octave. Doubled by the feminine Love (III) of Eve, who had been created from him and not outside him, the Androgynous ADAM–EVE represented the true and complete Microcosmos, called on to form a higher human race — a race of *Sons of God*,[13] or leaders responsible for the development of organic Life on Earth according to the *divine Plan of Creation*. This race, because of its particular nature, was not intended to participate in animal reproduction, nor in the alternating sequence of birth and death.

---

8. Vol. I., p. 135, fig. 47. Vol. II, p.119, fig. 9.
9. Genesis, ii: 2.
10. Genesis, ii: 7 (from the Slavonic text).
11. 1 Corinthians ii: 16 (from the Slavonic text).
12. We will notice that this passage from the narrative of Genesis appears in Chapter II, in verse 7.
13. Luke xvi: 8.

(2)

I n the next chapter we will come back to the question of the coexistence of the two human races *before* and *after* the Fall. For the moment, let us try to grasp the esoteric symbolism of the Major Numbers XIII and VII from the practical point of view.

If we now refer to figures 12 and 13, we will notice that the physiology of adamic man before the Fall was essentially different from that of the creatures of the VIth Day of Creation, pre-adamic man included. Whereas God had willed for these creatures an ephemeral existence, subject to the law of birth and death so that the interval between FA and MI of the Great Octave could be filled, Adam, the man of the VIIIth Day, was created and conceived under the law of permanence to which the breath of life received from the Absolute II entitled him.

In other words, whereas pre-adamic man was provided with only one nature, a human essence, adamic man was endowed with a dual nature: one part *human* but superior, coming from the finest expression of the notes LA and SI, and the other *divine*, coming from the Ψ or breath of God.

Incidentally, we may note that this throws light on the Christian dogma of the dual nature of Jesus Christ.[14] As the Son of Man in the midst of a corrupt and degenerate mixed humanity, the Son of God represented the *New Adam*, the perfect prototype of adamic man before the Fall, possessing in full and manifesting the *eight powers* that enable one to dominate the nature of things.[15] Simultaneously, the deeper meaning of the word 'Gospel' is unveiled — the *Good News*, the written record of the divine revelation which offers corrupted adamic man a practical possibility of Redemption.

IV

(1)

W e will better understand now that figures 12 and 13 form two *Ennea-grams*. One (fig. 12), which we will call Enneagram 'A', refers to pre-adamic man; the other (fig. 13), which we will call Enneagram 'B', refers to adamic man — to the Adam formed 'of the *dust of the ground*,' as he was before receiving the *Breath of Life*.

---

14. (A dogma of considerable importance in the Eastern church. Ed.)
15. Cf. Vol. II, pp. 240.

Made of fine matter,[16] Adam's body was terrestrial, but the psyche was its dominant side—in this way it was different from the body of pre-adamic man, in whom the hylic side was dominant. Consequently, Adam's body was of a simpler structure than that of the Man of the VIth Day—a fact which stands out clearly when we compare the two enneagrams. But as well as its terrestrial nature, Adam's lighter body received the Breath of Life, a supernatural gift that is represented by an *independent* addition to the Enneagram 'B', derived from the first analysis of the Major Number VII. This addition, which expresses in esoteric terms the penetration of the divine breath into Adam's body, takes the form of a *Triangle* whose three vertices are placed at points 3, 6 and 9 of the circumference—points that are vacant in Enneagram 'B'.

Completed in this way, the figure appears like this:

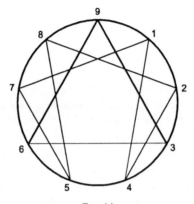

FIG. 14

We will immediately observe that without this *Triangle*, and so without *breath*, neither Adam nor any other adamic man would have been able to exist. Although simple and fine, the *natural* Enneagram 'B', when it is without the triangle, does not contain the necessary elements for even an ephemeral existence; this is why God put His *breath* into Adam's body as soon as He had formed it of fine matter—the *dust of the ground*. For in the original divine plan, adamic man, produced from the Ψ of the Second

---

16. When studying the Holy Scriptures, one must never forget that their object was to express sublime truths in the language of the times, and with ideas that were accessible to the intellects of that time. It is possible to speak of 'fine Hydrogens' or of 'fine Matter' to the readers of 'Gnosis', but to translate the same ideas into the language of those times, Moses used the expression 'dust of the ground' because the men of that day considered this dust as the finest element on earth. For the same reason, when he addressed 'exterior' men, Jesus said, the sun which 'rises' and which 'sets', but to His disciples who were already far ahead in their evolution, he said: '*I stand in the centre of the Cosmos*' (Thomas, Log. 28, Ibid. pp. 19, 89, 20), that is, at the level of the note SOL of the Great Octave.

cosmic Octave and from the finer layers of the notes LA and SI, was supposed to live under the rule of the law of permanence.

Pre-adamic man was intended for a purely ephemeral existence, and even this would not have been possible without the triangle 3-6-9. As we can see in Enneagram 'A', two sides of this triangle, 3-9 and 6-9, were already naturally derived from the analysis of the Major Number XIII: only the side 3-6, the base of this incomplete triangle, was missing. This base was added artificially, that is, from the outside — just as was the whole triangle for Adam — but this time, it was not by a direct breath from God, jointly communicated by the Absolute I and the Absolute II — '*I and my Father are one*,' said Jesus[17] — but by the Absolute III, or Sathanael, making Sex and the force of earthly Love contribute to this end.

(2)

This difference between the triangles inscribed in the two Enneagrams is full of esoteric significance. Before the fall, adamic man was an *Individuality*, thanks to the breath received directly from God. He was truly placed at the level of man seven, and in any case, he was immortal. After the fall, identified with his Personality and enclosed in a body that was becoming coarser, he became mortal.[18] Yet he retained in latent form the power to 'redeem' himself, especially after the redemptive work of Jesus Christ, who came to announce the *Good News* to him and to reveal the possibility of his becoming an Individuality again by mastering first his Personality, then his body, and finally, by the Second Birth, regaining his original immortality in the bosom of the Lord.

Thus, although adamic man in his corrupt condition — that state that is generally falsely considered as 'normal' — has become a Personality like the pre-adamic, he still remains an Individuality because of the Breath he received. But he is only an Individuality in potential, and his real goal in life, which is the objective of esoteric work, is to realize this potential.

(3)

Pre-adamic man was never an Individuality. Created as a Personality on the VIth Day, he is deprived of every possibility of *direct*, 'individual'

---

17. John x: 20.

18. In the early years after the fall, adamic man lived several centuries. According to the Bible, this longevity progressively diminished until it stopped at an average age of 80 years, (which became the normal span). It is interesting to note that during the period immediately following the fall, reproduction took place only a short time before the death of the patriarchs. One is led to believe that this subordination to reproduction, which became equally obligatory for adamics after the fall, was the direct cause of their mortality.

individuation—if one may put it thus—for his existence was placed under the law of *collective Individuation*, which is governed by the Absolute III with the aid of a whole hierarchy of spirits who are subject to his authority. This hierarchy forms an octave and, seen from below, is composed of the spirits of hearth and home (the couple and their children), of the family (brothers, sisters, uncles, aunts, nephews, nieces and first cousins), of the *folk*, of the tribe, of the nation, of the caste, of the race, and, in the lateral octaves, of the spirit of corporation and corps, and of the spirit of different clans and orders, of the spirit of snobbery and still more.

V

(1)

We will now describe the two symbols relating to pre-adamic and adamic man respectively, as they are taught in the Tradition. First, let us take Enneagram 'A':

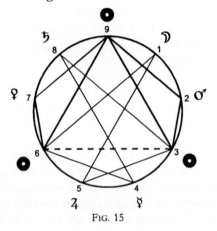

FIG. 15

Then Enneagram 'B': (fig 16, opposite)
The reader may notice that in both cases the symbol is accompanied by the astrological signs that later passed into astronomy. While, in Enneagram 'B', the three suns are white as they symbolize the *suns of the seeing*, in the Enneagram 'A', where they symbolize the *suns of the blind*, they are black.

For the moment, we will leave Enneagram 'A' aside, and make our principal commentaries on Enneagram 'B'. The latter interests us most, since it symbolizes adamic man, who, even in his present corrupt condition, is capable of esoteric progress.

We know that in most western languages the sun — situated at the top point of the Enneagram, and the six ancient planets, have given their

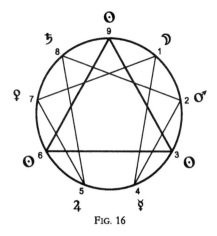

FIG. 16

names, slightly modified, to the days of the week. In Latin, the succession of terms is perfect:

Dies Solis
Dies Lunae
Dies Martis
Dies Mercuris
Dies Jovis
Dies Veneris
Dies Saturni

The traditional syllables that designate the musical notes also show their connection with the Great Octave,[19] which shows clearly that the Enneagram preserved in the Tradition was well-known in ancient times.

Enneagram 'A' is a symbol with limited significance, confined to the organic Life of soma and psyche on Earth, vegetable, animal and human; Enneagram 'B', whose place is in the centre of the Cosmos, is a universal symbol. It has a multitude of aspects and meanings that it would be vain to try to describe in detail, for as St John said, even the world itself could not contain all the books that could be written on this subject. Besides, such a work would be of little use, since Enneagram 'B', which contains the whole *Gnosis*, provides a kind of *universal instrument* that enables us to penetrate everything, providing, of course, that one uses it correctly in the search for Knowledge and Savoir-Faire. For example, without a single exception, all the schemata which appear in the volumes of 'Gnosis' are derived from it, and, conversely, each of them reflects one or other of its aspects.

The Enneagram has many other aspects, each of which can provide the elements for one or more esoteric symbols. The traditional esoteric

19. Vol. I, pp. 90, 91.

teaching is not concerned with the detailed description or commentary on these aspects or symbols, but with showing disciples how to use the universal instrument, provided in the Enneagram, as a way of solving problems they are considering, whether these concern *being* or *action*.

(2)

W e will now give the reader of 'Gnosis' an idea of that aspect of this symbol which is most necessary for the kind of esoteric work described in the present volume.[20] This aspect is the one which determines the transmutation of Hydrogens in the organism of adamic man, whether perfect or corrupt.

In both cases the symbol is the same. The only difference in the second case is with the application — following its loss by forgetting or by mental laziness — of the capacity to bring into play at a chosen moment *the two conscious and voluntary shocks* that ensure the complete functioning of the symbol, and consequently of the whole body, psyche, and pneumatic organism of the adamic man 1, 2 or 3. This allows him to free himself of his corrupt condition. For man 4, other aspects of Enneagram 'B' become immediate and necessary: they will be revealed to him directly parallel to his evolutionary progress through the VIIIth, IXth and Xth stages of the Way, represented by the notes MI, RE and DO which correspond to his progressive initiation to the levels of Man 5, 6 and 7.[21]

(3)

L et us now study Enneagram 'B' in that aspect which governs the transmutation of the hydrogens in the organism of adamic man — 1, 2 or 3 — according to the three scales of nutrition that the reader of 'Gnosis' already knows.[22]

---

20. The readers of 'Gnosis' may consult the *Stromata* for other aspects of the two Enneagrams. (This refers to planned additional publications which were never completed before Mouravieff's death. Ed.)

21. Vol. I, p. 216, Vol II, p. 249.

22. Vol. II, Chapter XI.

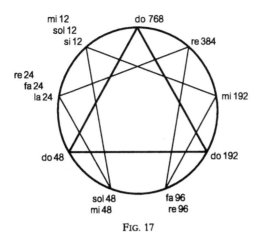

FIG. 17

In the Tradition, the lighter line 1-4-2-8-5-7 ... etc. is called the *Line of Periodicity*. Every *organic* cyclic movement evolves following the law expressed by the succession of these Major Numbers, and at the end of each stage in turn, the following stage is assigned to these same Numbers. Everything in this *cosmic Symbol* is full of significance: the circumference as a whole, the three great arcs and the 3 x 3 = 9 subordinate arcs; the inscribed figures and their sides as *chords*; all the points of intersection of the lines inside the circle; all the geometrical connections between the whole lines and their subdivisions, and this in every direction. The whole should be visualized starting from the 9 points of the circumference and the 7 + 7 + 1 inner points of intersection, which makes 9 + 7 + 7 + 1 = 24, a number which signifies DESIRE and is derived from RENEWAL (2 + 4 being equal to VI).

After what we have just said, the reader will understand that a complete description of this symbol, with the necessary commentaries, would be of practically no use. This is why the traditional esoteric teaching confines itself to *ad hoc* commentaries that are introduced according to need. For the rest, disciples are taught how to make use of this symbol as a tool enabling them to make certain analyses or syntheses methodically, in strict conformity with cosmic laws.

We will continue our study of Enneagram 'B' from the point of view of the transmutation of Hydrogens in the process of adamic man's nutrition on the three planes: hylic, psychic and pneumatic.

If we divide the series 1-4-2-8-5-7 into two parts, one part 1-4-2 and the other 8-5-7, we will obtain two groups of numbers which determine two large complexes of organs whose totality constitutes the complete organism of organic man viewed in terms of his hylic, psychic and pneumatic functions.

We may recall that each of the nine points of the circumference of the Enneagram corresponds to a number, from 1-9, which indicates its sequential order, to an astrological sign, and to one or several notes. These are accompanied by the numbers specifying the seven groups of Hydrogens, and it is these that maintain the vibratory movements of the organs of adamic man at the different rates needed to ensure the integral expression of the phenomenon of life in him. This is the general meaning of Enneagram 'B', which is the cosmic symbol appropriate to 'terrestrial-celestial' adamic man. The scale of Hydrogens that relates to this contains six degrees, from H 768 to H 12, and we must not forget that the *Zero*, with the Hydrogen 6 that corresponds to it, is hidden behind the number 9.

This aspect of the Enneagram deals with adamic man in his terrestrial and celestial constitution. It would be different if we were visualizing other cosmic entities superior to man, of which there are only two big groups in the Cosmos;[23] here, the geometric outline of the symbol would remain the same. Neither the figures showing the order of the points, nor the notes would change, but the astrological signs and the type-substances of the Hydrogens would be different.[24]

(4)

The first big complex of organs, governed by the series 1-4-2 and the notes RE-FA-MI, consists of the three groups of organs of the human body that ensure, respectively, the digestion[25] – RE, the circulation – FA, and the respiration – MI. The order in which these three notes of the first octave of nutrition[26] have been taken corresponds to that of the first three figures of the decimal fraction 0.142857... and indicates the course followed in the organism by the transmutation of the fine matters: H384 — H96 — H192. At first sight, this seems paradoxical. To understand the process better, the reader should refer to chapter XI of the second volume of 'Gnosis'. He will then see that the transmutation of Hydrogens takes place according to several parallel processes, some of which follow the circumference of the Enneagram in numerical order, while the others, in the epicyclic sequence, continue by using previously accumulated reserves of Hydrogens. Here a group of *linear* transmutation processes follows the numerical order: RE H 384 — MI H 192 — FA H 96, while another group follows an *epicyclic* course: RE H 384 — FA H 96 —

---

23. Cf. Vol. II, Ch. VII, fig. 3.
24. Cf. Vol. II, Ch. X, p. 115: the three scales of hydrogen.
25. This term should be interpreted in its widest sense, going beyond the common notion of metabolism (anabolism and catabolism) as well as basal metabolism.
26. Cf. Vol. II, Ch. XI, fig. 10.

MI H 192 which, in a healthy human organism, ensures the balanced functioning of the groups of organs in question.

We may say, *roughly*, that in a certain sense the three groups of organs governed by the figures 1-4-2 and the notes RE-FA-MI of the first octave of nutrition together form the instrument for the Hydrogen-*producing* transmutation. In a normal healthy organism, whose activity reaches *optimum*, the note FA 96 gives out a clear and powerful *sound*. Hydrogen FA 96 is the animal magnetism which radiates in the interior of the organism as the *fire of the blood*, and passes out to the exterior through the skin, after which it obeys the law that governs all radiating energy. It is important for every man — and even more so for every student of *Gnosis* — to closely observe the way his FA 96 'behaves', for if the disciple is to cross the First Threshold easily and embark on the Staircase with any chance of success, its resonance must have both purity and strength.

(5)

The three groups of organs governed by the three other figures of the decimal fraction 0.142857… that is, 8-5-7, and by the notes of the first octave with the Hydrogens that correspond to them: SI 12, SOL 48 and LA 24, form a second ensemble within which the transmutation continues, but its output of fine energies is destined to be expended rather than accumulated. This definition, however, is made with certain reservations. It demands circumspection, as we must not forget that this concerns an organism and not a mechanism. In the first group, the transmutations are almost exclusively intended for internal use: only the surplus Hydrogen H 96 radiates to the outside. In the second group, however, a great part of the energies produced, above the minimum required to maintain the physical body in good condition, serve the psychic life of the 'I'. This is how the energy SOL 48 serves as matter for thought, while the energy LA 24 makes the motor and lower emotional centres function—the former completely and the latter in part, that is, only the negative part. Lastly, the sexual group is activated in its direct functions by the energy SI 12.

But we must not forget, here or elsewhere, that this transmutation also has a direct or linear path: SOL 48 — LA 24 — SI 12; and an epicyclic path that begins from previously accumulated reserves of energy SI 12, and that it is also subject to an indirect pressure coming from the breath. This epicyclic sequence, which follows the line 8-5-7, goes from SI 12 to SOL 48 and from SOL 48 to LA 24. When reserves of LA 24 energy begin to fall below a certain level, we feel hunger. At that moment a certain quantity of this energy is projected to RE 384, to give it the impetus that will set it moving and, through adequate glandular secretions, will make it prepare the organism for the absorption and digestion of food.

(6)

The transmutation of the Hydrogens in this first octave can continue beyond SI 12 in two ways: ordinary and extraordinary. The ordinary, direct transmutation of SI 12 into DO 6 takes place in a natural way in the normal sexual act, which fills the interval between these two notes. When the act ends, the transmutation is completed by conception, where, united in the genetic orgasm, the male SI 12 and the female SI 12 conceive a new, independent embryonic life, which will follow its own way and develop through a descending scale.

In the second case, the extraordinary transmutation, all the surplus SI 12 energy, which is ejected from the organism for the price of the pleasure obtained by carnal love, can be accumulated in the organism and undergo an internal transmutation.

This extraordinary transmutation is indirect. It does not take place in an instinctive, natural way, as with conception. It can only result from the conscious efforts of those who are progressing on the Staircase and have attained the third step. We will come back to this important question in more detail toward the end of the present volume. For the moment we will leave aside the question of 'how', and will only describe the alchemical technique of the process.

Like the first, this second mode of transmutation has three stages, which we can regard as analogous to *betrothal, marriage*, and *conception*. It is true that we are still dealing with Love, but here it acts on the higher plane of the *Courtly Love* that unites the Knight with the Lady of his dreams.

During the first stage of this Love, instead of being ejected from the physical and psychic organisms of the man and woman, the energy SI 12 is preserved in them both by being associated laterally with SOL 12, the fifth note of the octave of respiration.

The happy climax of this process is felt like an irresistible sexual attraction, but of a higher, purely psychic order, and the fresh energy of the SI 12, uniting *synchronously* with SOL 12 in the two organisms, communicates a new impetus to the latter; the couple feel a wave of high *inspiration* flowing through them and opening up surprising perspectives.

Apart from very rare cases, the couple — the Knight and his Lady — realize this state of higher inspiration only after they have practised courtly Love for a more or less prolonged period; for only courtly Love can provoke this new impulse that comes from SI 12 turned towards their interior. This is because the SOL 12 is already the fifth note of the respiratory gamut, so that the loss of charge at this distance, in the 'fallen' condition of the couple, is such that it barely responds any more. But, under the effect of this powerful impetus coming from the SI 12, the couple experience a union of the psyche which can be compared with nothing else, a foretaste of the androgynous consciousness. In this way the Knight and his Lady reach the stage of the mystical *betrothal* and receive a benediction from Above through the mediation of the higher emotional Centre.

If the couple attains the desired degree of emotional tension through courtly Love practiced in this way, the SOL 12, aroused by the strength of the SI 12, will communicate an inflow of energy to MI 12, the third note of the octave of impressions. Keeping in mind the epicyclic currents, the reader will understand the power of this *triple* Hydrogen 12 that comes from the two sexes and combines in itself the SI 12s, the SOL 12s, and the MI 12s, all three vibrating fully in both partners.

The successful unfolding of this process can provoke a state where the masculine and feminine energies coming from the SI 12, aided in both the man and the woman by two other Hydrogens 12, unite in an ecstasy — in the consciousness of their bipolar real 'I', which is ONE and indivisible for the two elements of the couple.

In this way the *marriage* of the psyche, which is the crowning of courtly Love, is consummated: after this, the Knight and his Lady will be forever fused together in their androgynous consciousness, whatever the outer circumstances and even in spite of death. On the *Fifth Way*, this is the first tangible result obtained through a sustained and conscious effort for the sublimation of sex.

(7)

It is necessary to state here that the sublimation of sex is not an aim in itself, but a means. It has four degrees, of which the three that follow the ecstasy of the mystical marriage appear in an order opposite to that in which courtly Love had led the couple to the androgynous consciousness. The second is the synergic and synchronous passage from MI 12 to FA 6 in both the man and the woman, a passage which is instantaneous and has an effect analogous to *conception*. The third degree is the passage from SOL 12 to LA 6 which happens gradually and demands time: we can compare this with the stage of *pregnancy*; lastly, if nothing happens to stop the process, the couple reach the fourth degree, the simultaneous passage from SI 12 to DO 6: this is the *Birth*, the *Third Birth* which, with the crossing of the Third Threshold, opens up the way that will lead the Knight and the Lady of his thoughts towards the empyrean of the *Pleroma*.

(8)

It is easier to understand now why it is such an error for the evolved adamic man and woman who have reached the third Step of the Staircase and are about to climb the fourth, that of Love, to continue to eject the SI 12 energy from their organisms for the sake of ephemeral pleasure, when its accumulation, its mastery, and its judicious orientation toward the act of courtly Love, can open the door to the lost Paradise for them.

The reader may now also understand the deep meaning of *platonic Love*, something that is so often misinterpreted.

VI

(1)

To outline the possibilities for the transmutation of higher Hydrogens within the organism of adamic men and women, we have already in a small way anticipated our explanation. But now let us return to the study of the evolution of the gamut of respiration with the aid of the Enneagram. We have already seen[27] that without the intervention of DO 192, the evolution of the first octave of nutrition will not go beyond the level of MI 192. If respiration stops, the death of the organism follows, and the first act of the newborn is the cry that begins the process of respiration which is the affirmation of life. But to activate the MI 192, the DO 192 must surrender a part of its energy to it. Now, in spite of the weakening effect this has on the latter, it must still give an impetus to the evolution of its own gamut. In the case where living conditions are natural, that is, where we work in the open air — an air that is pure and rich — and where our muscles are well exercised, the circulation will be stimulated so that the quantity of DO 192 energy introduced into the organism with the breath will be enough to meet both needs in full. But when we live in the conditions of a 'civilized' life, which is an unhealthy way of life from all points of view—especially in towns—respiration is generally incomplete and uses polluted air, so that the amount of DO 192 energy taken in is far from adequate. For the same reasons, because of the bad quality of our food, the first gamut of nutrition is inadequately developed, so that the motor centre must draw additional DO 192 energy from the breath to alleviate the chronic shortage of MI 192. This even further reduces the transmutation of the Hydrogens passing through the gamut of the breath, which is already very much below the normal level. Adamic man in his corrupt state no longer knows how to actively draw the energy DO 48 from his

---

27. Vol. II, p. 121, 122.

impressions. This energy is intended to fill the interval between MI 48, the energy of active thought, and FA 24, the energy of attention, which are both practically exhausted every day. This means that adamic man can never accumulate a sufficient reserve of the energy SOL 12 to pass spontaneously to LA 6 following the linear steps of the transmutation of Hydrogens.

The epicyclic movement between the three groups of organs takes place in the order 8-5-7, that is, SOL 12—MI 48—FA 24. Obviously, with this chronic deficiency of SOL 12, this movement does not bring any substantial aid. Yet the epicyclic action of SOL 12 is necessary to activate the third gamut of nutrition, that of impressions. By communicating a complementary impulse to MI 48 and FA 24, SOL 12 creates the conditions necessary for a man to pass to the practice of constatation of his own impressions—an *indispensable* condition for DO 48 to begin to act. The transmutation of the Hydrogens can then begin: from DO 48 it passes without difficulty to RE 24, then from RE 24 to MI 12; once there, it stops before the interval that separates MI 12 from FA 6. We have already seen how this stage in the transmutation of Hydrogens can become active through the practice of courtly Love on the Fifth Way.

(2)

It follows that the disciple who wishes to connect his higher centres with his waking consciousness must possess a vigorous and healthy organism, and must be in conditions where he can obtain the best food and air to breathe, and will be nourished with abundant impressions of good quality. Besides this, he must produce in his organism a sufficient quantity of Hydrogen 12 and Hydrogen 6 — one being of a different shade[28] from the other. We must underline the fact that we can never obtain this result in a *natural* way; it is necessary to make sustained and conscious efforts oriented towards:

a) The constatation of one's everyday impressions, and above all, those that flow from the relationship uniting the Knight and the Lady of his thoughts in courtly Love — (first *voluntary shock*).

b) The redirection of the SI 12 sexual energy produced through the sexual attraction felt by the couple, from the act of carnal love to that of courtly Love — (second *voluntary shock*).

In the third part of the present volume, which is dedicated to the LIFE, that is, to real life, we will give a few indications that will enable the disciple to make a practical approach to this double, and doubly vital, problem.

---

28. The French is *nuance*, which in the context appears to refer to the fact that the Hydrogen 12 and Hydrogen 6 are derived from different sources. (Ed.)

(3)

The complete design of Enneagram 'B' includes certain indications placed around the circumference. Besides the numbers from 1 to 9, these are the notes of the three octaves of nutrition, the cosmic atomic weight of the Hydrogens corresponding to them, and the astrological signs corresponding to these octaves. In order not to overcrowd figure 17, we have marked all these indications on a separate schema reproduced below, but we must point out to our readers that, in their meditations, they should study figures 17 and 18 *together* and superimposed.

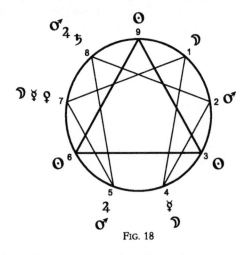

FIG. 18

Again we emphasize that this symbol, even in this form and with the commentary just given, is far from complete. However, it is an adequate working instrument for any experienced and diligent *student of Gnosis*. It will enable the seeker who meditates deeply on problems which preoccupy him to discover the treasures that are so carefully hidden in it. In this, the reader must not forget the maxim inscribed in the *Golden Book*:

Gnosis has to be conquered![29]

---

29. Cf. Matthew xi: 12. (Ed.)

THIRD PART
THE LIFE

CHAPTER XV

(1)

B y identifying himself with the 'I' of his Personality, Adam lost consciousness of his real 'I' and fell from the Eden that was his original condition into the same condition as the pre-adamics. Before the fall, the adamics came under the sole authority of the Absolute II, and they played their part in the note SI under the impulse of the ψ of the second cosmic octave.[1] The two humanities, coming from the two different creative processes, later mingled on the level of organic life on Earth, which comes under the authority of the Absolute III. From then on, the coexistence of these two human types, and the competition that was the result of this, became the norm. Now, '*as the children of this world are in their generation more able than the children of light*'[2] we can see that throughout the centuries, even in our own day, adamics in their post-fall condition, have been and are generally in an inferior position to the pre-adamics.

Further on, this situation, with its practical consequences and problems, will be the object of a deeper study. This is necessary because the Era of the Holy Spirit is approaching, at the end of which the question of the separation of the *tares* from the *good seed* will arise. For the moment we will restrict ourselves to repeating that contemporary adamic man, having lost contact with his higher centres and therefore with his real 'I', appears practically the same as his pre-adamic counterpart. However, unlike the latter, he still has his higher centres, which ensure that he has the possibility of following the way of esoteric evolution. *At present*, pre-adamic man is deprived of this possibility, but it will be given to him if adamic humanity develops as it should during the Era of the Holy Spirit.

(2)

T he third stage of the Creation of adamic humanity, when Woman appeared, is like the second in that we find a process totally different from the one that gave birth to pre-adamic humanity. In the latter case, woman was created independently of man but in a like manner;[3] Eve was created *after* Adam, and *after* he had received the Breath of Life. She too was not created directly *from the dust of the earth*,[4] but indirectly from an

---

1. Vol. II, p. xxxvi.
2. Luke xvi: 8; after the Slavonic text.
3. Genesis i: 27.
4. Genesis ii: 7

Adam who was already living, but asleep, so that she also appeared on Earth as a *living soul*. This is an essential difference. For the moment, we will only note Adam's reaction when, coming out of the sleep into which God had plunged him, he saw the woman who had been drawn from his side: '*This is now bone of my bones, and flesh of my flesh.*'[5] By these words, the Bible underlines the fact that the man and woman of the VIth Day (the pre-adamics) were of a different race from Adam and Eve.

Moreover, the pre-adamic man and woman were not given names, but Adam, which signifies the *red man*, or *man of the red earth*,[6] was named *by God*.[7] Obeying the Lord's orders, he gave a name to the Woman, his wife, as he had to all creatures.[8] He called her Eve, which means *Life, Living* or *Lifegiving*.[9]

This symbolic and esoterically significant story finds a certain echo in modern physiology. Studying the two races mixed together, scientific knowledge today shows us that man has female hormones as well as male ones, and woman has male hormones as well as female. In contemporary man, the proportion of female hormones is only 1 percent; while in woman the percentage of male hormones is about 5 percent: we see therefore, that woman is more man than man is woman. It is probable that, after the thousands of years during which the two races have mixed, this proportion is now balanced between pre-adamics and adamics. It would be worthwhile to verify this in all the different races of contemporary humanity. It is possible that, originally, the proportion of the hormones of the other sex in both men and women of the VIth day was equal, while in the adamics the disproportion must have been even greater than it is today.

'*The sons of God*,' says the Bible, '*saw the daughters of men, that they were fair; and they took them wives of all which they chose.*'[10] The mingling of the two races which resulted was contrary to the Plan of Creation, and God decided to partially exterminate the humanity that had become corrupted in this way by means of the Flood.[11] But the mixing of chromosomes was already an accomplished fact, so that the hormonal asymmetry of the adamics has naturally diminished through the generations until it has become stabilized at the point it has now reached. Since certain indications in the Gospel lead us to believe that the two human races that coexist on the earth are numerically equal,[12] it may be supposed that in early adamics the hormonal

---

5. Genesis ii: 23.
6. *Concordance*, op. cit., p. 618.
7. Genesis ii: 15.
8. Ibid., ii: 23.
9. Ibid., iii: 20; *Concordance*, p. 645.
10. Genesis vi: 2.
11. Ibid., vi: 7 and following.
12. Matthew xxiv: 40; Luke xvii: 36 and others.

asymmetry was about 1 to 10. Probably the adamics should regain this proportion during the Era of the Holy Spirit, so that, their physiology being restored in this way, they may once again be, like Adam and Eve before the fall, liberated from the servitude to reproduction which was originally imposed only on pre-adamics. It was to the pre-adamics that God said: '*Be fruitful and multiply.*'[13] Adam and Eve were not given this mission; their union was purely androgynous, and it was only after the fall that Eve conceived and gave birth to her sons. The first indication that God imposed the obligation *to multiply* on the adamics appears much later, notably in these words addressed to Jacob: '*Be fruitful and multiply; a nation and a company of nations shall be born from thee, and kings shall come out of thy loins.*'[14] One may place this around 1760 years before Jesus Christ,[15] and it is probably from that moment, when God had accepted the 'fait accompli' and resolved to make a new start with Jacob, that the hormonal proportion 1 to 5 began to become general.

We have already said that this new beginning was to the advantage of the pre-adamics, for whom it opened up the perspective, (distant but real), of an evolution that would operate during the cycle of the Holy Spirit, when, if all goes well, they will be allowed to take the place of the *corrupted adamics*, when the latter obtain their Redemption — the integrated harmonious state in which they were before the fall — which they must now regain by conscious efforts.

Faced with the 'fait accompli' of Adam's fall, God, whose will is that nothing should ever be entirely lost,[16] was obliged to modify His Plan to make the best of the situation: first, after Abel's death, which threatened the continuity of His Tradition, He made Eve conceive Seth, and then, after the Flood, He undertook to reconstitute a new humanity with Noah and his sons. But the latter were mixed from the beginning, which is how the pre-adamics were too often able to dominate the adamics in the years that followed.

II

(1)

The adamic man who has even a vague consciousness of his real '*I*' finds that this is a source of internal conflict that he cannot solve on a purely human plane. This conflict becomes more acute from the moment he actively enters esoteric work. It is then that he becomes weak and falls

---

13. Genesis i: 28.
14. Genesis xxxv: ll.
15. *Concordance*, op. cit, p. iii.
16. Matthew xviii: 4.

a prey to uncertainty, doubt, and mistrust toward himself, for the road that leads to Truth always passes through doubts. Throughout this work, we have seen several times the considerable sum of efforts and superefforts that are demanded of the adamic man, who, after having recognized his real position in life, resolutely crosses the First Threshold and climbs the Staircase to attain and pass the Second Threshold with its promised Redemption.

Pre-adamics are not subject to these fits of anguish and these permanent inner conflicts; not that they live in perfect peace, or are never troubled by conflicts — far from it — but in most cases their conflicts take place in *the interior of the Personality*, between different groups of the little 'I's which produce these conflicts. As a result, the character of their conflicts is purely psychic, and they are generally resolved by some kind of compromise.

The more acute conflicts that take place in pre-adamic man occur between the 'I' of the Personality and the 'I' of the body. We have dwelt at length on this subject in volume II of *Gnosis*, emphasizing the fact that the 'I' of the body usually wins over the weak, changing Personality, which capitulates without much of a struggle whenever it is a question of satisfying the stomach or the sexual appetites.

Justification is then sought in slogans such as those which allow us to think that it is normal to 'act like everyone else,' or in a maze of paradoxical reasons that are simply lies to oneself.

But the inner conflicts of adamic man, who often enters esoteric work because he has reached the last extremity of moral bankruptcy, cannot be resolved by compromise, as there is no place for this kind of solution in the consciousness of the real 'I' from which he receives his calls. In him, it is the ensemble formed by the entire Personality, with the 'I' of the body, an ensemble which, directly or indirectly, is often made to act by the sexual centre, which flees from the voice of conscience, i.e. of the real 'I'. He then has a choice, either to obey his real 'I' and triumph over himself, or to flee from this *invisible Combat* into self-calming and the powerful illusions offered by a life of lying to himself.

In every case, if he triumphs over himself, which is what will enable the adamic man to resolve the inner conflict of the moment, this will inevitably involve a modification of his attitude towards outer life. Generally, the result will be conflict with those closest to him, unless the latter follow him step by step in his esoteric evolution, which is rare.

This does not mean that those who are near and dear to him wish him any ill; on the contrary, it is nearly always his good that they have in view: the conflict arises simply from their different *conceptions of what is real*. If those who surround the individual in question are pre-adamic, they could never agree with him, being incapable of understanding the reasons for his change of attitude and unable to grasp the nature of the ends he pursues. They will therefore automatically become instruments of the General Law, which makes sure that those who step out of line are brought back to the fold. This is how '*a man's foes shall be those of his own household.*'[17]

Pre-adamic man, as we said, cannot be subject to inner or domestic conflicts of this kind. He rarely receives 'B' influences. If he vaguely senses their existence, they only appear as a curiosity to his eyes and do not have the power to trouble him right to the depths of his psyche. In him, the sexual centre reigns supreme, whether by its direct action that takes the form of carnal love, or by an indirect, 'psychological', action of the psyche to which his Personality submits. Like adamic man's, his Personality contains the three lower centres, but that is all. Equally underdeveloped and unbalanced, but sheltered from the troubles provoked by 'B' influences, this Personality lives and acts obedient to the commands of the sexual centre. Nothing in him withstands the latter, which is known in contemporary language as *temperament*.

In the arena of the 'exterior' life of human society, dominated by 'A' influences, the adamic man who has crossed the First Threshold proves to be weaker than his pre-adamic counterpart — just as good seeds sowed on ploughed land are weaker than tares; and the greater the strength he acquires during his progress on the Staircase, the greater is his weakness when faced with life.

This was the main reason why monasteries existed—so that the monks or nuns could be sheltered from 'exterior' life. But now greenhouse cultivation is outmoded; what is needed today is cultivation in the open air — entirely exposed to the elements. However, let the sincere, untiring and *useful* worker know that he will receive the means to protect himself against these storms.

(2)

Pre-adamic man does not reincarnate. Not having any individualized element in himself, (in the esoteric sense), he is born and dies but he does not incarnate, and consequently he cannot reincarnate. He can be *hylic* or *psychic* but not *pneumatic*, since he does not have the *Breath of Life* in him, which is manifested in adamic man through the medium of his real 'I', which can be realized or potential. The individualization of pre-adamics is *collective*, and is directed in groups by certain spirits of the hierarchy of which we have spoken above.[18] This does not, however, prevent pre-adamics from entering the evolutionary field that forms the *films* of adamics in great numbers, and as adamics suffer from a lack of discernment

---

17. Matthew x: 36.
18. *Infra* in chapter XIV.

because of their corrupt state, this disturbs and sometimes slows their evolution.

(3)

As we have seen already, because of the Principle of Equilibrium, humanity on this earth is divided into two equal parts; adamics and pre-adamics. The equilibrium between them is automatically adjusted to follow fluctuations of the incarnations of adamic souls. However, if the adamic race, by casting its pearls to the swine, denies its divine nature to an inadmissible degree, this balance will be broken in favour of the *tares*. In the parable of the talents, Jesus foresaw the possibility of such a degeneration — where the slave buried the one talent entrusted to him, and, on returning it to his master without having made it multiply, was told: *'Thou wicked and slothful servant ... and cast ye the unprofitable servant into outer darkness: there shall be weeping and gnashing of teeth.'*[19] Is there any need to emphasize the esoteric meaning of this terrible penalty?

We have seen that, when creation took place, the two humanities were placed under different authorities. Essentially created, with organic Life on Earth, in the note LA of the second cosmic octave, pre-adamics come under the Absolute III. Essentially created in the note SI of the same octave, and receiving the breath of the Ψ, the mission of the adamics was to govern organic Life on behalf of the Absolute II, and under its direct authority. The fall necessitated a new beginning, and God provided for this through *Purgatory*, which is represented by the Staircase between the Two Thresholds. From then on, like the Man of the VIth day, subject to the law of birth and death, adamic Man appeared on the Earth below the First Threshold. He has kept a dim consciousness of the real 'I' in spite of the almost complete obstruction of his channel of communication with the higher Centres which still exist in him, and this still gives him the possibility of a choice. If he hears the *Voice of the Master* and resolutely steps onto the Staircase, and if he reaches the Fourth Step and resists the Trial by Fire, then, when he crosses the Second Threshold, he will be welcomed as a *prodigal Son* by the Absolute II himself.

III

(1)

If the adamics *en masse* abandon the combat that leads to Redemption, and if this desertion goes beyond the tolerance allowed, the good seed

---

19. Matthew xxv: 26; same as the Slavonic text.

could be progressively stifled by the tares, since for cosmic reasons the general potential of organic Life on Earth must be maintained in any circumstance. The world would then go straight toward catastrophe, which this time would take the form of a Deluge of Fire. On the other hand, if the equilibrium, which is already jeopardized, were reestablished, then, with the integral and simultaneous incarnation of adamic souls, the Time of transition would end and humanity would enter the Era of the Holy Spirit. Then would follow a thousand years consecrated to the perfecting of the two races, and after a second millennium, the reign of the Androgyne, the Last Judgment would definitively separate the tares from the good seed. The latter, by integrally regaining the note SI of the second cosmic octave, and now inspired by the breath of the Ψ, would then enter the bosom of the Lord to undertake a higher evolution and at last attain the *Pleroma*. The tares of yesterday would cease to be tares. Promoted to the rank of good seed, they would begin the long evolutionary course that the adamics would have already covered. Then they in their turn would receive the higher centres of consciousness, which, given them in potential, would be the *talents* that they must make fruitful.

(2)

We must add that the adamics who had previously degenerated into pre-adamics would have the possibility of taking up their abandoned evolution again, while an equivalent number of the most able pre-adamics would receive the *talents* that were initially given to the former, and this would help them leap forward on the road of esoteric evolution. They may be compared with gifted, hardworking students who get a double promotion while the incapable and lazy ones do another year in the same class. But in this case, one can fail only once.

(3)

When we consider this leap forward, it would be useful to meditate upon the parable of the *unjust Steward*,[20] a clever man in the domain of the 'A' influences, who knew how to find a new point of application for his cleverness, with good timing.

However, apart from rare periods and rare exceptions, characterized by the direct intervention here below of higher forces coming from the Absolute II, the faithful stewards of the Absolute III generally occupy an important position in the different groups and layers of human society. It would, nevertheless, be impossible to give any precise indications that

20. Luke xvi: 1–9.

135

would enable adamics at the level of men 1, 2 and 3, to objectively recognize pre-adamics, because the latter are also men 1, 2 and 3, with the sole difference that they have no possibility of individual esoteric evolution. Thus, as long as the higher centres in adamic man remain in a lethargic state, he will be without the psychic instrument by which he could objectively recognize his pre-adamic counterpart, so that society remains mixed.

Therefore it is only with the approach of the Era of the Holy Spirit, and the appearance of the New Man, that the progressive formation of a new elite in all groups of human society will end the chaotic state, from the esoteric point of view, in which humanity has found itself since the fall of Adam.

Meanwhile, the two races are totally mixed: not only nations, but even families can be, and generally are, composed of both human types. This state of things is the belated result of transgressing the Biblical prohibition against mixed marriages because of the beauty of the daughters of pre-adamics.[21] The dominant position of the pre-adamics that is a result of the esoteric failure of the adamics is now creating a critical situation of unprecedented gravity. The remainder of the Time of transition offers the last chance for humanity to reestablish the threatened equilibrium and so avoid a general cataclysm.

If we do not take this opportunity, the tradition of 'Solomon' will finally overcome the tradition of 'David' — that is, it will overcome the Christian tradition in the planetary sense of this term. Then, deflected from the Absolute II, and even going beyond the limits of what is necessary and useful in the mission of the Absolute III in the deification of the Personality, the false prophets and their followers, thinking that they are right, will hurl pre-adamic humanity — the children of this world — against the adamics — the children of light — and will provoke a final frightful and useless struggle.

If this should happen, and if then, the new adamic elite does not manage to quell the revolt against the Love of the Absolute II and, paradoxically, against the authority of the Absolute III, a resistance that would ensure victory, the balance will finally be broken, and humanity will be destroyed in the Deluge of Fire.

---

21. Genesis vi: 5 and 12.

CHAPTER XVI

(1)

We will now look over our analysis and study it from a different point of view: that of the possible correction of this dangerous situation. We will recapitulate what was set out here and there in our earlier text, so as to sketch in the complete picture.

The Book of Genesis, which teaches that pre-adamic man and woman were created, simultaneously but distinct, on the VIth Day, at the same time as the animals, does not give us any details about the process used.[1] As for the creation of Adam, this was after the VIIth Day, the divine day of rest, that is, when organic Life on Earth was already complete in its three notes, FA, SOL and LA.[2] In this case the process is described. It is written:

'*And the Lord God formed man of the dust of the ground, and breathed into his nostrils the breath of Life; and man became a living soul.*'[3]

Thus, while the creation of the two sexes of pre-adamic humanity took place as a single stage, as with the animals, that of adamic humanity took place in two stages. Adam was created:

1) First, as a *human* being, in the proper use of the term, analogous to his pre-adamic predecessor, and like him, mortal, though of finer substance.

2) Then, as a living Soul, by the addition of the Breath of Life, of the divine essence that was introduced into his *psyche*, and through that into his *hyle*, which rendered him immortal.

Readers of 'Gnosis' already know that at the second stage, Adam was endowed with the real 'I', which was divine in nature, and the consciousness of which was established in him from that moment through the intermediary of the higher emotional centre. He was given this in addition to the 'I' of the body and the ephemeral 'I' of the Personality, which also exist in pre-adamic man.

We repeat: 'Before the fall, Adam had in him three 'I's: the 'I' of the body (hylic), the 'I' of the Personality (the psyche), and the real 'I' (pneumatic), whereas his counterpart of the VIth Day only had, and still only has, the first two: the 'I' of the body and the 'I' of the Personality.

It is through the higher centres, the means of access to the real 'I' and to Consciousness, that Adam participated in the higher spiritual life: that of

---

1. Genesis i: 27.
2. Ibid., ii: 1–6; after the Slavonic text.
3. Ibid., ii: 7.

Paradise, the 'geometric place' of the divine consciousness, to which pre-adamic man had no access as he lacked the necessary means.

(2)

From the Book of Genesis it is evident that, before the fall, Adam was clearly conscious of his real 'I', which enabled him to be in direct contact with God. On the other hand, he only had a rudimentary consciousness of the 'I' of his Personality, which may be compared with contemporary cultured man's consciousness of the 'I' of his body when involved in his daily activities. In other words, before the fall, Adam was *confluent with God*. From the moment that he *became confluent with his Personality*, the fall came about.

Technically speaking, if Adam had played the role initially assigned to him, he would have maintained the balance between the divine plane and the human plane by adhering to the androgynous race. Instead of that, when the Serpent ensnared Eve, and when she gave him the fruit of this ensnarement to taste, he went over to her side. That is when a magic sleep overcame him, and his descendants after him. Ever since then, adamic man has taken for reality the dreams that the sleeping *little Serpent*,[4] curled up in his *sacrum*, produce in him. This state, which is normal for all the species of organic Life on Earth including the humanity of the VIth Day, is entirely abnormal for adamic man, who contains higher centres of consciousness within him. It is therefore necessary for him to awaken this *little Serpent* to recover the consciousness of his Real 'I', for the most part forgotten and, even at the eleventh hour, to fulfill his true mission on this Earth, the one that the Lord God entrusted to him.

(3)

A small indication in the Book of Genesis, which seems trivial and strange, shows us that, before the fall, Adam and Eve had a waking consciousness that was different from ours, for it tells us that they were not conscious of their nudity. They became conscious of it, and experienced a feeling of shame after the fall, that is, at the moment when, turning away from the consciousness of their real 'I', they identified themselves with their Personality.

From then onwards, this *consciousness of nudity*, and the feeling of shame attached to it, have remained among the characteristics of their descendants. It is only recently — since the beginning of the twentieth century — that men, and especially women, either instinctively or for reasons which

4. Cf. Vol. I, pp. 142; Vol. II, 7, 91 (note), 92, 108, 110, 256.

have nothing to do with the approach of the Era of Truth, seek to eliminate this kind of shame, which belongs to the corrupt state of fallen man, and contrasts vividly with the boundless moral effrontery of the 'civilized'.

We may grasp the whole significance of this symbolic indication on shame and nudity if we consider it in relation to the words that Jesus used to define the spiritual condition of human beings who regain consciousness of the real 'I', and through that, the Kingdom of God. In his *Stromata*, Clement of Alexandria quotes a passage from the Gospel according to the Egyptians, as follows:

'... *When Salome asked when these things about which she asked would be known, the Lord said: "When you would have trampled on the clothing of shame".*'[5]

And in the Gospel according to St Thomas, we find the following:

'... *His disciples said to him: "Which day wilt thou reveal thyself to us, and on which day shall we see thee?" Jesus said: "When you will lay yourselves bare without any shame, and when you take off your clothes like little children and trample them underfoot".*'[6]

II

(1)

When Adam and Eve lived in Paradise, they were in a state of androgynous beatitude in the bosom of the Lord. It was a perfect but unconscious beatitude, in other words it was not realized intellectually. Incidentally, we must again emphasize the fact that because of the meaning of the Major Number VI, which is *Rebirth*, *Renewal*, and *Reproduction*, the man and woman of the VIth Day were entrusted with the mission of *being fruitful* and *multiplying*. As long as Adam and Eve were in Paradise, they were exempt from this servitude: it was only after the fall that Eve conceived Cain, Abel, and later, Seth.

The organic unity of the androgynous consciousness, that is, of the real 'I' which, being bipolar, is ONE for the couple, was subjectively disassociated in the Psyche of Adam and Eve at the very time that they became conscious of the *objective* bipolarity of their respective Personalities with which they were identified — a bipolarity which faithfully reflects that of the created Universe, and the cause of Death.

---

5. Clement of Alexandria, *Stromata*, III, 13, 92. (Literal translation from the French).

6. *The Gospel according to St Thomas*, or the secret words of Jesus, by Jean Doresse, Paris, Plon, 1959 (42), p. 99. In the edition of the Presses Universitaires de France, quoted elsewhere, the same passage is given as: '... *His disciples said: Which day wilt thou reveal thyself to us and on which day shall we see thee? Jesus said: When you will lay down your shame, and take your clothes, and put them under your feet like little children and trample on them.*' Log. 37, p. 23. (Literal translation from the French).

This was the effect that the fruit of the Tree of *logical* Knowledge, called Cartesian, that of Good and Evil, produced in them. Logically, Adam's identification with the 'I' of his Personality must have produced a psychological fall in him first, and then a fall of the psyche. Further, it must have made him attribute a character of reality to the world of 'A' influences and to his Personality, while his real 'I', the divine gift he received as the Breath of Life, was relegated to the domain of probabilities or even of improbabilities or just pure fantasy.

Because of this, for the fallen Adam as for the pre-adamics, the conditions of psychic and physical life became an end in themselves, instead of having in their eyes only the value of a *means* — a means of acting in the domain of organic Life on Earth without confluence with it, to fill the role of regulator of the pulsation of organic life — a function of the needs of the First Cosmic Octave, and especially those of the interval between FA and MI of this Octave.

(2)

B y taking the means for the end, adamic man endangered the natural evolution of organic Life on Earth, which had been conceived as a hierarchy starting from so-called inanimate matter, and ascending to the humanity of the VIth Day, the latter being guided by the humanity of the VIIIth Day, adamic humanity.

We have seen that, in the notes LA, SOL and FA, organic Life on Earth, including a pre-adamic humanity charged to '*be fruitful and multiply*' and subject to the law of birth and of death, was placed under the authority of the Absolute III. In the original plan, however, it was destined to be governed by adamic humanity which, because it had higher centres, came directly under the authority of the Absolute II, and should have served as an *organic* link between the Third and Second Cosmic Octaves. If it had happened like this, the growth of our Ray of Creation and the development of the system of the corresponding cosmoses would have followed a harmonious ascending curve. The fall of Adam and Eve, by causing a rupture in the chain of interdependence, caused a deviation in the onrushing current of Love proceeding from the Absolute I, infused on the way by the creative tenderness of the Absolute II, and became an obstacle to the manifestation of this Love in an angelic (androgynous) form in the midst of terrestrial life.

The androgynous consciousness — that of the real 'I' that is now relegated to the background of waking consciousness, (which we incorrectly call clear consciousness), has nevertheless not been finally lost despite the fall; for if it is possible to lose the *relative*, which belongs to the 'A' world, the phenomenal or ephemeral world, it is impossible to lose the *real*. We can lose the feel of it, but even that can only be temporary; we can forget it, but in the real sense of the word, the *real* cannot be lost. Thus, ever since the fall, the androgynous consciousness lives on in adamic man, although only in potential. In other words, as elements of the noumenal world, the higher centres of consciousness are always in full strength and continually act within him, but as he has diverted his attention from them and concentrated on the three lower centres, he has no 'ears to hear' the divine Voice, which nevertheless ceaselessly transmits the Word to him.

(3)

The last chance to reestablish the equilibrium — from DO up to RE inclusive — between the two directions of the current of Love which vibrates all along the Great Octave of *our* Ray of Creation, depends on the attitude of the adamic men and women who *today* face the approach of the Era of the Holy Spirit. To exercise a salutary action, these men and women must exert themselves and make *conscious* superhuman efforts aimed at reviving the androgynous consciousness of their real 'I' and, in so doing, at renewing the organic link that was intended between the Second and Third cosmic Octaves, which was broken by the Fall. It is important not to lose sight of the fact that there remains scarcely half a century in which to accumulate an energy that is quantitatively and qualitatively sufficient to restore the endangered equilibrium and harmony. The Time of Transition is already considerably advanced.

The importance and urgency of individual and collective esoteric work thus appears in all its fullness. Today, the method of research pursued in the silence of scientific laboratories or monastic cells — research that progresses slowly, step by step, from one generation to the other — is out of date. To save humanity from the Deluge of Fire, we must in future have recourse to rapid means and direct our esoteric work to the very heart of our *Mixtus Orbis*, which is in danger of being destroyed.

Now, by the nature of things, we must place all our hopes and confidence in the couple, the Knight and the Lady of his dreams. They alone, strong in their awakened androgynous consciousness, will be capable of creating a change of direction which, in the name of Jesus, will launch the Ark of our planet towards the fullness of the Era of the Holy Spirit.

Then, and only then, the sacrifices of the One who was Beheaded and the One who was Crucified will be justified.

CHAPTER XVII

(1)

It is important to remember that — except of course for adamic man — every creature taking part in organic Life on Earth, whether it has one centre to its psyche, two, or three as in man of the VIth day, has only one higher centre — the sexual centre. Indeed, on the hylic plane, the sexual centre is analogous to the higher emotional and higher intellectual centres, since it is by nature and structure *whole*, that is, indivisible.

Except when its energy is usurped by the three centres of the Personality, the sexual centre in its direct function, which is carnal love, has a goal that is well defined by the words: *Be fruitful, and multiply*. In other words, in a healthy organism, this centre, like the higher emotional and intellectual centres, knows neither doubt, nor hesitation, nor sadness, which is quite the opposite of what is too often the case with the three lower centres: it either participates in action, filling the psyche and the body with joy, or else it is in repose, accumulating energy SI 12 in the *cream of the blood*,[1] which is the highest point of the transmutation of Hydrogens through the first octave of nutrition. This is the 'fuel' of carnal love. The reader may recall that, by filling the interval which separates SI 12 from DO 6, the carnal act causes resonance in the latter and so finds its raison d'être in the conception of a new being.

However, if the Creator willed that all that made up organic Life on Earth should reproduce and multiply, this was not the mission of Adam and Eve before the fall, for, by virtue of its dual nature, adamic humanity was originally called on to serve as a link between the two planes.

(2)

The fall of Adam and the loss of consciousness of the real 'I' had the essential result that they led the adamics to a new, essentially logical attitude towards the sexual centre. Adam, we have said, was initially intended to play a pivotal role between the Second and Third cosmic Octaves, a role in which he was not intended to participate in human reproduction, but to preside over the evolution of all the creatures of organic Life on Earth, including the Man of the VIth Day. This was so that the fashioning of primitive types would pass through progressively foreseen changes along the ladder of general cosmic evolution.

---

1. Expression used by Aristotle to specify sperm.

(3)

Now we must try to see what role the sexual centre would have had to play in adamic man if he had not fallen. This question has a practical aspect, as it touches the heart of every seeker who is engaged in esoteric work and whose goal is to return to the condition of adamic man before the fall, as well as taking up the neglected task and the rank he lost on the scale of cosmic evolution.

(4)

Just as Adam and Eve did not procreate before the fall, so, through their *redemption*, the androgynous couple of polar beings will be exempt from the servitude of reproduction. In this instance, we simply refer to the texts quoted in the previous chapter.

What then was the original role and use of sex in Adam and Eve, and what will it be in their descendants when the latter, having brought about the necessary rectification of the situation, have recovered their original dual nature in the image of Jesus Christ, when they will see the doors of the *Covenant of Love* opening in front of them, where, according to St Paul, the Son of God will be the *Firstborn among many Brethren?*[2]

Above all, we must not think that redemption will eliminate the sexual centre or the psychosomatic nature of adamic man. This is a point that must be underlined, as the human mind always has a penchant for extremes, and it has happened that an erroneous understanding and application of the theory of asceticism has pushed the faithful towards mutilation. This is how Origen, despite his lucid and enlightened mind, fell into the trap laid for him by the Absolute III and, sticking to the letter of the Gospel, castrated himself.

This is how Eusebius describes the incident:

'When Origen was working as catechist in Alexandria, he accomplished an action which is a very great proof of an inexperienced and juvenile heart, but one that was full of faith and temperance. He interpreted the following words of Jesus in a very simple, naïve manner: *"And there be eunuchs, which have made themselves eunuchs for the kingdom of heaven's sake"*,[3] and thought that he was obeying the Saviour, and that, preaching divine things at a young age not only to men, but to women also, he would deprive the unfaithful of every pretext to shamefully slander him, by carrying out the Saviour's word.'[4]

---

2. Romans viii: 29.
3. Matthew xix: 12.
4. Eusebius, op. cit., Book VI, ch. VII, 1, 2, 4.

We must add that Origen later regretted his mutilation.[5] In any case, after Hadrian, the civil laws of the Empire forbade castration, which was punished very severely. It is unthinkable that the Church ever permitted it. It is true that, at the time, the ecclesiastical law forbidding the ordination of the castrated did not exist, and that the eunuch Meliton was Bishop of Sardis. In fact, the most reputable bishops in Palestine, those of Cæsarea and of Jerusalem, having judged Origen worthy of the highest distinction, conferred priesthood on him.[6]

We can form an idea of the heights which Origen could have reached in his esoteric evolution, for the greater benefit of the Church, if we consider the wide scope of the work he managed to accomplish in the transmutation of Hydrogens and the production of SI 12 energy in his organism in spite of the castration he had suffered.

The reader of 'Gnosis' must keep this example ever present in his mind as a terrible example of the determining influence that the general Law can exercise over the Personality. Origen, who came into the world with uncommonly rich and strong predispositions, and who was animated by an ardent faith, even so sadly fell into the trap that had been laid for him, and committed an irreparable error through a momentary lack of discernment which made him confuse planes, the *Letter* with the *Spirit*.

(5)

At the time of his Second Birth, man acquires a permanent consciousness of his real 'I', which is a monad of the Absolute II. He reaches this through his higher emotional centre. Strong in this consciousness, he becomes capable on the one hand of progressively creating a link with his higher intellectual centre, which gives him access to the *mind of Christ*,[7] the consciousness of the Absolute I, and on another hand, of establishing his authority over the motor centre. Then the lower emotional centre, which has already been absorbed by the magnetic centre, but without losing its individual structure, takes its place within the higher emotional centre.[8]

Thus man 5, thanks to the permanent consciousness of his real 'I', benefits from a double current of Love — the Love from the Absolute II, to which the Love from the Absolute I is gradually added, and which pervades him through his higher centres. In this way he escapes the

---

5. Eusebius, op. cit., (note), Vol II, no. 41, p. 96, French original edition; Cf. *In Matth. comment.*, XV, 3, pp. 104–5, English manuscript.

6. Ibid.

7. 1 Corinthians ii: 16. (In the French the word used is 'intelligence', and in the Greek New Testament νοῦν *(nous)*. Ed.)

8. Vol. I, fig. 26, p. 61.

authority of the Absolute III, and because of this, from the domination of carnal love. But the current of the latter, charged with SI 12, does not cease to penetrate the 'I' of the body and the 'I' of the Personality.

Here there is no motive for fear or *scandal*—on condition, naturally, that one remains master of this energy and avoids the two extremes: the first, the ejection of SI 12 from the organism, can be remedied by appropriate exercises; the other, of which Origen gave an example, is irremediable. The current of carnal love which invades the body and the Psyche of man 5 is a beneficial phenomenon, appreciated and desired after the passage of the Second Threshold, for, from that moment, Hydrogen SI 12 serves as a *raw material* for 'manufacturing'. We have seen that the energy SI 12, diverted from its usual destination and surrounded by the SOL 12 and MI 12 acting as higher auxiliaries, formed the essential factor in the general transmutation. The DO 6 of the *inner* octave, or octave of redemption can, indeed, only be obtained starting from SI 12 for, in any case, the transmutation of the MI 12 stops at FA 6 and that of the SOL 12 at LA 6, the Hydrogens 6 are the finest that the human organism can produce or capture. Indeed, FA 6 and LA 6 are not capable of creating an inner octave, since this must necessarily begin with the note DO. DO 6 can only be obtained by a process of transmutation that follows the first octave, that of nutrition — the only complete octave in the human organism — which starts from the DO 768 and arrives naturally at SI 12, which, to be precise, is sexual energy. This is the real reason for the continence observed in monastic practice as well as in the courtly Love which unites the Knight with the Lady of his dreams.

(6)

In order to give an idea of the technique of creation which ensured the diversity of the species that form the notes LA, SOL and FA of organic Life on Earth, we may mention that this diversity is due to the density of the Hydrogens which form the sexual energy specific to particular species. Each type of Hydrogen contains a whole series of Hydrogens of the same type, just as, for example, the vitamin-type 'B' contains vitamins B1, B2, ... B12, etc. It is thus that, in all the diversity of the species that are part of it, organic Life on Earth is fertilized by the sexual energies which, in the order of density of the Hydrogens, form an uninterrupted scale: SI 24 for a great part of the fauna, SI 48 for cereals, SI 96 for the perfumed flowers and plants, and so on.

It is important to remember this, especially because of the modern tendency to treat certain illnesses by introducing into the human organism living sexual or other cells which have been drawn from animals. We

146

can understand without much difficulty that it would be useless to expect the sexual hormone of a pig or of a sheep, which is comparable to human testosterone, to have a direct effect on the plane of SI 12 of the individual who is being treated, since the animal hormone is Hydrogen SI 24. All that one can hope for would be a passing resonance on the plane of LA 24, giving a light shock to the SI 12 — short, and of an impure resonance. In addition, the human organism defends itself against the intrusion of living cells, especially from lower organisms, for this intrusion *draws man towards lower levels* so that he *regresses* due to the fact that it constitutes a bestialization of his body, which immediately has a repercussion on the Personality in one form or another.

Let us recall: the fine is always the cause; the coarse is only the consequence. Thus, starting from the sexual Hydrogen, which is always the SI of the first scale of nutrition, it is easy to determine the basic Hydrogen which forms the food of the species being considered: for man, it would be Hydrogen 768, whereas for a dog it would be H 1536 in its most varied expressions. It is the same for the respiratory scale and the scale of impressions: the dog draws the coarsest elements from the air; the more refined enter its lungs but pass out of them again without being assimilated; and as for impressions, it is obvious that the great mass of those which are received by human beings escape the dog.

This explains why, in spite of all the artistry he brought to it, Professor Voronoff's grafts produced only a temporary effect on the sexual plane, although sometimes they had unfortunate repercussions on other planes. We may go even further and say that the introduction of human cells in the organism, or in such and such organ or group or organs, could produce a durable curative effect only if the Hydrogens which govern the working of the organ or group of organs concerned were the same in the donor and in the patient — not only of the same type, like SI 12, for example, but of the same degree of this type, which would presuppose a psychosomatic diagnosis taking into account the blood group of the two individuals, the degree of the development of their Personalities, and the specific nature of this development.

We will close this digression here, leaving to specialists the task of drawing practical conclusions from the wider considerations developed below.

(7)

We have seen that when the act of carnal love comes to a head at DO 6, the sign of conception, a new gamut—that of pregnancy—begins to develop on condition that the orgasm communicates a willing impulse to the spermatozoa — an impulse sufficient to impel them in search of the ovule until one of them manages to penetrate it. We also know that the gamut of pregnancy is necessarily a descending one. This being so, the first interval to be filled is the one which separates the DO from the SI. This filling must take place during the lapse of time between the moment of ejaculation and the moment when the ovule is penetrated, and it demands, on both sides, high and complete harmony in the will of love; *the will of man and the will of the flesh.*[9] This explains why, especially in human beings, pregnancy only occurs in a very small percentage of cases even though the couple may perform the act of carnal love many other times.

The number of spermatozoa contained in every discharge of semen — half a million — and the enormous amount of those which are pouring out every month in the direction of the ovule, lead one to think that through this abundance nature tried to multiply the chances of conception, which are generally very slim. This is why, at least for adamic humanity, a *successful pregnancy* demands harmony between the types of the father and the mother, as well as a sufficiently high tension of the will of love in both partners, so that ecstasy may arise — not only sensual, but emotional as well.

For obvious reasons, pregnancy is more frequent in contemporary pre-adamics. And, as the esoteric evolution of the adamics presses on at an accelerated pace which is necessary for the successful ending of the Time of Transition — and there is a parallel diminution of births — pregnancy will take place more and more often among pre-adamics, so that the incarnation of the totality of souls attached to our planet may be assured.

(8)

Let us come back to the process of inner transmutation of Hydrogens H 12 and H 6. This is produced by the series of phenomena which the reader will find described in Chapter XIV of the present volume.

In order to avoid any misinterpretation of the postulates put forward in 'Gnosis', it is useful to emphasize once more that the psychosomatic technique of esoteric evolution depends essentially on the appropriate treatment of sexual energy.

If the FA 96 does not give forth a pure, strong sound, the resonance of the SI 12 which it commands will be defective, and the student's esoteric evolution will be seriously handicapped. Sex and health, therefore, play the same kind of role in esoteric evolution, and this is even greater than in reproduction.

---

9. John i: 13.

We have seen the process of direct and lateral transmutation by which the opening of the higher emotional centre operates in man, and how the possibility of receiving its messages enables him to arrive at the consciousness of the real 'I'—a consciousness which is itself androgynous, that is, bipolar. It is the passage of the Second Threshold which unites the Knight and the Lady of his dreams forever in a celestial marriage which crowns their first exploit. Having reached the bosom of the Absolute II, and being One together and ONE with Christ, they experience at that moment the state which is defined by St Paul in the following words which we have quoted several times already: '... *neither is the man without the woman, neither the woman without the man, in the Lord.*'[10]

It would be vain to try to describe in human language the stages of esoteric evolution between the Second and Third Thresholds. The more the Knight and the Lady of his dreams, now *androgynous Initiates*, progress along the stages MI and RE of the Way, the more completely they trample on the *clothes of shame*. Entrusted with missions corresponding to their strength, and allowed to contribute toward the building of the *New Jerusalem*, they will build themselves at the same time. They will do this while they advance towards the Third Threshold, moved by the desire which inspires an ardent love in them to reach the Door which leads to the *Pleroma*.

(9)

A useful indication may be given to the Faithful who unhesitatingly continue to climb the Staircase. This concerns the transmutation of the Hydrogens along the gamut of the *inner pregnancy*, starting from DO 6. As soon as the latter sounds, a powerful current of Love from the Absolute I invades the androgynous being of the Knight and his Lady and makes their pneumatic body tremble with joy, while their psychic bodies, filled with the love of the Absolute II, overflow with an intimate and holy affection. Their physical bodies, purified and glorified, become capable of directly receiving the maternal tenderness of the Queen of Heaven. Then, with the *Cloud of Virtue*, comes the consecration of the sublimation of sex, and the Absolute III, in its aspect of Sathanael, comes to greet the Androgynous Conqueror.

It is therefore clear that the process of inner pregnancy, just like the physical pregnancy, follows a descending scale in which the salvation of the Absolute III marks the Birth of the *Androgynous-Man 8*. This is the end of the esoteric evolution possible on Earth for the fallen ADAMEVE, who in full consciousness then takes up again the rank that was his before

---

10. 1 Corinthians xi: 11.

the fall and the task which was entrusted to him. He does this without confluence either with the divine plane or the human plane, between which he is called to maintain the balance.

Only then can he say with certainty that he is happy to be born on Earth, and can cry out in the fullness of his heart: Hosanna! Glory to the Lord Jesus Christ, Son of Man, Son of God, Saviour, First-Born amongst many Brethren! Glory to the *Covenant of Love*, the life-raft afloat on the stormy sea of human passions. *Maran-Atha!*

III

(1)

We would like to end this chapter by an *Appeal* reproducing the following two texts. We will begin with the sermon traditionally attributed to St John Chrysostom — *Golden Mouth* (374–407), which is recited in all Orthodox churches at midnight in the Easter matins. In the eastern Church, the resurrection of Jesus who, according to the Easter hymn, *conquered death by His Death*, is the *Feast of feasts and the Triumph of triumphs*; and every year after this cry of victory: *Khristos anesti! Christus resurrexit!* the Faithful, filled with emotion, listen to *Chrysostom's* words:

Let every pious man who loves God rejoice in this beautiful and
    glorious ceremony!
Let the devoted servant delight to share the joy of his Master!
Let him who has fasted diligently now receive the promised reward!
Let the labourer of the first hour come forward to receive his due.
Let him of the third hour also render thanks and be joyful!
Let him of the sixth hour have no doubt:
    nothing will be held back from his wages!
Let him who waited until the ninth hour
    approach without hesitation or fear,
and let him who appeared only at the eleventh hour not be afraid,
for the Lord is generous! He welcomes the last as the first.
He gives rest to the labourer of the eleventh hour,
as to the one of the first hour.
He is full of mercy towards the former,
and of kindness towards the latter.
He commends the completed work
and appreciates the intention.
He esteems the act, and he lauds the desire.

Enter ye all to the joy of your Master!
First come or last, now take your reward!
Rich man or poor, you can celebrate together!
You who have abstained, and you who have neglected to do so,
   honour this day!
Whether you have fasted or not, exult today!
The banquet is ready: come all and sit down;
the calf is fat: let no one go hungry!
Enjoy the banquet of Faith, gather the riches of mercy!
Let no one deplore his poverty, for a Kingdom has appeared which
   belongs to us all!
Let no one lament his faults, since pardon has sprung from the tomb!
Let no one fear death: for the death of the Saviour has liberated us!
He who was its prisoner has vanquished it.
He who descended into hell has overcome it.
He has struck down the death which tasted His flesh.
Isaiah prophesied about it:
'Hell was brought low by death when it met You under the earth.'
Hell was brought low by death because You have annihilated it;
brought low by death because You have laid it low;
brought low by death because You have enchained it.
View yourself as flesh, you will find yourself before God;
View yourself as earthly, it is Heaven you will see.
Regard yourself as visible,
and you will find yourself face to face with the invisible.
Where then is thy sting, O death? Hell, where is thy victory?
Christ is risen, and thou art brought low!
Christ is risen, and the demons are fallen!
Christ is risen, and the Angels rejoice!
Christ is risen and Life remains.
Christ is risen and the tombs are emptied of their dead,
Christ has risen from the dead;
For He is the first of them all![11]
To Him be glory and power for ever and ever. *Amen*!

And here is the second text: the prayer of St Ephraim the Syrian (320–
379), which is read in Orthodox Churches from the first to the last day of
Great Lent:

My God, Lord of my Life!
Drive out from me the spirit of laziness, despondency,
of domination, of levity:

---

11. Translated from the Slavonic text.

Give me, grant to Thy faithful servant the spirit of chastity, humility,
  patience and love;
Make me see my sins; help me not to judge my brothers,
Since Thou alone art blessed, for ever and ever.[12&13]

Amen.

---

12. *Idem.*
13. This is the normal English translation of this prayer:
    O Lord and Master of my Life!
    Give me not a spirit of sloth, despondency, lust for power and idle talk;
    Grant to me, Thy servant, a spirit of sobriety, humility, patience and love; etc. etc. (Ed.)

CHAPTER XVIII

(1)

At this point in the Third Part of the esoteric Cycle of the Doctrine, we humbly think it necessary to give a few details about Jesus, Son of God, Son of Man, and Son of David.

During His lifetime His Personality was already the object of lively controversies. The Gospel tells us that: '... *there was much murmuring among the people concerning Him: for some said, He is a good man: others said, Nay: but he deceiveth the people.*'[1] We do not know the outcome of these differences.

Above all, we must not believe that this controversy has lost any of its force after all these centuries. Jesus is *Alive*, and earthly Time has no hold over Him. He remains eternally present, and the controversy continues, even if it has taken new forms. By changing more and more in its form, it has taken a different shade but its content has not changed with its appearance, and the opposition to Jesus continues as before. Students of the Doctrine should keep this fact in mind, or else they will be unable to recognize the *scandals* that multiply on the road which leads to the First Threshold, and which can be explained by the continual action of the General Law. There are many formulae to lead one astray: some uphold 'liberty of opinion'; others demand 'proof' (sic) of the historical existence of Jesus; still others say that He existed, but that the true Saviour was John the Baptist, or even Simon Magus.[2]

The word *Christic*, which is in vogue now and replaces the word *Christian* in certain minds and in certain circles, bears witness to a greater refinement. It appears more conciliatory, more attractive even, but it is not so innocent as it appears at first sight, for, if we look closer, we may easily discern a subtle manoeuver that is intended to eliminate the Saviour by 'modernizing' Christianity.

The name *Christian* — which goes back to the first century, since the disciples first received it in Antioch when Paul and Barnabas preached there[3] — is not in any way ambiguous, while the adjective *Christic* has no proper definition: it is vague, elastic, and even as a neologism it lacks an academic definition.[4] Because of this, it permits deviations that are easy but dangerous, and which can lead, if this verb can be used in this context,

---

1. John vii: 12: in the Slavonic text, the word 'deceiveth' is replaced by 'seduceth' or 'ensnareth'.
2. Acts viii: 13-24.
3. Ibid. xi: 26.
4. One cannot find it in the *Littré*, in the *Robert*, or in the *Larousse*, nor in the dictionaries of religion.

toward a Christianity without Christ, which is perfectly acceptable to the General Law.

(2)

As for the doubt about the historical existence of Jesus, for centuries this has been paving the way for propaganda in favour of all sorts of philosophico-religious systems which claim to be initiatory, and which are Christian or rather *Christic* in appearance, that is, pseudo-Christian and 'independent'.

The search for the Truth naturally began long before the Advent of Christ. It was pursued in different parts of the world, including the Hellenistic perimeter which especially interests us, where it took different forms. At the time of the Advent, certain cults were dying out; others, like the cult of Mithra, which some historians claim was a serious rival to the propagation of the Christian Doctrine, were at full strength.[5] Two great traditions attracted the attention of the Apostles: the declining one of the chosen people, and one that was nurtured in the heart of the Greek nation which was called upon to be the *cornerstone*,[6] and to bring forth the *fruits of the Kingdom*.[7] With a striking gift for synthesis, St Paul defined the two traditions in these terms: '... *the Jews require a sign, and the Greeks seek after wisdom*':[8] then, passing on to a higher plane, he added: '*But we preach Christ crucified, unto the Jews a stumbling block, and unto the Greeks foolishness.*'[9] We can find the pre-Christian attitudes of the Jews and Greeks in our contemporary society which wishes for 'proof' and demands 'freedom of thought'.

Further on in his epistle, after having glorified the power and wisdom of God, the Apostle addresses the Corinthians who had been converted, as follows:

'*Consider, brethren, that amongst you who have been called, there are not many wise men after the flesh, nor many mighty, nor many noble. But God hath chosen the mad things of the world to confound the wise: God hath chosen the base things of the world and those which are despised, those which are not, to bring to nought those which are, so that no flesh should glory before God. Now it is by him that you are in Jesus Christ, who made himself for us wisdom, righteousness, sanctification and redemption so that, as it is written, he who glorifies himself, glorifies himself in the Lord.*'[10]

---

5. Cf. Prof. Thaddeus Zelinsky, *The Rivals of Christianity*, in Russian.
6. Matthew xxi: 42.
7. Ibid., 43.
8. 1 Corinthians i: 22.
9. Ibid., 23.
10. 1 Corinthians 26–31; after the Slavonic text. The Apostle refers here to the disciple who is conscious of his real 'I'.

The reader of 'Gnosis' will understand, without difficulty, that St Paul is referring to adamics and pre-adamics, the latter being the mighty, the noble, and the wise according to the wisdom of this world, for whom the crucifixion was, and still is, merely a myth, and who describe the Christian religion as the *opium of the people*. Only the adamics, or, in St Paul's terms, those who are 'called', can admit without a doubt that Jesus Christ, Son of God, Son of Man, and Son of David, was crucified and resurrected from the dead, for they possess the higher centres of consciousness in latent form.

Addressing the *perfect*,[11] who were scattered among the pre-adamics of that time, the Apostles, when preaching the *Good News* among the 'A' influences, strongly emphasized the absolute reality of the incarnation of the Word in the crucified and resurrected Jesus. In our days, a firm belief in the reality of this should be a definite sign for the seeker that he is on the right road, just as, for those who heed it, the preaching of this belief will be the sure sign that they hear the truth.

St John summed up this fundamental thesis in the following words whose meaning is as clear as it could be:

Beloved, believe not every spirit, but try the spirits whether they are of God: because many false prophets are gone out into the world.

Hereby know ye the Spirit of God: Every spirit that confesseth that Jesus Christ is come in the flesh is of God:

And every spirit that confesseth not that Jesus Christ is come in the flesh is not of God: and this is that spirit of antichrist, whereof ye have heard that it should come; and even now already is it in the world.

Ye are of God, little children, and have overcome them: because greater is he that is in you,[12] than he that is in the world.[13]

They[14] are of the world: therefore speak they of the world, and the world heareth them.

We are of God:[15] he that knoweth God[16] heareth us; he that is not of God heareth not us. Hereby know we the spirit of truth, and the spirit of error.[17]

---

11. In the real sense of the word: 1 Corinthians ii: 6; 2 Corinthians xiii: 9; Phillipians iii: 15; Colossians i: 28, etc.
12. The real 'I', the monad of Christ.
13. The Personality.
14. The pre-adamics.
15. The awakened adamics, conscious of their real 'I'.
16. Who has obtained the consciousness of his real 'I'.
17. 1 John iv: 1–6.

(3)

We can now clearly see the profound difference between the words *Christian* and *Christic*. The first demands commitment; the second demands nothing: it proposes an abstract Christ, at the most legendary if not imaginary; a Christ who is in no way an obstacle to 'freedom of opinion', even where this includes the deification of the Absolute III and, at the same time, of the human Personality, bearing aloft the banner on which this misleading motto is inscribed: Liberty, Equality, Fraternity.[18]

II

(1)

Let us now try to establish the facts.

The first question that arises is the following: is Jesus an historical figure or a myth? As an historian, the author of 'Gnosis' is always deeply surprised by the prejudice that exists against evidence about the Saviour's life. We can constate a very marked difference between the way in which people treat other sources from which we get our knowledge of the ancient world and those which inform us about Jesus' life. Yet the scientific value of both sources is usually the same. It is very difficult to explain this phenomenon, but we can say that one reason is because, added to accounts of the 'normal', historically certain side of the Saviour's life, there are many other aspects that emphasize the miraculous side of His passage on Earth. Because the Cartesian spirit, the basis of the Western science of yesterday, could not admit the truth of the miraculous, the ordinary events were also seen as open to doubt.

In our days, however, science officially recognizes the reality of cures just like those that make up the greater part of the miracles performed by Jesus. This kind of miracle was known at all times, just as were other phenomena like clairvoyance, the partial disappearance of gravity, levitation, etc. In addition, modern physics has opened up perspectives which are categorically opposed to the Cartesian spirit, so that only yesterday they seemed to belong to the realm of pure fantasy, and the life and actions of Jesus appear in a new light to today's scientists. The gap between traditional science and positive science is becoming narrower every day, and in this new light it is possible to reevaluate certain testimonies that were once well-known but were systematically set aside in years gone by. The most significant is the one found in the *Ecclesiastical History* of Eusebius of Cæsarea, which is our

---

18. Boris Mouravieff, *Liberté, Egalité, Fraternité* in *Synthèses*, Brussels, 1957, No. 129.

principal source of information on the early centuries of Christianity. This deals with the correspondence between Jesus and King Abgar *the Black*, a genuine historical character who reigned in Edessa in 7 BC, and then again, from 13 to 50 AD. This is what Eusebius tells us about him:

'... King Abgar, who was reigning in a distinguished way over the nations beyond the Euphrates, was then consumed by a terrible physical illness that caused him acute pain and was known to be incurable, at least by human methods. When he heard the illustrious name of Jesus, and of the miracles the latter was performing, which were attested by all, he sent Him a letter asking Jesus to cure him of his disease. Jesus did not answer his calls by going to him, but honoured him with a personal letter promising him that He would send one of His disciples to cure Abgar of his illness and to save him and all his subjects. The promise to the King was fulfilled shortly afterwards. In fact, after Jesus was resurrected from the dead and rose to heaven, Thomas, one of the twelve Apostles, by divine inspiration sent Thaddeus to Edessa. Thaddeus was one of the seventy disciples of Christ sent out as heralds and evangelists of Christ's doctrine. All the Lord's promises were accomplished through him: we have written proof of this in the archives of Edessa, which was the royal city in those days. This was found among the public documents of that country, which contain ancient records that go back to those of Abgar's time. It has been preserved there up to the present day. There is nothing like verifying the letters themselves, which we borrowed from the archives and translated literally from the Syriac as follows:'

Copy of the letter written by the Toparch Abgar to Jesus, and sent to the latter in Jerusalem through the messenger, Ananias.

Abgar, son of Ushmanas, Toparch, to the good Saviour Jesus appearing in Jerusalem, greetings:

"I have heard people talk of you and your cures, which you perform without remedies or plants. From what they say, you make the blind see and the lame walk; you cleanse lepers; you drive away unclean spirits and demons; you cure those with long illnesses; you raise the dead. Having heard all this about you, I have come to the conclusion that: either you are God, and having come down from heaven, you perform these wonders; or else you are the Son of God performing these wonders. This is why I write to you now and ask you to take the trouble to come to me and to cure the infirmity that I have. For I have also heard that the Jews murmur against you and wish to do you ill. My town is very small, but honourable, and it will suffice for both of us."

'This is the letter written by Abgar, who was then partially enlightened by the divine light. It is interesting to read the letter that Jesus wrote, which was brought back to Abgar by the same messenger. It is, undoubtedly, short, but it is full of meaning. Here is the text:

Jesus' reply, sent to the Toparch Abgar through the messenger Ananias.
"Blessed are you to have believed in me without having seen me. For it is written of me that those who have seen me will not believe in me, so that those who have not seen me may believe and live. As for what you write to me, to come to you I must first accomplish here all that I have been sent for, so that after having accomplished all this, I may return to him who sent me. But when I have been lifted up, I will send you one of my disciples to cure you of your infirmity and give you life, to you and to those who are with you."

'With these letters were the following texts in Syriac:

'After the ascension of Jesus, Judas, called Thomas, sent to Abgar the apostle Thaddeus, one of the seventy. On his arrival, the latter lodged with Tobias, son of Tobias. When they heard about him, certain people informed Abgar that an apostle of Jesus was there, just as He had promised. Thaddeus had therefore started to cure every illness and every depression by the power of God, so much so that everyone was astonished. And when Abgar learned about the wonders and the miracles that he was performing, and the cures that he was accomplishing, he thought that this must be he of whom Jesus had written: "... When I have been lifted up, I will send you one of my disciples to cure you of your infirmity ..."

'Abgar asked Thaddeus: Are you in truth a disciple of Jesus, the Son of God, who told me: "I will send you one of my disciples who will cure you and will give you life?" Thaddeus said: As you have strongly believed in the one who has sent me, I have been sent near you as you would have expected. And Abgar replied: I believed in him so much that I would have taken an army and destroyed the Jews who crucified him, if I had not been prevented by the Roman Empire. And Thaddeus said: Our Lord fulfilled the will of his Father, and after he had fulfilled it, he returned to the Father. Abgar said to him: And I also believed in him and in his Father. And Thaddeus said: Because of that I stretch my hand over you in his name. As soon as he did this, the king was cured of his sickness and the pains he endured.

'This is what we thought would not be useless or inopportune to report, and which we have translated literally from the Syriac.'[19]

There is no doubt that, imbued with the Cartesian spirit, yesterday's men of science, who discredited the miraculous aspect of Jesus' work, have extended this attitude by discrediting even the positive evidence of this work. And about this discrediting, it is surprising to note the ease with which phenomena that appear supernatural are accepted in Hatha Yoga, as well as in other eastern teachings which are more and more in vogue in Europe and America.

---

19. Eusebius of Cæsarea, *Histoire Ecclésiastique*, Greek text, taken from the French translation and annotations by Gustave Bardy, Paris, les Editions du Cerf, 1952, Book I. ch. XIII, pp. 40–6. Available in English: *An Ecclesiastical History to the Year 324 of the Christian Era*, translated by C. F. Cruse. London, 1838.

III

(1)

R eferring to the testimony of Eusebius of Cæsarea and Clement of Alexandria, we have already shown that the *Gnosis* based on the Doctrine revealed in this work had been revealed by Jesus, after his resurrection, to the three *Taborites*, Peter, James and John, his favourite disciples, who transmitted it to their spiritual descendants. At first it was taught to the faithful in the heart of the early Churches, and then in the *Didascalia*, where teaching was free and the only limits were defined by the capacity of the students to assimilate it. During the persecutions of the third century it became 'clandestine'. From that time on, it spread as an underground movement, just like a stream of water that in this way avoids obstacles on the ground so that it can continue to flow until a suitable place allows it to reappear on the surface, as it is doing today.

Repeatedly we have said that Jesus' teachings, summarized in the Gospels, and those of the Apostles, which appear in the thirty-two books of the New Testament, were founded on this *Gnosis* which, since then, has formed the object and the subject of the Holy Tradition. The attentive reader of 'Gnosis' would have observed that it provides the mind with a key that allows us to discover the triple meaning of the Holy Scriptures: narrative, symbolic, and hieroglyphic. It also permits the 'disoccultation' of the latter, conforming to the following words pronounced by Jesus: '*Unto you it is given to know the mysteries of the kingdom of God; but unto them that are without all these things are done in parables.*'[20]

It is now time to subject the text of the Lord's Prayer—the *Pater Noster*— to a critical analysis made in the spirit of the study that is the object of the third part of the present volume. We must first consider it in the form in which it has reached us, and then, after reestablishing its original form, we must try to recognize the central point of the Saviour's teaching as it was bequeathed to the Faithful and to their posterity.

(2)

In modern languages the Lord's Prayer appears in the following forms:
9. Our Father which art in Heaven, Hallowed be thy Name,
10. Thy kingdom come. Thy will be done in earth, as it is in Heaven.
11. Give us this day our daily bread.

---

20. Mark iv: 11; from the Slavonic text.

12. And forgive us our trespasses,[21] as we forgive them that trespass against us.

13. And lead us not into temptation, but deliver us from evil:
For thine is the kingdom, and the power, and the glory, for ever and ever.[22]
Amen.

In making a critical analysis of this text, we will follow the general rule which should be applied to every interpretation, to interpret it in relation to its context.

Saint Augustine wanted passages from the Gospel to be annotated in this way, and he protested strongly against the bad faith of certain commentators who, he said, 'choose a few isolated passages from the Scriptures, with which they can mislead the ignorant by not linking them to the statements that precede or follow them, and through which the author's will and line of thought can be understood.'[23]

We will therefore study the Lord's Prayer in the framework in which it appears, namely, in the context of the five verses which precede it:

5. And when thou prayest, thou shalt not be as the hypocrites are: for they love to pray standing in the synagogues and in the corners of the streets, that they may be seen of men. Verily I say unto you, They have their reward.

6. But thou, when thou prayest, enter into thy closet, and when thou hast shut thy door, pray to thy Father which is in secret; and thy Father which seeth in secret shall reward thee openly.

7 But when ye pray, use not vain repetitions, as the heathen do: for they think that they shall be heard for their much speaking.

8. Be not ye therefore like unto them: for your Father knoweth what things ye have need of before ye ask him.

9. After this manner therefore pray ye:[24]

and the twenty-one verses that follow contain a commentary on these verses, 5–9, and repeat the recommendations which appear in them.

This is why the eighth verse is repeated and widely commented upon in verse 31 and the verses that follow:

31. Therefore take no thought, saying What shall we eat? or What shall we drink? or Wherewithal shall we be clothed?

32. For after all these things *do the Gentiles seek:* for *your heavenly Father* knoweth that ye have need of all these things.

---

21. The Biblical version is as follows: 'And forgive us our debts, as we forgive our debtors.' But we have reproduced the version that is currently used in the Churches, and by most English-speaking Christians. (Ed.)

22. Matthew vi: 9-13. Revised version of 1611 AD. Published by the British and Foreign Bible Society, 146 Queen Victoria Street, London, and printed by Eyre and Spottiswoode, Ltd.

23. 'Bene Augustinus contra Adimantum: Particulas quasdam de scripturis, eligunt, quibus decipiant non connectentes quae supra et infra scripta sunt, ex quibus voluntas et intentio scriptoris possi intellegi ...' C4 (c. 14).

24. Matthew ibid., 5–9.

33. But seek ye first the kingdom of God, and his righteousness; *and all these things shall be given unto you.*

34. Take therefore no thought for the morrow: for the morrow shall take thought for the things of itself. Sufficient unto the day is the evil thereof.[25]

It is obvious that, through these words, Christ was trying to turn the attention of human beings away from the 'necessities' in which they were absorbed, and to inculcate in them a desire for a higher bread, for *the one thing necessary.*[26]

(3)

If we return to the text of the prayer quoted above, we will see that four of the five verses, including the request not to be led into temptation but to be delivered from evil,[27] are related to divine things; thus, the prayer itself, and the whole of the VIth chapter of the Gospel according to St Matthew, seem to be dedicated to the principle of the importance of living on the noumenal plane rather than on the phenomenal. While they encourage man to concentrate his efforts on the application of this principle, they also promise him *everything else,* that is, the daily needs of life. These will also be given to him if he respects this priority.

Only one of the five verses is out of keeping with the four others and with the twenty-nine that complete chapter VI; this is verse eleven, which is as follows:

11. Give us this day *our daily bread.*[28]

This sounds strange when we see that Jesus twice said (verses 7 and 32) that this kind of prayer is the prayer of a pagan.

We can therefore conclude that, in this form, verse 11 directly contradicts the prayer as a whole and its context, that is, chapter VI as a whole.

The Slavonic and Greek texts do not contain this contradiction. In them, there is no question of *daily bread,* but of *supersubstantial bread*[29] — in other words, *heavenly bread,* or *bread descended from heaven,*[30] of which Jesus speaks so often.

---

25. Ibid. The italics are the author's.

26. Luke x: 42.

27. That is, the Absolute III.

28. The italics are the author's. We must mention that, in esoteric commentaries, the words *this day* or *today*, are usually used in relation to the whole life of the individual.

29. НАСУЩНЫИ in Russian, ἐπιούσιον in Greek.

30. John vi: 32, 33, 34, 35, 41, 48, 51, etc. And then: Labour not for the meat that perisheth, but for that meat which endureth unto everlasting life, ibid., vi: 27.

(4)

Now, we must try to find out how the idea of *daily bread* supplanted that of *supersubstantial bread* and became so firmly anchored in the minds of the mass of believers in the West. This appears even more enigmatic when we consult the *Vulgate* and find in it the expression, '*Panem nostrum supersubstantialem da nobis hodie,*'[31] which is correct. The original expression also appears in the first translations of the Gospel into modern languages. For instance, a French edition, published in Lyon by Nicholas Petit in the year 1540, contains a correct translation of the eleventh verse; it appears in the following terms: '*Donne-nous auiourdhuy nostre pain supersubstantiel.*'[32] Continuing our research, we came across another copy of the Gospel that appeared in the following century, at La Rochelle in 1616, where this formula had already become:

'*Donne-nous aujourd'huy nostre pain quotidien.*'[33]

The edition came out in a place and date that lead us to think that this innovation was due to the rationalism of the Huguenots — at that time, La Rochelle was their citadel. If this rationalization of the mystical formula, though erroneous, was logical for a Calvinistic spirit that was true to itself, we still fail to see how this Protestant version and certain variations of it found a place in the Catholic gospels that appeared in proper form under a Bishop's *Imprimatur*. For example, we have before us a copy of the Gospel printed in Paris in the Augustinian printing works, which carries the following *Imprimatur*:

'In view of the report submitted by Canon Ferry, Doctor of Literature and President of the Commission for the study of Books in the Diocese, the Bishop of Nimes is pleased to state that he approves the translation of the holy Gospel according to Saint Matthew, submitted by the TT.RR.PP. Augustinians of the Assumption.

Le Vigan (Gard), on pastoral tour, the 30th August, 1891
(S) † Jean-Alfred, Bishop of Nimes.'

In this Gospel, the 11th verse of the VIth chapter appears in the following form:

---

31. *Novum Testamentum*, Vulgatae Editionis. Ex Vaticanis Editionibus Earumque correctorio. P. Michael Hetzenauer O.C. Prov. Tirol. sept. Approbatus lector S. Theologiae et Guardianus. Cum Approbatione Ecclesiastica Omnipote, Libraria Academica Wagneriana, MDCCCIC, Secundum Matthaem, Caput VI, II.
The *Vulgate* was translated from the Hebrew by St Jerome (circa 331–420) towards the end of the IVth century, on the demand of Pope Damase. It is the only Latin version recognized as canonical by the Council of Trent.
32. *La Première Partie du Nouveau Testament*, en françay, nouvellement reveu & corrigé, Nicolas Petit, Lyon, 1540, p. 7 (translated by Le Fèvre).
33. *La Bible qui est Toute la Sainte Ecriture du Vieil et Nouveau Testament*. At La Rochelle, printed by Corneil Hertzmann, at M. H. Hauttin's Printing Press, 1616.

11. '*Donnez-nous aujourd'hui le pain necessaire a notre subsistance.*'[34]

What a gulf there is between this formula and the actual terms that Jesus employed when He spoke of *supersubstantial* bread. No doubt the reader of 'Gnosis' will recognize the results of the action of the General Law, which is busy neutralizing those still active 'B' influences that represent a danger to a world where 'A' influences rule.

(5)

If we have taken the trouble to explain all these things that are almost self-evident, it is because the Lord's Prayer, the *Pater Noster*, is the core of the Doctrine. It is no exaggeration to say that there never has been, and never will be, on Earth, a prayer that surpasses or even equals it.

This prayer expresses a yearning towards the *Light* and towards *Love*, for God is both *Light* and *Love*.[35] Because of his identification with his Personality, adamic man is submerged in blinding obscurity and, in formulating this prayer, Jesus wanted to teach him to implore the aid of the warm Light of Love of which he had been deprived ever since the Fall. From this didactic point of view, the five verses of the Prayer summarize the whole of the Gospels and Epistles, which form a commentary on it. What is more, this prayer offers the adamic man a mystical means of working his way up the stream of Love emanating from the Absolute I, which undergoes a considerable loss of pressure as it descends toward our planet. It follows from this that, on every rung of the Ray of Creation, life is a resultant specifically characterized by the conjugation of the vibrating Love of the Absolute I, whose action progressively weakens as it crosses the different planes of the Cosmos, with an inversely proportional quantity of feminine Love, the will of the flesh, the inert, passive love coming from the Queen of the Heavens. In pre-adamic man the proportion of these two elements is 25% and 75% respectively, while in Adam it was 50:50.

By the Fall, adamic man broke this divine equilibrium, and, by deliberately abandoning his light body, made of the 'dust of the earth', for a gross envelope resembling that of pre-adamic man, he sank another step deeper into the *Darkness*. The prayer that Jesus taught gives him a marvelous instrument thanks to which he can strive to 'go upstream' and reestablish the broken balance of these forces.

This prayer is built in what might be called transverse form. Attentive study will lead to the discovery of nine autonomous elements in the five verses of the *Pater Noster*. These correspond to the notes of the Great Cosmic Octave:

---

34. 'Give us this day the bread necessary for our subsistence.'
35. John i: 6–9.

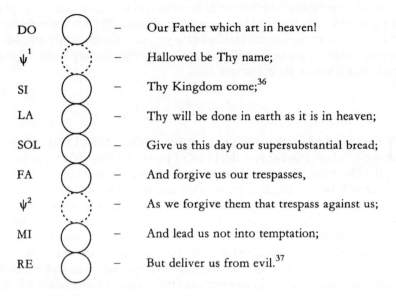

DO	◯ –	Our Father which art in heaven!
ψ¹	◌ –	Hallowed be Thy name;
SI	◯ –	Thy Kingdom come;[36]
LA	◯ –	Thy will be done in earth as it is in heaven;
SOL	◯ –	Give us this day our supersubstantial bread;
FA	◯ –	And forgive us our trespasses,
ψ²	◌ –	As we forgive them that trespass against us;
MI	◯ –	And lead us not into temptation;
RE	◯ –	But deliver us from evil.[37]

FIG. 19

Let us now try to analyse the prayer from this angle, to grasp the meaning of each of its elements:

We will quickly notice that, from the top and working downwards, these elements form four groups which contain four, two, one, and again two verses.

The first group has a general character, with a preparatory role which is to clear the cluttered heart of the faithful so that the fine current of Love emanating from the Absolute I (the Father) can easily penetrate it. This operation is the first condition *sine qua non* for the effectiveness of the prayer. It is difficult to practice in the tumult of world 'A', and it was to make it easier that Jesus made the following recommendation: '... *when thou prayest, enter into thy closet, and when thou hast shut thy door, pray to thy Father which is in secret; and thy Father which seeth in secret shall reward thee openly.*'[38]

---

36. We have already established that the *Father* is the Holy Spirit; one prays here, therefore, for the coming of the Era of the Holy Spirit.

37. The Absolute III.

38. Matthew vi: 6; identical to the Slavonic text. One will notice that this text appears in verse *six* of Chapter SIX: a number chosen twice, and which signifies the *Resurrection*.

164

(6)

The preparatory work mentioned above is necessary to isolate the heart from the hubbub of life, and to make it receptive to calm, inward contemplation. If this isolation is effective, the disciple can tackle the elements of the second group — the fifth and sixth — in an active and fearless '*mantric*' spirit.[39] He will then solicit the intervention of the Absolute II: the Christ; the supersubstantial bread by whose Grace he can obliterate his karmic burden, and by doing so can obtain his purification.

Christ's attitude toward the supplicant who shows courage is invariably positive. He himself exercises constant pressure on the human heart, as the following words show: '*Behold, I stand at the door, and knock.*'[40]

(7)

Thus, a possibility of purification is freely offered to him who, by following the transverse course of the prayer and, through this, creating the desired atmosphere within himself, first by passive concentration then through active concentration, knows how to implore this cleansing through Grace which is the supersubstantial bread of the Christ. This is offered to him 'today', that is, in this very life.

All the conditions required for effective prayer are thus brought together. Yet these *necessary* conditions are not *sufficient*: a second *sine qua non* condition remains to be fulfilled. This demands of the human will the effort to anticipate the divine will, which is always ready to help the man who aspires to Redemption. This condition is defined in the seventh element of the prayer: '... *As we forgive them that trespass against us.*'

Through this *human* act, which is divinely inspired, the faithful fills the interval that separates the notes FA and MI and, in this way, opens the 'sluice gate' for the current of Christ's redeeming Love, which flows here to join that of the Father. It is easy to imagine the importance of this act, on which the crossing of this interval depends.

If this second condition *sine qua non* is effectively fulfilled, the faithful can pass to the fourth group of elements, and it is then that he will pray usefully, in the note MI, to be preserved from another fall even worse than the first, and, in the note RE, to be forever delivered from the yoke of the Absolute III.

This is the first of the hieroglyphic meanings of the Lord's prayer, which is the pillar of the Doctrine centered around the problem of individual

---

39. Jesus once said: 'Courage, woman, Thy faith hath cured thee!' (Matthew. ix: 22; literal translation from the Slavonic).
40. Revelation iii: 20.

salvation. But there remain two others: the reader of 'Gnosis' who has reached this point of our detailed study must first discover the second, then the third. He must try to do this by studying the indications given earlier with the schemata diagramming the universal cosmogony, especially the system of the Three cosmic Octaves. This discovery demands a great *emotional* assimilation of the Doctrine. The only way this is possible is by individual revelation, and knowledge acquired in this way cannot be transmitted in human language.

Whoever — man, woman or child — manages to have a vision of the architecture of the *Pater Noster*, immediately enters, if only for a split second, into direct contact with the plane of the divine *Gnosis*. He must then apply all his strength to keep alive in his memory the impressions he felt during this instantaneous revelation...

IV

(1)

The only thing that remains to us now, for this chapter, is to consider the miraculous side of Jesus' work.

We will begin with the Nativity as the Gospel describes it. It is known that Eastern Orthodoxy does not accept the dogma of the Immaculate Conception of the Virgin Mary. This theory, which was upheld by the Franciscans and opposed by the Dominicans, was presented before the Catholic Council of Basel (1431), which decided to recognize it as part of the doctrine of the Roman Church, but it was only in 1854 that Pope Pius IX declared, *ex cathedra*, in the Bull *Ineffebilis Deus*, that the *Immaculate Conception* was a dogma whose acceptance was obligatory for every Catholic.

According to this dogma, from the moment of her conception by Saint Anne, the Virgin Mary was protected from every trace of original sin. To the Eastern mind, this theory seems contrary to the very meaning that the Western theologians wished to give it. Apart from the fact that the Orthodox Church does not recognize any dogmatic evolution after the VIIth Council, which had a truly œcumenical character, to qualify the conception of the Mother of God as *immaculate* does not appear to the Orientals so much as an attack on the High Fact of the incarnation of the Word as Son of God, but more on his nature as the Son of Man. For them, this damage has a monophysite implication, since it takes away from the *human* nature of Jesus its *humanity* in the strict sense of the word. What is more, since the Catholic dogma regards the Saviour as born of the Father, who is the Holy Spirit, and of the Mother, miraculously preserved from any trace of original sin, one could maintain that, if the nature of Jesus, as the Son of Man, was not really human, terrestrial, and integrally inherited from his Mother, His sacrifice and Passion have no intrinsic value. Orthodox dogma recognizes a dual nature in Jesus: divine and human, in which each of the two elements has its full reality and strength. The Virgin Mary was pure, chaste, and innocent, but wholly terrestrial and adamic; she conceived Jesus by the Holy Spirit, and therefore without the intervention of man, by the grace of an immaculate conception, but this sinless conception was that of her Son and not of herself.

Briefly, the Orthodox belief is that the divine intervention in a genuinely terrestrial feminine body is precisely what makes the greatness of the birth and passion of Jesus. Not only this but, with the current progress of science, parthenogenesis has now lost the nature of absolute unbelievability it had before. Tomorrow, sceptics will no longer claim that the story of the Gospel is 'impossible' with the ignorant certainty which they possessed yesterday.

(2)

Let us suppose that, his scepticism silenced, man finally admits the greatness of Jesus' work, it would still have to be explained how His passion was in fact able to save humanity. We might say that Jesus was neither the first nor the last innocent man to be executed, and that judicial errors and abuses of power are as old as the world. This reasoning, however, is false because it is incomplete. The fact is that Jesus was not only innocent, but without sin.

Let us try to analyse this fact in mathematical form by representing it in an equation:

Let us say that the aggregate value, physical and moral, of the average earthly man is equal to x, that the sum of his faults, again physical and moral, is equal to y, that his karmic burden is equal to z, and that all three elements are variable. In this case, the value of the ratio:

$$\frac{x}{y + z} \quad \dots \dots \dots \dots \dots \text{(I)}$$

would show the remainder of man's general balance-sheet drawn up at a given moment.

Now, every human being is born with a certain reserve of vitality and with a particular karmic burden, so that:

$$x > (y + z) \dots \dots \dots \dots \text{(II)}$$

During the course of life, this ratio is modified. Generally, y and z increase, whereas after a certain time, x decreases. However, as long as the ratio (I) remains positive, that is, as long as:

$$\frac{x}{y + z} > 1 \quad \cdots\cdots\cdots\cdots \quad \text{(III)}$$

the man remains alive and is capable of *producing*, that is to say, of using as physical moral or spiritual strength, the excess of x − (y + z) for ends pursued on the corresponding planes. When, because of age or fatigue, the formula (III) takes the form of the following equation:

$$\frac{x}{y + z} = 1$$

the man lives like a business operating with neither a profit nor a loss.

When, later in life, this ratio continues to be modified in the same direction until it looks like this:

$$x < (y + z)$$

or

$$\frac{x}{y + z} = 0,n,$$

the 'n' being an infinitesimal that has zero for its limit; and when this limit is reached, and our formula becomes:

$$\frac{x}{y + z} = 0$$

then the man dies.

If we now take the case of Jesus, we will see that our equation takes quite a different and even unique aspect. In Jesus, by definition:

x   was a constant of his perfectly developed Personality and body;

y   was equal to zero;

z   was also equal to zero.

Even without considering the strength of his divine nature, the human equation is as follows:

$$\frac{x}{0 + 0} = \infty$$

This means that the voluntary sacrifice of the Son of Man, He who was without fault or sin, and without the liability of a karmic burden, released a moral and physical force of *unlimited* greatness.

During the twelve millennia between the fall of Adam and the Advent of Christ, the general karmic burden of organic Life on Earth had become so great that the *Tritocosmos* was threatened with disintegration, since the accumulation of hate, jealousy and violence was too great for the new Commandment: '*Love one another.*' And the call to adopt the ultimate saving attitude: *Love your enemies*, could no longer be understood nor even heard. Since it had become impossible, because of this, to save the 'A' influence world by an inflow of the 'B' influence of divine Love, there only remained the formidable substitution formula: to achieve this salvation through suffering '... *For God so loved the world that He gave His only begotten Son that the world through Him might be saved.*'[41]

(3)

Apart from what has just preceded, it would be impossible to pass by in silence the very widespread belief according to which *the prayer of a just person can do much.* We need to explain this.

This is the royal formula of Jesus:

$$\frac{x}{0 + 0} = \infty$$

for the just, it becomes the following:

$$\frac{x}{\Delta y + \Delta z} = P$$

where

Δy = traces of sin
Δz = traces of faults
P = real Power

this enables us to appreciate the words of St Paul about the Covenant of Love, which we have quoted more than once, in a new light:

'*And we know that all things work together for good to them that love God,*[42] *to them who are called according to his purpose. For whom he did foreknow he also did predestinate to be conformed to the image of his Son that he might be the first born among many brethren.*'[43]

In the end, that is, at the passage of the IIIrd Threshold, where the traces of faults will be erased and all traces of the karmic burden burned, the infinitesimals y and z will become equal to zero. The androgynous equation of the Knight and the Lady of his dreams will then take on a significance equal to that of the royal equation given above:

$$\frac{x + x'}{0} = \infty$$

---

41. John iii: 16, 17. We may now better understand the profound meaning of St Paul's words: '*For we are saved by hope ...*' (Romans viii: 24). The meaning is that humanity will remain safe from destruction along with Organic Life on the Earth. This allows everyone to work with a hope of salvation.

42. The adamics as compared to the pre-adamics.

43. Romans viii: 28.

(4)

How vain and insignificant appear the ambitions and pretensions of the human Personality, puffed up with self-deification, if we consider them in relation to the hierarchy of *Conquerors*, the only real power that keeps world 'A' standing, although not without pain despite the methodical destructive efforts made in profusion by *human wisdom* — which, we can now understand, really is folly before God![44]

It is because he could measure this vanity and this insignificance in all its fullness that St Paul said:

'I bow my knees unto the Father of our Lord Jesus Christ, of whom the whole family in heaven and earth is named, that he would grant you, according to the riches of his glory, to be strengthened with might by his Spirit in the inner man; that Christ may dwell in your hearts by faith. That ye, being rooted and grounded in love, may be able to comprehend with all the saints what is the breadth, and length and depth, and height; and to know the love of Christ, which passeth knowledge that ye might be filled with all the fullness of God. Now unto him that is able to do exceeding abundantly above all that we ask or think according to the power that worketh in us, unto him be glory in the church by Christ Jesus throughout all ages world without end. Amen.'[45]

---

44. 1 Corinthians iii: 19.

45. Ephesians iii: 14–21; from the King James text. Slavonic text originally used by Mouravieff translated from the French as herewith:

I bow my knee before the Father of our Lord Jesus Christ, from Whom all fatherhood in the heavens and on the earth takes its name. That He may grant you through the richness of His glory, to be powerfully strengthened by His Spirit in the inner man, so that by faith Christ may come to dwell in your hearts, so that being rooted and grounded in Love, you may be able to comprehend, with all the the saints, what is the breadth, the length, the depth and the height, and to know the love of Christ which surpasses all knowledge, so that you may be filled even unto the fullness of God.
Now, to Him Who can do, by the power that acts in us, infinitely beyond all that we ask for or to which we aspire, to Him be glory in the Church and in Jesus Christ, throughout all generations, for ever and ever, Amen!

CHAPTER XIX

(1)

Before the Earth can enter the Era of the Holy Spirit, the Time of Transition must reach a successful outcome, and this outcome will in turn depend on a positive answer to a whole group of problems which will be solved by the appearance of the New Man.

We have already studied these problems from different points of view: now let us try to consider them all together. This will give us an opportunity to observe the behaviour of certain elements on different planes; elements which play a role in humanity as a whole and should in principle make an active contribution to the positive evolution of mankind.

The better to grasp all the problems that interest us, because they are in a certain measure autonomous, it is useful to examine their elements one by one. The positive and synchronous development of these will contribute to a satisfactory outcome of the Time of transition, and then to the establishment on Earth of the Era of the Holy Spirit.

From this point of view, we can distinguish four principal elements in human society:

1. *The population of Earth*, which today has over 3,200,000,000[1] inhabitants. The annual percentage growth, according to UN publications, is 1.3%, which should make it reach about 7,000,000,000 people by the end of the century.

2. *The ruling elite of the world*, those in different countries who hold the reins of command on political, economic and social planes, and which, by the force of events, begin to be penetrated by the planetary consciousness.

3. *The family*, the reproductive cell of the body of humanity.

4. *The couple*, androgynous or not. At every level, this is the fundamental unit of humanity.

We are going to consider this whole group of problems that concern us by visualizing them in action, that is, by observing their evolution in the past and then extrapolating it into the future.

We know already that the only motive strong enough to make living beings rise out of their somnolence is Love, pure or mixed, in all the ways it acts—positive or negative. In the light of the manifestation of this creative and at the same time perturbing force, we are logically brought to study the four elements—mentioned above—at different levels. This will lead to a final synthesis, from which we will draw some general conclusions.

---

1. In the 1960s.

In outline, this is the plan for the final chapters of this part of the present volume of 'Gnosis', which is dedicated to THE LIFE, and which is finally followed by an Epilogue.[2]

(2)

The human species, adamic and pre-adamic, is at present very degenerate. The Bible tells us that man was created in the image and likeness of God, that is, in a perfect physical and psychic form. According to the Book of Genesis, the physical degeneration of the adamics began with the Fall, and the degeneration of their psyches with the fratricide committed by Cain: because of the close interdependence of the psyche with the physical, this latter phenomenon had an influence on the beauty of their descendants that was as powerful as it was pernicious, and this is how *Cain went out from the presence of the Lord.*[3]

A stranger to the Fall, pre-adamic humanity evidently did not suffer its effects. In contrast with the ugliness of the adamics, which grew worse and worse as time went on, their beauty became more and more striking, and: ... *the sons of God saw the daughters of men that they were fair; and they took them wives of all which they chose.*[4] The mixture of the two races which ensued — and which included Seth's posterity — dragged the pre-adamics towards a degeneration which then became general.

The more this degeneration progressed, the more the physical ugliness and the corruption of the psyche progressed: beauty as it was at the beginning became very rare, and was no longer fully expressed. The print of ugliness was visible even in the most beautiful girls, but men, whose spirit had become deformed as they degenerated, ended up by finding beauty even in the 'stylized' ugliness of their companions; then the Eternal said: *My Spirit shall not always strive with man, for that he also is flesh.*[5]

After having lost contact with the higher centres, the corruption of the heart having persisted over millennia, being successively tainted by fratricide, genocide, the murder of the prophets and the crucifixion of the Saviour, despising the possibilities of salvation offered him and mocking

---

2. For an understanding of the *natural* evolution of the organization of human society, see: *Le Problème de l'Autorité super-étatique*, Boris Mouravieff, Paris-Neuchâtel, La Baconnière, 1950, 133 pp.
3. Genesis iv: 16.
4. Ibid., vi: 2.
5. Genesis vi: 3.

at God, how can one be surprised that adamic man became no more than a pitiable caricature of the image of the Most High?[6]

(3)

We know that the Personality of adamic man was originally the instrument through which the real 'I' manifested on the psychic plane. To manifest itself on the physical plane, the Personality had the use of the instrument that was the hylic body. But when it lost consciousness of the real 'I', on the contrary, it became to a great degree enslaved by the body. This reversal of roles led to the anarchistic psychosomatic confusion which characterizes the human species today.

In spite of everything, in the depths of his heart adamic man still preserves a vague recollection of his origin, which clings to the continuation of the chromosomes and their genes. Humanity's chance lies in this fact, which not only allows us to hope for regeneration, but to depend on it; without this, contemporary man, who in his present state is a caricature of God, would certainly never inherit the Kingdom of Heaven.

Let nobody be mistaken, the adornment of the body is neither a luxury nor a concession to coquetry. It is a condition that is necessary if we are to obtain a positive outcome of the Time of Transition. Yet we must not see a reason for despair in this rigorous imperative, nor think that the process of regeneration would require millennia. If we became clearly conscious of the necessity for attractiveness, this would be a great help. The indispensable minimum could be achieved in two or three generations. If the process is effectively begun by the end of the Time of Transition, the perfecting of both human races during the millennium of the Era of the Holy Spirit will become the responsibility of the families and couples of whom we will speak further on.

In the meantime, compulsory education for the new generations contributes more and more every day to the selection of talent in all the races of the world, while technical progress ensures the necessary improvement of living conditions.

---

6. Man does not generally take account of this. In order to see himself as he is, he must look at himself in two mirrors, because the image reflected in a single mirror is inverted. He must observe himself in this way for ten minutes, while simultaneously practicing *presence in himself*. By repeating this exercise every day, one will progressively eliminate all compromise with oneself. Of course, this demands strong nerves.

II

(1)

We know that man can reach the consciousness of his real 'I' by working on his under-developed and unbalanced Personality. The same kind of work can also act in the opposite direction, enabling him to beautify his body. It is important to understand how this can be done in practice, since the improvement of the human race, which is the object of our study, depends on this possibility. We will therefore discuss it briefly.

The real 'I', the Monad of Christ, is so beautiful that it defies all description. When the human Personality, which is dull by nature, becomes an Individuality by uniting with the real 'I', it begins to shine with the light communicated to it by the latter, and it then transmits the beauty it has gained to the physical body. This, in a few words, is the process of improving the human race, and it can lead to what Tradition calls *the glorification of the body*.[7]

Is there any need to say that we are still far from this? For the moment, let us see what modern man can do to move towards this goal.

(2)

To sum up, we can say that in order to become an Individuality, that is, in order to identify itself with the real 'I', the Personality should already have acquired a minimum degree of beauty; and the hylic body should be prepared for the establishment within it of the Individuality that is born of this union. In order to give our bodies this indispensable minimum of beauty, we must work on our Personality, for we know what an influence the psychic exercises over the physical; and we must do this without further delay, as very little time remains.

Man has an instinctive feeling which pushes him in this direction, only he confuses the idea of *being* with that of *appearing*, so that, while exerting himself on the plane of *appearance*, he makes no deliberate effort on the plane of *being*, not daring to believe that it may be possible to obtain tangible results in this, so much is he the slave of his scepticism. This is why, in spite of his ingenuity, imagination, and energy, there are no lasting results, and hardly any contribution is made to the improvement of the race. This is because these efforts are applied rightly in detail, where their aim is to aid nature, but are badly conceived in terms of the essential, where they too often run counter to the divine call by substituting fantastic

---

7. Vol. II, pp. 239–240.

stylization for the culture of true and healthy beauty. Indeed, the problem in the improvement of the human race, both adamic and pre-adamic, is precisely that of the cultivation of beauty: physical beauty and beauty of psyche, which are closely interdependent.

Everybody generally agrees that, in animated and visual form, the highest expression of divine Beauty on Earth is the human body, especially that of woman, for nothing can equal the harmony of perfect feminine forms. The male form cannot equal it, as we can see in even the most beautiful masculine forms left us by ancient Greek art: those of Apollo and Narcissus, which have never been surpassed but which are nevertheless effeminate. This is normal. It is a question of balance in the polarity of the sexes: Woman's strength lies in her beauty, whereas Man's beauty lies in his strength.

(3)

A beautiful mother who gives birth to beautiful children: this is the natural and feasible way in which we can improve the human race. If we leave aside the spiritual, pneumatic factor, which is not within everybody's reach, we can say that the solution of the problem we are examining here demands a synergy of properly oriented, conscious efforts, psychic and physical. Later, we will talk more fully about these psychic efforts, but here we will confine ourselves to saying only what is necessary about the participation of the motor centre in this aspect of culture.

(4)

It is no exaggeration to say that the question of pure physical beauty, which occupied an important place in ancient Greece, was later gradually relegated to the background until it was finally lost in the recesses of human consciousness. There is no doubt that for ancient peoples, especially the Greeks, physical beauty was of burning topical interest: we need no better proof than the penalty to which the civic oath of the Chersonese condemned traitors and perjurers, namely: *No longer to have beautiful children*. The desire to impart divine beauty to the human body made the Greeks give birth to an artistic expression whose proof to this day is in their unparalleled marble statues. Of course attempts were also made elsewhere, and Egyptian, Greco-Buddhic, medieval Christian and Renaissance art — to name only a few[8] — give us admirable examples; but these marvels are different from the Greek models because of their stylization,

---

8. We do not mention ancient Rome here. Except for *portraiture*, at which they were past masters, the Roman artists remained pupils of the Greeks.

which happened because the intellect intervened, imposing its own 'considerations' onto the realism of pure Art. The realism of Greek art, which created such beautiful images of the human body, with such a perfect knowledge of its harmony and its anatomy, has never been surpassed or even equalled. We must consider these images as proofs of a divine revelation of a very high degree, which placed those artists who were blessed with it on the same level as the prophets. Works like this, made by the hands of *epoptes*,[9] such as Praxiteles, Phidias and other great masters, will forever remain the objects of study and admiration.

The divine nature of these revelations may also be recognized by the fact that these ancient Greek masters generally represented perfect human beauty in the form of nude or semi-nude bodies. This nudity did not shock them, neither did it offend those who contemplated these masterpieces later, whether they were men or women, initiates or non-initiates, for they were all impregnated with the very high religious spirit that reigned at the time.

To be ashamed of nudity is a logical consequence of the Fall. It is a result of comparing the ugliness that has been acquired with the beauty that has been lost because of it. This shame was effaced before the classical nudity of the marble gods and goddesses, which were images of divine perfection and, as such, were objects of chaste contemplation and sacred veneration. These nude bodies were very real expressions of perfect Beauty, and thus of the divine essence, and this meant that they were free of the stylization which comes from intellectual interference.

The divine purity of masculine and feminine forms really depicts adamic humanity before the Fall. It presents us with the original types and subtypes of sinless men and women, without vices and without karmic burden. From this point of view, the pantheon of Greek gods and goddesses gives each of us a practical means of recognizing our original type or subtype and thus discovering our own physical deformation and, through this, learning the nature of our psychic deformation.

The attentive study and regular contemplation of these images, exposed in the temples and on the public squares of Greece, explains to a great extent what is called the 'Greek miracle.' And if people in our cities today could admire the statues of the gods and goddesses of the Greek pantheon, perhaps it would be easier for them to understand the oracle of the Pythia of Delphi which Socrates transmitted to posterity, but which is so little understood in its true sense;

GNOTHI SEAUTON![10]

---

9. Initiates to the Mysteries.
10. Know thyself.

External contemplation of this kind, accompanied by simultaneous introspection (constatation), and pursued in a spirit that we might properly call religious, would be a powerful factor in the improvement of the human race which is the object of our study. And the higher the degree of contemplation, the greater[11] the influence of this factor.

III

(1)

We must make it clear that we are not advocating naturism or nudism. It is obvious that to constantly look at imperfect, flabby bodies could only augment the ugliness of future generations. But if it is true that the majority of human beings have imperfect bodies, it is still possible to favour the regeneration of the human race, and we are going to propose at least one way in which this can be done.

'One nail drives out another,' they say. It is this that we are suggesting, but the nail we insert must be up to standard! We are, indeed, spectators of a terrifying show which is a result of the deformation of our degenerated mind: the pathological taste which is spreading through the Arts, and which deforms faces and bodies until they become monstrosities which are a veritable offence to God and a blasphemy against the Holy Spirit.[12] Not only do we come to terms with ugliness, but we even admire it as long as it is 'in style'. The general quest is not towards the *Beautiful* and the *True*, but towards the *New at any cost*, so great is our fear of being left behind! In ancient times, was it not this frantic search for the 'sensational' that urged Erostrates to burn the Temple of Artemis at Ephesus, one of the Seven Wonders of the world.[13]

What else could replace this enormous nail? The framework of the present chapter does not allow us to examine in great detail the effects of this illness of the psyche from which our civilization suffers; we must limit ourselves to consider one aspect of the vast question which is at the centre of our interest: that of feminine beauty. We will try to show that women's clothing, conceived in an appropriate manner, could play a significant role in (solving) the problem of the improvement of the human race.

This faces us with a new principle which is at first sight paradoxical: if it is not possible to rely on obtaining this improvement by means of individual beauty, which is rare and never complete, then could this not be

---

11. This is on all planes. One must also see here the deep meaning of the veneration of icons in Eastern Orthodoxy.

12. Matthew xii: 31; Mark iii: 28.

13. In 356 BC Erostrates was condemned to be burned at the stake.

obtained on the basis of what might be called a 'collective' beauty, wisely applied *to each individual case*, to hide the ugliness and emphasize the partial physical beauty which each woman and each girl possesses. This question undoubtedly deserves the attention of the masters of couture.

(2)

W e will digress here to make it clear that, because chromosomes and their genes are perpetuated, *ugliness* never completely supplants beauty in the human body. The proportion of beauty and ugliness which are the lot of every newborn person are the expression of the *integral* content of that human being, who comes into the world with a certain total of physical and psychic predispositions and also with a karmic tare. In each case this proportion is strictly determined by the Principle of Equilibrium as it applies to human nature, so that it is possible *for he who knows how* to judge, according to the observed deformations of its beginning, the original value of any Personality.

(3)

L et us close this thought without taking it any further, and return to the question of what could be asked from artists and fashion-designers. For the latter, haute-couture and its ready-to-wear imitations, designs should be created not only appropriate to the situations the designers have in view: for daily activity in office or store, travel by car, sports, socializing, celebrations etc., but also, above all, based on the different partial expressions of feminine physical beauty. If we leave out particular cases, we can say that the proportion of beauty that is retained by the feminine body is in general from 25% to 50%, it is rare that it reaches 75%. In no case does it reach 100%. Thus it is a question of increasing the percentage of beauty and reducing the proportion of ugliness.

The beauty which enters the feminine body has a limited number of expressions: beautiful shoulders, beautiful arms, beautiful legs, beautiful feet, pretty neck, lovely hands, pretty throat, pretty waist, etc. If what is ugly is cleverly hidden, the distinctive elements of each human type can be made prominent, together forming *an integral expression of the sought after feminine beauty*, no longer expressed in marble, but in flesh and bone.

The realization of this objective would naturally require the creation, for each category of clothing, of a whole series of designs carefully studied for the precise aim of revealing the case types of *partial beauty*. The spectacle of the collective beauty of women and girls thus dressed, to which each would bring her part of the divine heritage, can only be imagined, so that in this way clothing would again find its authentic aesthetic role, which is precisely to emphasize the femininity of the weak sex.

We can only suspect that over time the impressions produced on pregnant women by the collective beauty thus offered to their eyes would have an effect on their children which would spread the artistic effort that we have just described.

(4)

Let us repeat, so as to clarify our thought, that women's clothing, studied from this angle, should be conceived in a manner corresponding to each case type of partial manifestation of the perfect Beauty in the imperfect human body. It is thus — a second paradox — that 'appearance' put to the service of 'being' could effectively contribute to the general enhancement of the beauty of the human species, and that in the exceptional circumstances of the Time of Transition, the art of dressing women would take on the character of an esoteric mission.

However, in the accomplishment of this mission, which requires a synergy of science and talent, the artists and designers of women's clothing should not lose sight of what should be emphasized, and not concealed, *femininity*. This is a constant aesthetic imperative, which, moreover, the national costumes of all peoples have obeyed throughout the centuries. In the general framework of a new Fashion, whose characteristic would be precisely — divine reflection — the issue today is to create a *unity* of femininity in the *varied* interpretation of types.

One could object that if, in applying the proposed method with the design of putting partial beauty into evidence, we would achieve a total exposure of the integral beauty of the feminine body, it would have to be the same for faces, of which nothing could be hidden. That is true, but the beauty of the face and beauty of the body arise from different planes: whereas the body is the principal expression of the divine beauty on the physical plane, the face essentially reflects the interior content of the individual. The beauty of the body is affirmed by the beauty of its members, by the harmony of proportions and lines, all things which are exterior, while the face is the expression of interior things. And when the psychic and spiritual content of an individual is really beautiful, this beauty is translated by the captivating *charm* which emanates from the face.

IV

(1)

I f we now pass from the dressing of the body, which has an ornamental function, we will ascertain that the care of the body has been the object of a growing attention since the beginning of this century. Much has already been done in this respect, particularly for women, and a healthy and fit body, with muscles that are well developed through physical exercise, is today the ideal of every woman and every girl. This tendency, as long as it does not go beyond moderation, is healthy and even excellent: swimming, horsemanship, mountain-climbing and the exercises of classic dance, for example, whose practice is more and more widespread, are among the best means at our disposal to contribute to the harmonious improvement of the race.

(2)

A ll this concerns the exterior care of the body, using methods whose beneficial effects join with the progress that hygiene has realized in the whole world, and which, already, have increased the expectancy of life at birth and favoured longevity. These two factors, by augmenting the chances of procreation on the one hand and diminishing infant mortality on the other, act toward the incarnation of the totality of souls attached to our planet, a condition which must be fulfilled at the time of the coming of the Era of the Holy Spirit.

About the internal care of the body we must admit that, except for surgery, this still leaves much to be desired. Yet outer and inner care should go hand in hand to produce the maximum result, which leads us to mention two vast domains which are closely related: those of diet and medicine.

The problem of diet has a dual aspect: the production of foodstuffs, and rational choice from amongst them to meet the needs of nutrition.

The progress of the chemical industry in the manufacture of fertilizers, as well as the mechanization of agriculture, have led to very great results. Yet it is generally agreed that, while they have improved in quantity and even in appearance, the products of that agriculture have lost a great deal in terms of quality. What is more, most of the time we drink water which has to pass through filter stations before it becomes drinkable, and we breathe air which is more and more polluted by the emanations of all kinds of factories and vehicles, to say nothing of atomic tests. The problem that this state of affairs poses is beyond solution not only on the individual and collective planes, but even on that of the State: indeed, this is one of the most pressing international problems.

(3)

In this light, the creation of the INTERNATIONAL HIPPOCRATIC FOUNDATION on the Island of Kos, in Greece, is of œcumenical significance, and the message addressed to the Crown prince of Greece (now King Constantine II[14]) in the name of the Goddess Hygieia, appears moving. This message was addressed to the prince when he was presented with the keys to the future *Palace of Health*, and we reproduce it here in full:

Η ΘΕΑ ΥΓΙΕΙΑ
ΠΑΡΑΔΙΔΕΙ ΤΗΝ ΚΟΥ ΔΕΙΘΝΟΥΣ ΙΠΠΟΚΡΑΤΕΙΟΥ ΜΕΛΑΘΡΟΥ ΕΙΣ ΤΟΝ
ΔΙΑΔΟΧΟΝ ΚΩΝΣΤΑΝΤΙΝΟΝ

Ἡ λιπαρόμματος πραΰγελως, ὑγιεία,
ἡ βασιμεία ἡ ποθηνή, ἧς χωρὶς
οὔ τις εὐδαίμων ἔφυ,
Σοὶ τῷ κλεινῷ τῆς Ἑλλάδος Διαδόχῳ
τὴν κλεῖν ταύτην παραδίδωσι
καὶ τοῦ ἐνθάδ᾽ ἰδρυθησμένου
Διεθνοῦς Ἱπποκρατείου Μελάθρου, τοῦ
φαίνοντος τὴν παλαίμαχον τῆς Ἑλληνικῆς
Ἰατρικῆς δόξαν, πύλας εὔχεταί σοι
ταύτῃ διανοῖξαι καὶ
τὸ τῆς ὑγείας Μέγαρον εἰς εὐκρασίαν
τῆς ἀνθρωπότητος παραδοῦναι.

Translation:
To thee, renowned Prince of Greece,
The serene and smiling goddess, Health
With eyes full of light, and without whose
Protection none can be happy.
To you we entrust the key of the International Hippocratic Foundation,
Which will emerge here to testify
To the ancient glory of Greek medicine.
May thou, O prince, open its doors,
And may those who will work
In this Palace of Health
Pledge themselves to the happiness and the unity of Humanity.

---

14. At the time when the book was written, in the 1960s.

V

(1)

Let us now leave the psychosomatic plane for the moral plane and study the behaviour of women—especially that of young women of the new generations—those who are no longer destined to become the inspirers of a fall, as was their Mother Eve, but instead must inspire a triumphant regeneration in the Era of the Holy Spirit.

Woman's entry into the arena of public life is not deplorable in itself: on the contrary, we can only be glad that this tendency is now well-rooted in the cultured classes of all peoples, who recognize the young woman's right to try and affirm herself like any young man. However, we must be careful not to adopt extreme attitudes, even if they are understandable on the morrow of the victory won by women in the bitter struggle that they have had to wage to win the right of free determination, as well as their place and their new role in human society.

The main danger for women, and above all for young girls, lies in the frequently observed attitude of *copying men*, for then woman loses all the specific assets that give her her charm, so that she betrays her mission without any reason or benefit. By this, we mean that if woman helps man according to the precepts of the Book of *Genesis*,[15] and even if she replaces him, she does not lose her specific qualities, but this loss is inevitable from the moment she forces herself to be *like* a man instead of being *polar* to him.

In the following chapters we will come back to this question which is of paramount importance. In the meantime, let us end by an illustration which expresses the depth of our thought: let us try to imagine a child who, through one of Nature's caprices, is born with a left arm ending in a right hand! Can we think, even for a moment, that this malformation will not have an effect on the whole life of this unfortunate child? It is the same for young girls who cultivate a masculine spirit in a feminine body: by deforming themselves psychically, they also lose their charm, so that they fall into the ranks of a third, psycho-pathological sex: *the neuter sex*.

If it is not stopped in time, this tendency to copy the other sex — which can be found in men as well as in women — excludes both from any possibility of esoteric[16] evolution!

---

15. Genesis ii: 18, 19.
16. 1 Corinthians vi: 10.

CHAPTER XX

(1)

To study the esoteric meaning and mission of the Family during the Time of transition, we must first give a definition. When we refer to the *family*, we mean the group consisting of a couple and their children, excluding all the paternal and maternal relations. We do not class couples without children in this category, but will dedicate later chapters to them.

(2)

Profiting from scientific discoveries and technical progress whose scope increases every day, man improves the material side of his life more and more, while he neglects the psychic and spiritual sides to a surprising degree. It would be difficult to claim that the magnificent efforts he has made in the exploration of nature have led to a general reassessment of moral values, or to a reformation of our scale of values. Because this has not happened, against all reason the old and now obsolete scale of values continues to influence our behaviour. This means that the progress of positive science only acts on the material elements of life and has no influence over its essential parts. This in turn means that, underneath, the human condition remains to all intents the same. Men are born and die today as they did in the past, and they continue to be subject to incurable diseases of body and psyche. The increasing numbers of those who do not fit into the new ways of life has led to delinquency of unprecedented proportions, not to mention the widespread use of drugs, which leads to moral suicide. Finally, in the most economically advanced countries, the pace at which all means of transport are developing results in so many fatal accidents that we sometimes wonder if Nature is not taking revenge on us for the destruction of its wild animals.

In short, in spite of all the conquests that man has made through the development of his intelligence, he has not become fundamentally happier. He tries hard to convince himself to the contrary, but this is a sign of his weakness. In his heart of hearts, he knows perfectly well that he is mistaken. In addition, does not Cartesian wisdom itself teach him that happiness is only illusory; that it only lasts as long as the illusion lasts?

(3)

Though man is willing to exhaust himself in feverish activity — not to mention the compromises, so debilitating to the psyche, to which he lends himself — to secure a job, build up a fortune, and to satisfy his self-love and especially his vanity, he would straightway reject as false the idea that the conquest of happiness demands methodical efforts — a struggle even harder than that for material wealth. He simply believes that happiness is his due, and then, paradoxically, he just waits for it to come to him, ready-made, from the world of 'A' influences. And as this world begins from the relative Zero, it is an illusory world, in which Life is characterized by an exhausting instability which makes it a very rough sea![1]

Is it not unreasonable to hope that perfect and lasting happiness can come to us from such a world? Yet man becomes indignant — or he cries in the silence of the night — when he sees that he cannot realize this hope.

(4)

The reader of 'Gnosis' will notice the illogical nature of this attitude. He knows that without the practice of esoteric work, which demands an almost permanent state of introspection and presence in oneself, as well as uninterrupted conscious efforts, man passes his life in a continual state of *mechanical confluence* varying in degree between x% and 100%, the absolute so-called 'normal' value of 'x' being at least 75%. In these conditions, it is correct and realistic to say that happiness lasts only while the illusion lasts.

(5)

This is because man lives without a goal, or, more precisely, without a goal that transcends the domain of 'A' influences. Instinctively, however, he aspires to true and permanent happiness, but instead of applying all the strength of his soul to conquer this, he wastes it running after the will-o-the-wisps that pleasure makes shine before his eyes. He dreams of pure gold, but he is satisfied with tinsel like the great child that he is. Real happiness is inaccessible to him because its conception is beyond the mental horizon of a being whose spirit is oriented in this way.

Even when, animated by the best intentions in the world, man resolutely tries to create a happy home and hearth and to realize a satisfying life, he never entirely succeeds; but then, how could he when, in world 'A', nothing lasts, everything breaks, and everything tires...

---

1. Vol. I, p. 32.

The conditions of life in Russia a hundred and fifty years ago inspired the writer Pushkin with a formula for the maximum happiness possible in such a world. At that epoch, on the lands of the squires, life flowed on with no complication. Every evening, on going to bed, one made the sign of the cross and said: 'Yet another day has gone by: God be praised Who has made it so!' It is in this sleepy atmosphere, where hearts beat slowly, that Pushkin makes a faithful old servant say: 'Habit is given us from on high to take the place of real happiness ...'[2]

This sovereignty of habit supported by religion gave a great stability to the families of peasants and squires alike: from generation to generation, the former provided the latter with servants and nursemaids who became real members of their families. Everything followed its daily round, today as yesterday, and tomorrow as today... But it is not possible to idealize this past, nor a habit so mechanical that, with rare exceptions, one got married without knowing why, had children without knowing why, and got them married in turn without asking their opinion, so that it continued over and over in the same way, without any specific goal or reason other than the peremptory commands of *manners and customs*.

II

(1)

Since then, the revolutions that have successively brought us steam, electricity, mechanization and atomic energy have transformed the face of the world, and *habit* as a substitute for *happiness* has disappeared during these upheavals. This means that, although we hear people claim happiness with growing fervour in the feverish atmosphere of our times, we find ourselves in a void. If a few 'last of the Mohicans,' with their outdated mentality, raise their voices to call for a return to the 'normal' state of things, in their naïve sincerity they appear like mediaeval knights leading a cavalry charge against armoured cars!

(2)

In spite of everything, the need for happiness not only continues, but drives human beings, now deprived of the passive solution of habit, to look for other infinitely more dynamic or even explosive solutions. The character of these is particularly appropriate to the generally accelerating pace of life in the world of 'A' influences. Since happiness cannot be found

---

2. Pushkin, *Eugene Onegin*.

in this domain, for reasons that the reader of 'Gnosis' knows, one falls back on the ephemeral substitute; pleasure, in all its forms. The more violent and easy this is to find, the less it endures, yet this is what we ask for today, and progress makes it possible for us to attain it in ever greater measure. There are also healthy elements, in the rising generation of our youth, who still demand to be shown ways that lead toward authentic and lasting satisfactions.

Gnosis shows the best Way, and there are many paths that lead to it. We will now briefly consider the path reserved for the group we have called the *Family*.

(3)

Let us take the classic case of a young man and a young woman who have tender feelings toward each other. Usually they think of marriage without having the slightest foreknowledge of the esoteric possibilities that this offers. They will simply be filled with vague and blinding ideas on what has come to be called the *Great Love*. This is an expression used by those who do not know its esoteric significance, and who are ignorant of the union of polar beings in the triumph of the Second Birth. Certainly our two young people know nothing of this, but, fascinated by what is no more than a mirage, every day they come closer and closer to marriage.

Leaving aside details of the stages of this approach, which contain elements of a *free romance* between the future partners, we will only say that the process takes place following an ascending gamut of which it occupies the first three notes: DO, RE and MI, as shown in fig. 20 (opposite):

DO^1: the meeting between the two young people and the manifestation of a reciprocal attraction with varying intensity and quality;

RE: the young man and the young girl see each other more and more frequently. They end, rightly or wrongly, by convincing themselves that they are made for each other;

MI: the process unfurls unhampered, and the young people decide to get married, to create a home, and to lean on each other for the rest of their lives;

Ψ^1: now they face the interval whose crossing demands a decisive action: marriage.

A commentary is necessary here. The aspiration that leads to the decision to unite with the chosen being can take either of two directions which form a fork in the path: ignoring marriages contracted 'without rhyme or reason', it may be a *hylic* marriage or a *pneumatic* marriage, understood as meaning that the psyche is present as an element in both cases, although in different degrees.

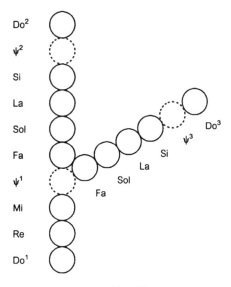

FIG. 20

A pneumatic marriage will ensure the direct development of the gamut reproduced above, and will enable the happy partners to *attain Love*[3] at the level of DO^2 at the time of their Second Birth: this will be a union for Eternity, in the consciousness of their real I, bipolar in itself but ONE and indivisible for them both.

In the following chapters we will study the evolution of this direct gamut through the notes FA, SOL, LA, SI and Ψ^2, until the crowning point. For the moment, we only want to call the reader's attention to the following detail, before going on to the analysis of the fork. While the goal of the pneumatic marriage is a union for Eternity, that of the hylic marriage does not go beyond the limits within which the *hyle* exists; that is, of the physical body of one of the partners. In this way, the possibilities for spiritual evolution of each of them remains intact, and this is why the Orthodox Church, which admits divorce in principle, also foresees cases where one or the other may enter a religious order during the other's lifetime, since he or she then becomes '*dead*' to world 'A'.

The pneumatic marriage imposes special conditions, notably abstinence, which provides the *complementary shock* necessary to cross the interval between FA and MI of the direct gamut. Besides this, the husband and wife are called on to make a series of successive efforts which, taken together, represent the vow they undertake to respect to the end of time and even beyond. This vow gives them what one may call a certain amount of 'credit'. It is this that enables them to pursue direct development of this

3. 1 Corinthians xiv: 1.

gamut, on condition that they gradually repay this debt at each of the notes that follow, which take the form of trials that they must overcome.

In the hylic marriage, the vow of the couple ties them to each other only for the duration of the existence of one or other of them. The marriage sacrament only destines them *to be one flesh*:[4] All Christian churches agree on this point. According to the words of St Paul, after the death of the other, either partner is free to contract a new marriage.

The hylic marriage, therefore, does not require a conscious effort by either of them to dominate nature and master the demands of the 'I' of the body. Because of this, and because of the Law of Seven, in choosing the hylic direction, the gamut of the terrestrial marriage deviates by dividing itself *at this very place*, as shown in our diagram, and from then on the part which forks off develops very differently from the way the same notes unfold in the direct part.

FA: this note should sound until it reaches the Ψ^3, that is, its vibrations should extend over the remainder of the gamut. It corresponds to FA 96 of the first gamut of nutrition, from which it derives. If its resonance is good, it governs the hylic action of the notes SOL, LA, SI, and Ψ^3, up to and including orgasm and ejaculation.

It is necessary to point out another correspondence here — this time with the Third cosmic Octave — it being understood that this is a generalization for the whole of organic Life on Earth. The present case concerns an internal, individual gamut, which concerns only the two partners. For this reason, it is oriented in the opposite direction, and develops alternately according to the will of the man or according to that of the flesh (woman),[5] to end at the 'birth of blood'.

If the note FA of the diverging part of the marriage-octave produces an impure sound, or even a pure sound without harmony between the couple, then on the plane of the psyche the development of this gamut comes to a stop. But it continues on the hylic plane, where it takes on an exaggerated degree of bestiality; in this case the note SOL cannot sound in full.

SOL: This note of the diverging part of the gamut commands the prelude in the physical union of the couple in carnal love, a prelude that normally falls under the aegis of the third sun of the food diagram, DO 48, or the Hydrogen of visual and auditory impressions in its passive form. When there is harmony between the partners, this is helped by SOL 48 and MI 48.

LA: the carnal act. This act falls under the aegis of LA 24, which makes the affective sector of the motor centre vibrate, the positive part if there is

---

4. Genesis ii: 24.
5. Gnosis Vol. I.

agreement, the negative part if not. In the latter case, the act provokes a feeling of aversion but does not prevent conception — an important fact that we will return to later. Let us note that in the present case, the LA 24 involves only a faint vibration of FA 24, and practically nothing of RE 24; we may well understand why.

SI: in this note the couple, normally impregnated with Hydrogen SI 12, should reach a harmonious orgasm. In practice, however, this happens only too seldom because of the lack of strength and clarity of resonance of the notes that follow Hydrogens 48 and 24, not to mention the lack of SOL 12, and above all of MI 12, of which we spoke at length in Chapter XIV of the present volume of 'Gnosis'.

Ψ^3: ejaculation. We repeat that the lack of the psychic element in carnal love is no obstacle to the fertilization of the ovule. We must recognize this as a sign of divine wisdom, for, without this, the reproduction of the species would gradually diminish.

DO^3: conception. If conditions are propitious, the spasms that accompany ejaculation enable the crossing of the interval Ψ^3. In DO^3, impregnated with Hydrogen DO^6, conception takes place.

(4)

A new gamut starts with conception, when the spermatozoon, propelled by the energy released in the orgasm accompanied by ejaculation, crosses the interval and goes on to penetrate the ovule, uniting with it in DO^3. The gamut of conception is naturally a descending octave: in its notes, SI, LA, SOL and FA, the pregnancy follows its four stages; the interval from FA to MI is filled by the pains and efforts of the woman in labour; in the note MI the breaking of the waters occurs, and the actual birth of the child takes place in the note RE. Finally, with the first cry of the newborn, the life of an independent organism begins in DO^4.

III

(1)

That is a brief account of the different stages of development in the gamut of a hylic marriage, and that of the fœtus from the moment of its conception to the child's first cry announcing its arrival in the world. We will now leave it to specialists to find out how the different notes of our gamuts link to the physiology of the organs in the couple whose synergy ensures carnal love and conception in conjugal life. To produce concrete results, we must base our analysis on the food diagram, within the general framework of the complete Enneagram.

We will now tackle the obscure problem of the influence of the psyche on the physical in the development of the gamut of hylic marriage, as well as the possible action of this influence on the kind of conception that occurs. In this way, we will come back to the question that interests us most here, which is the meaning and eventual mission of the Family and how it relates to successful evolution through the Time of Transition.

(2)

Several times we have emphasized the urgent need for children endowed with pronounced esoteric predispositions in the coming generations. With sufficient work, they could take their places among the new ruling elite whose task is to materially realize the passage of humanity into the Era of the Holy Spirit. We must now see how the Family, and especially the parents, can ensure their presence. This naturally requires efforts, and as always when we deal with esotericism, these must be *conscious* efforts.

We must first have a clear idea of the nature of these efforts, then of their point of application. This is a question of the possible influence of the psyche as a factor in the incarnation of a particular category of souls attached to our planet: in other words, a sort of *birth-control*, but in quite a different sense than the one given to this word by organizations that are preoccupied with demographic increase in the world, and are anxious to stop it.

If we refer to the *Introduction* to the second volume of 'Gnosis', and especially to the schema dealing with the supersensory world, which we reproduce here, we can easily realize that, for the success of the Time of transition, it is very important to arrange things so that the incarnation of souls of the Ψ zone is favoured more than the incarnation of souls of the SI zone:

FIG. 21

190

All the souls attached to Earth must reincarnate before the beginning of the Era of the Holy Spirit, but it is obvious that the incarnation of the most developed souls first offers more chances of success. Selective incarnation will make sure that coming generations will contain the greatest possible number of polar beings who are able first to recognize each other, then to form couples who will pledge themselves to a marriage that follows the direct gamut, with the intention of rapidly reaching the Second Birth. These are the cohorts — of all races and all colours — who, at the head of a really United Nations, will lead humanity along the road of esoteric evolution, through the Cycle of the Holy Spirit, up to the thousand years without war, and the Last Judgement.

This should enable all races and nations in the world to measure the importance of *birth-control* in the form that we have defined it. We must not forget too that the SI zone of the supersensory world contains in its lower part souls — who are unhappy and to be pitied — who are loaded with a frightful karmic burden, full of negative emotions and rancour, who are driven to incarnate by an unfulfilled will to dominate. The horrors perpetrated during the Second World War enable us to foresee what will happen on earth if we allow these dregs of the disincarnated to prevail over the developed souls and so spread over our planet. Even if such a mass invasion does not take place, there is a column of anti-Christs that continues to infiltrate into the ranks of humanity.

(3)

In short, the control to which we are referring amounts to the selection of souls, allowing the more developed to pass before the backward ones. This enterprise gains its full importance if we consider that the long-predicted struggle between the two humanities[6] seems imminent: the two world wars and the balance of terror which followed them, and under which we continue to live, are only a prelude to this.

When will this collision between the two humanities take place? Will it be in twenty, thirty or fifty years? Nobody can tell; but there is no doubt that a triumph of the dark souls would bring about the *defeat of the Holy*

---

6. The reader may find a contradiction here if he remembers that we said above that pre-adamics do not re-incarnate. We therefore emphasize that, even if they are not re-incarnated *individually*, due to the lack of the real 'I' even in the potential form in which the adamics possess it, pre-adamics do, however, incarnate from the *collective* real 'I' which belongs to each group of pre-adamic humanity: first, the races, then the sub-divisions which exist in the heart of the latter, according to the group of civilizing agents to which one belongs. We referred to this in the second Volume of 'Gnosis' when we spoke of Danilevsky's theory.

It is therefore, really a struggle between the two humanities, adamic and pre-adamic, but, while adamic souls can be *individually* dark or evolved, pre-adamics, who cannot reincarnate individually, are reincarnated in vast groups coming from the 'I' of the *collective* Personality. This latter can also be dark or evolved.

Spirit's final attempt to raise humanity out of the abyss, where it is held by the fratricidal spirit that has dominated it ever since Cain.

IV

(1)

Let us now come to the technique by which we can make this selection of souls awaiting incarnation. First, it is important to note that the more evolved are generally in less of a hurry than the backward ones, who are burdened by the spirit of Evil. While the latter greedily seize every occasion to be incarnated, the former *choose their parents*, seeking for an atmosphere of love, for conditions that will ensure that they have a body that corresponds to their degree of evolution, and for an adequate education.

Normally, the FA of the part which diverges from the direct gamut spreads over all the other notes of this part. This is why conception takes place regardless of the psychic climate in which the carnal act is accomplished. And this is why, in the great majority of cases, these are children of 'chance'. A conception where love between the progenitors is absent, or when they are under the influence of negative emotions, or worse still, under the influence of alcohol or of drugs, gives a good opportunity for dark souls who are looking for an opportunity to be incarnated, and they rush to make the best of it.

(2)

When the fusion of the two sexual centres takes place, conception is accompanied by a reduction of the chromatic material of the male and female gametes, so that the child inherits only half of his father's chromosomes and half of his mother's. Even if we suppose that every block (chromosome) of genes always presents the same variety in each of the partners, nothing guarantees that in all the successive conceptions the reproductive cells of the child will always receive the same mixture from one or the other. The fact that children from the same parents are never alike, even when they are twins, simply shows that this is not what really happens.[7]

In its present state, positive science is not able to tell us what factors govern the selection of the 23 chromosomes contributed by each progenitor from the 46 found in each. But esoteric science gives us precise

---

7. According to the Tradition, beauty spots are just like finger-prints: there are never two exactly alike; and these are signs which distinguish one body from another.

traditional indications about this: it is the soul that wants to be incarnated which chooses from among the genetic characteristics offered by the couple. But, by conscious efforts, the couple can exercise a certain influence over this choice.

Ever since the fall of Adam, and the mixing of the adamic and pre-adamic races that resulted from it, the chromosomes of the one are mixed with the other in us, and each of them is stained with karmic burdens accumulated during former incarnations. *Blue blood* is therefore not something that one can inherit by birth: it can only be regained at the Second Birth, which depends on the fulfilment of successive tasks imposed during the climbing of the Staircase.

As far as the chromosomes are concerned, the role of the couple can be compared to that of a window-dresser who arranges his merchandise so that the passer-by cannot help going in to buy. The assortment of chromosomes that each of us possesses carries a great diversity of genes. Normally, esoteric evolution starts by ridding the chromosomes of the karmic burdens which stain them, then it operates to sort them according to their adamic or pre-adamic origin. This is intended to enable their appropriate use.

We must also note that all the chromosomes are not stained with negative karmic burdens, and that the latter, when present, can differ quantitatively as well as qualitatively. On the other hand, as intermediaries between the supersensory plane and that of living matter, the chromosomes are in danger of being subject, and are in fact subject, even if the fact cannot be constated, to the influence of the psychic (moral) life of the individual in the succession of all the good or bad, noble or evil acts that he may perform. This is a very mechanical reaction, but, by conscious and well-oriented efforts, the couple can progressively cleanse their chromosomes of their karmic burdens, and bring to the fore those that will be sought by developed souls. It is through the play of this psychosomatic mechanism—a play that can be the result of conscious[8] action, or simply of circumstances[9] — that children can surpass their own parents in countless ways.

We repeat that, to enable developed souls to be incarnated, it is necessary to produce conditions which meet their needs, and this makes the following demands on the couple:

1. sexual harmony that ensures the full blossoming of carnal love;
2. a psychosomatic attraction;
3. a psychic love capable of transporting the three lower centres *simultaneously*, even if only for a few moments;

---

8. Prayer, for example.

9. As an example of the influence of circumstances, we can quote the case of Laetitia Ramolino, Charles-Marie Bonaparte's wife, the mother of Napoleon. When she was carrying the latter during the war, she joined with the men in shooting in the Corsican mountains.

4. a love of children in general;

5. the passionate desire to raise beautiful, gifted children;

6. finally, through their conscious attitude toward love, the will to offer to a developed soul a body worthy of his incarnation.

This enumeration of the minimum conditions is not, by definition, exhaustive; other requirements will arise in the minds of the couple once they choose this way.

(3)

In short, one must arrive at a point where the act of carnal love is not simply a source of sensual pleasure. Along with the desired psychic elements, it must become an act that occurs on different planes and is thus a true sacrament, touching the mystery. If the two partners are animated by an ecstatic desire to be the artisans of this transformation, they will reach an orgasm of full abandon, in direct contact with that zone of the supersensory plane that is bathed in the Love of the Absolute II, and this will be the point of culmination.

Preparation for the *sacrament of conception* should begin with betrothal and continue right through married life. By contributing toward the success of the Time of transition as they favour the incarnation of evolved souls, the couple will also contribute toward their own esoteric evolution. If they prove to form a polar couple, this progress will be greatly accelerated. In the opposite case, each of them will powerfully magnetize his or her respective polar being.

To be fulfilled, the mystery of the desired incarnation requires a conjugal atmosphere free of all lies — expressed or thought — as well as a common interest in the Doctrine, the assiduous study of the latter and finally, a consciousness of the importance of the accepted mission, a consciousness that will make carnal love a source of joy and of unsuspected satisfaction.

It was in just such a communion of ideas and feelings that Zachariah and Elizabeth conceived John the Baptist.

CHAPTER XXI

(1)

The world is suffering from a lack of harmony which gets deeper on every plane, and this is a serious danger to the moral and spiritual recovery of humanity. It also involves a serious risk of failure in the last stage of this Time of transition that we are now entering. If this risk is not overcome, the Deluge of Fire awaits us. We will have to make an immense effort to ward off this fate, and we have very little time in which to do it.

Man has only himself to blame for the greatness of the effort needed: this is a result of his obstinate refusal to heed the warnings that have been addressed to him time and again by the Divine Voice, just as he continues today to blind himself to the fact that the Deluge of Fire is being made ready; that it is now technically feasible and — it must be said — morally possible.

(2)

This final cataclysm, towards which humanity is advancing so blindly, can only be avoided by the *conscious* superefforts of the spiritual elite, especially by young and enthusiastic elements of the present generation and those which follow it, whose esoteric predispositions will make them fit to assume key positions in all races and in all nations.

This is the present situation, stripped of every illusion and all lies to ourselves.

Neither the most marvellous technical progress nor greater refinement of the intellectual faculties will be enough to enable us to remedy this state of affairs, which is still deteriorating. The balance of terror — the only stability that men have reached by the combined development of the intellectual and motor centres of the deified Personality, leaving the emotional centre in an almost abandoned state — has led the human being and his civilization to chimerical results and to an imbalance in which the tendencies of 'Cain' weigh heavily.[1] A real and durable peace, that is, a stable international balance, cannot be realized on a planetary scale as long as the education of the ruling elite is limited to the development of their intellectual and motor centres: only a developed *emotional* culture, something that is sadly lacking today, could balance the Personality and thus

---

1. Vol. II, pp. 174–8, figs. 15–16.

bring the desired Peace and balance to our civilization and to the whole of human society.

Once this balance has been generally re-established, the elite will see, opening up in front of them, the road to a higher culture, that of *Gnosis* and Love; and as the success of the Time of Transition will by then be assured, it will become possible for the Era of the Holy Spirit to begin on the Earth.

For the second time—and let us emphasize that this will be the last time—the path that leads to the Kingdom of God is opening up before man: woe to him if he proves incapable of taking it and following it through to the end!

In this epoch, which is full of such marvellous possibilities as well as such frightful dangers, let him remember these enigmatic but powerful words that Jesus spoke:

And as it was in the days of Noah, so shall it be also in the days of the Son of man. They did eat, they drank, they married wives, they were given in marriage, until the day that Noah entered into the ark, and the flood came, and destroyed them all.

Likewise also as it was in the days of Lot; they did eat, they drank, they bought, they sold, they planted, they builded; but the same day that Lot went out of Sodom it rained fire and brimstone from heaven and destroyed them all.[2]

And they answered and said unto him, Where Lord? And He said unto them, Wheresoever the corpse is, thither will the eagles be gathered together.[3]

II

(1)

Let us stop and look in the mirror a moment. Have we not been too generous in saying that every individual has retained a minimum of 25% of divine beauty in his body, which in truth is generally ugly and sometimes monstrous?

Let us examine our own face: once youth has gone, it fades and is lined with wrinkles; later, it begins to look like a mask with a fixed expression. Most of the time this reflects the conceit with which we try to compensate for our profound nullity, as well as the fear, envy, and jealousy which haunt us. The older man grows, the more his once shining look loses its brightness. His mask changes. It is overrun by an expression of apathy. His desires become more and more elementary and, finally, he is happy to see the end of his terrestrial existence draw near. He sees this not as a final failure, but as a liberation from the meaningless labours that make up a life 'just like that of so many others.'

---

2. Luke xvii: 26–29.
3. Ibid., 37.

Now let us look around us: is there anything that is not destined to disappear sooner or later, even if some things survive for a time after the men who created them.

More than once we have said that the object of esoteric work on the individual plane is Victory over Death — the goal that all true religions preach, especially Christianity, since the Gospel is precisely the *Good News* of the victory over Death that was announced and promised by Jesus in these terms: '*in the world ye shall have tribulation; but be of good cheer, I have overcome the world.*'[4]

(2)

Seven ways are open to the courageous and persevering Faithful — and each one leads to the final Victory, where setbacks and falls are no longer possible.

Traditionally, the first three are intended for men 1, 2, and 3 respectively. They are called: the *Way of the Servant*, (of the fakir in the Orient), the *Way of the Monk*, and the *Way of the Scholar* (*Khoja* in the Orient and *Yogi* in India). These three ways, which ultimately combine in man 5, all lead to the state of man 4.[5]

We have also seen that there exists a fourth way which, by accomplishing the tasks of the first three ways combined, allows one to come directly and more quickly to the state of man 4: this is called the *Way of the sly man*, because the person who chooses it makes use of all his faults and negative emotions to assist his progress. This way has been dealt with in detail in the Tradition, especially in the teaching of John Climacus, who describes it concisely in the following words: '*The true wise man is he who turns everything to his benefit.*'[6 & 7]

(3)

The key words of the first four ways are the following:

I.   WORK: chiefly physical work, including special efforts aimed at mastering the body and its organs;

II. PRAYER: prayer having as a support the Love of God, cultivated by exercise, and leading to a limitless devotion to the Lord and to what is

---

4. John xvi: 39.
5. Vol. I, pp. 178–180.
6. St John Climacus (St John of the Ladder); cf. *Philokalia*.
7. Once rendered '*he who turns everything to a profit.*' Ed.

called contemplative prayer, at which stage, according to the Fathers of the Orthodox Church, *he who prays in this way never knows satiation*;

III. STUDY: study in depth in any branch of science, leading to the limit of pure reason in order to reach the contemplation of the thing in itself;

IV. CONTROL: control of oneself, by which the sly *man* forces himself to act, inwardly and outwardly, *as if* his magnetic centre were already passably developed and had assumed the general direction of the three lower centres — in other words, to act in all circumstances, using the three centres *as if they were already passably developed and balanced.*

(4)

Self control by means of *constatation* practised on all occasions is a particular characteristic of the fourth way. If the faithful has this attitude towards his Personality, he is led in his daily life to make almost uninterrupted constatations, and it is this that ensures his progress, providing that he makes *conscious efforts* and does not fall into somnolence in which he has only an illusion of practising constatation. This has a powerful influence on the underdeveloped and unbalanced Personality, and the disciple soon feels the beneficial effects. But in order not to drain the reserve of fine Hydrogens which we need for the practice of constatation, we must not go too fast nor make exaggerated efforts.

In fact, the same method is as good for constatation as for the physical exercises we practise to develop the body; if we do not want to exhaust all our strength, we must approach it gradually and with moderation; thus, constatation must be practised in such a way that the reserve of fine Hydrogens is not drained but conserved. If the disciple observes the required moderation in his progress on the fourth way, he will increase this reserve, and will gradually, and sanely, be able to intensify his efforts.

The exhaustion of our reserve of fine Hydrogens is accompanied — and this is how we recognize it — by a loss of interest in esoteric work. By making sure that this does not happen, we maintain this interest, and we feel it grow as we progress.

(5)

But, even though the fourth way offers us the possibility of rapid progress, it is not without danger. On this way, the student plays the role of a man 4 towards his Personality, even while he is not yet that. In these conditions, by immediately taking his fate into his own hands, without experience, it is almost inevitable that he commits errors of conception and judgement. These will naturally be reflected in his acts, to the greater profit of the General Law. The latter will supervise him much more closely than for the disciples who follow the first three ways, where progress is much slower. And the more he advances on the fourth way, the harder will be the eventual falls, especially if he continues his activities within the framework of day-to-day life: it is even possible that they will take on a catastrophic character to the point of bringing about disassociation of the Personality. Monastic life, which keeps the faithful isolated from the world of 'A' influences and its complications, is certainly more favourable for accomplishment of the tasks imposed on the fourth way.

The ultimate trial which awaits *man* on this way, when he is approaching the Second Threshold, will come to him from *Woman*, in the form of a mirage of his polar being. Whether the disciple works in the silence of the cloister or in the noise of the world, this trial is the same. For the monk, it is even more dangerous, since it offers him an image which borders on materialization, and which pursues him day and night until he falls or achieves Victory.

III

(1)

Even as the fourth way leads directly to the state of Man 4, the *fifth way* leads directly to that of man 5. However, there is a fundamental difference between this way and the other four: in the latter, the postulant (male or female), can reach the Second Threshold on his own. It is when he crosses this Threshold that he becomes conscious of his real 'I', which is androgynous by nature, and this then places him, *in spirit*, face to face with his polar being — his *true neighbour* — whether the partner is living or dead, for, as St Paul says '... *neither is the man without the woman, nor is the woman without the man in the Lord.*'[8]

This fifth way is open only to couples, especially to couples who *sincerely believe they are polar*, because, on this way, the *sine qua non* condition for success is simultaneous obedience to two commandments on which, according to Jesus' words, '*hang all the law and the Prophets*'[9]: *To Love God with all one's being*'[10] — an obligation which has to be respected very naturally on whichever way one wishes to advance — and '*to Love one's neighbour as oneself.*'[11]

8. 1 Corinthians xi: 11.
9. Matthew xxii: 37, 40.
10. Mark xii: 30, 31; Luke x: 27.
11. Ibid.

Knowing now that in the esoteric sense, the *neighbour* is the polar being, we may understand better that the bipolar real I, monad of the Christ, residing in His Love, (the Love of the Absolute II), which itself resides in the Love of God or the Holy Spirit, (the Love of the Absolute I), Jesus said that the second commandment is *similar* to the first, '*the greatest.*'[12]

(2)

If only human beings were not so heterogeneous in their substance, or in other words, in their Personality, they would recognize their polar being, whom they meet at least once during their lives, without difficulty. But because their hearts have become insensitive,[13] they generally pass them by without suspecting their identity.

Let us return to our calculation of the partial polarities that can exist between man and woman, or vice versa. We have seen that, starting from the twelve sectors of the two motor centres of a couple, we may reach sixty-six types.[14] Each of these sectors can become an organ of manifestation of the energy SI 12 of the sexual centre as it acts.

These sixty-six types represent the possibilities of more or less 'legitimate' relationships. Those that are formed outside this group belong to the vast domain of 'considerations' and of prostitution.

These sixty-six types, taken as a whole, express the different possibilities of *purely* carnal love. Four types out of the sixty-six associated with the 'I' of the body, which is essentially polygamous or polyandrous, are different from the others by nature and, *because they are distinct*, are not included amongst them, but are added to the list, thus carrying the number to seventy.

In the first place, it is a question of three cases in which one of the three centres of the Personality is wholly engaged — and so of three cases where hylic love is accompanied by psycchic love so that, from then on, it no longer simply represents three of the many possibilities of 'legitimate' mistresses or lovers, but the three possible husbands or wives allowed by the Orthodox Church in cases of widowhood or divorce in their recognized forms. It stops at this figure precisely because the natural possibilities of polarity of the psyche do not go any further.

---

12. Matthew xxii: 37–40.
13. Ibid., xiii: 15.
14. Vol. II, pp. 255, 256.

(3)

The distinctive signs of these three cases of polarity of the psyche, which can lead to three unions which are canonically and esoterically legitimate—but which only engage the couple for the terrestrial life of the psyche — are the following:

I.   When the polarization of the motor centres is complete, the attraction that the man and woman feel towards each other has its centre of gravity in the sense of *touch*, which prevails over the other sensory impressions: then there is, in the act of carnal love, such a deep confluence that the couple may momentarily lose consciousness of their intellectual and emotional functions.

II.   When the polarization of the intellectual centres is complete, the attraction is of another order: it is visual in the woman, and auditory in the man. These cases were relatively rare in past centuries, but they are multiplying in our days, now that intellectual formation is the same for the two sexes.

III. When the polarity of the emotional centres is complete, on the contrary, the attraction is visual in the man and auditory in the woman.

Of course, these distinctive signs exist in full only where, theoretically, the functions of the centres are not mixed; or in other words, when no centre interferes in the domain of the others. In addition, the sexual energy must not be previously usurped by one or two of the three centres, but must be discharged equally through them all, so that they may all be oriented together towards the act of carnal love, each taking its particular role.

(4)

The fourth example of the distinct cases mentioned above — and the seventieth of the total number—is that of truly polar beings.[15] Here the real 'I' is involved, and the couple's Love, while containing all the possibilities already described in the preceding cases, has a singularly

---

15. Regarding this, it is interesting to note a passage from Nestor's Russian chronicle *A Tale of Times Gone By*, in which he relates how, in the year 989 (AD) an Imam was called to the Court of the Great Prince Vladimir, who wanted to hear what were the principal dogmas of the Islamic religion. This is what he was told: '... Mohammed teaches that it is necessary to practise circumcision, not to eat pork, and not to drink wine. But after death, he will compensate each one with *seventy* beautiful girls, and when one has been chosen from amongst the others, he (Mohammed) would concentrate in her, the beauty of all the others, and she would become the wife of the one who chose her.' (RDTR, Academy of Sciences Publications, Moscow–Leningrad, 1950, in two volumes, Vol. I, p. 59). The italics are the author's.

emotional character of a higher order. It naturally follows that as this Love is hylic, psychic and spiritual at the same time, thus leading to an attraction that is visual, auditory and tactile, it is incomparably richer.

The chief characteristic of this so-called *Royal* case is the bi-polarity of the real 'I'—one for each couple. This orients their Personalities and their bodies[16] in such a way that *what each hopes for and awaits from the other is precisely, and very naturally, what the other desires to and is prepared to offer.*

It is only in a case of this kind that there can be absolute harmony between a couple, and even this is conditional on each of them trying progressively to liquidate his or her karmic burden and to establish a balance between the lower centres, whose development must be pushed to the limit. These are the combined objectives which the allegedly polar couple who enter on the fifth way must seek through their work. This means that, right from the beginning, the Knight and his Lady-elect must practice courtly Love, which unites in itself *Faith*, *Hope* and *Knowledge* (*Gnosis*). After the Second Threshold, this involves the acquisition of new faculties, and once this task has been accomplished, it comes to an end in the note MI of the Way.

(5)

After that, the couple will have to pass through the Sixth and Seventh Ways, conceived reciprocally in the RE and DO of the Great Way.[17]

The honours and high divine grades in Christ Jesus, of which St Paul[18] speaks, are traditionally defined as follows:

V.   THE MESSENGER, confirmed when crossing the Second Threshold through the Trial by Fire. He is a man of 'C' influence, affiliated in the second degree to the esoteric Centre 'E'.

VI. THE PROPHET, Master of Fire. A man of 'D' influence, affiliated in the first degree to the esoteric Centre 'E'.

VII. THE EQUAL OF THE APOSTLES, confirmed at the Third Threshold by the descent of the Holy Spirit. A man of 'E' influence. An active member of the esoteric Centre 'E': the Brotherhood of the *Alliance of Love*.

---

16. Vol. I, fig. 15; Vol. II, fig. 42.
17. Vol. I, fig. 57; Vol. II, fig. 42.
18. Philippians iii: 13–14. From the Slavonic text.

(6)

Everything degenerates in life. Everything is condemned to death. Everything leads to Nothing.

Towards the cold of *Zero degrees Absolute*, beyond which there is Nothing but the Abyss, the Great Emptiness which draws in and swallows everything *relative*; the *Outer Darkness*[19] into which everything falls with weeping and gnashing of teeth, giving out cries of distress. Only what is *absolute* will withstand their icy breath.

What is this Absolute? It is Love!

The Lord Love, who is the Lord God,[20] the true Light which shines in the Darkness — and the Darkness retreats, unable to contain it.[21]

It is Love in all its manifestations, on the whole scale of Creation, on all degrees of the Great Octave. In a perpetual reversible movement, Love, when descending, pours its seed into all creatures to make them bear its fruit afterwards by gaining Consciousness, by which they reascend the Ladder leading to *Absolute algebraic Zero.*[22]

Everything tends towards this *algebraic Absolute Zero*, having conceived the *Zero temperature Absolute* where every creature, on all the planes of the Relative, loses its relativity, to render up its absolute seed to Absolute Love, the Source of Life, enriched by the experience acquired during its ephemeral existence.

(7)

If Love were removed, organic Life on Earth would cease and our planet would become a cosmic corpse.

Man is placed at the head of organic life on Earth, and called on to lead it on the path of divine evolution. His failings, crimes, and the spirit of incompetence that govern him, which rejected Love and embraced Passion and Hate, have once again led the Earth to the edge of the Abyss.

Today — as two thousand years ago — the Lord Love is trying again to kindle our faint and hardened hearts with his sacred fire. He hopes to regenerate and revive us with his warmth, beauty, and truth, and lead us by his *Gnosis* toward the permanence of his Kingdom, which is approaching us again today!

---

19. Matthew viii: 12; xxii: 13.

20. 1 John iv: 8.

21. John i: 5.

22. Not used here as in the English sense in which Absolute Zero means Zero Degrees Absolute, but referring to the Absolute or original zero in the Algebraic sense of zero explained earlier. This principle applies throughout this chapter. (Ed.)

It is by multiplying our conscious efforts, laid out in hope of receiving Love and its installment in us as Absolute Lord, that *at the last moment* we can take straighten ourselves out by taking up again and completing the mission assigned to Adam and Eve before their fall.

This is a question of conquering the Darkness which has established itself in us; of conquering it through the strength of the Conqueror, which is Love. It is also a question of saving the Earth by saving organic Life on our planet — by raising it up from the downward slide of degeneration which it now follows, which is approaching the Abyss of Zero degrees Absolute at an ever faster pace.

(8)

We know that it is necessary to descend to a temperature of $-273.16°C$ to reach Zero degrees Absolute. On the other hand, we know that the temperature of the external layer of the sun is about $6000°C$. This temperature reveals the level of intensity of organic Life on our Star, the SOL of the Great Octave.

Thus, in degrees of temperature, the pitch of the pulse of Life in this segment of our Ray of Creation, situated between the Sun and the outer Void, is equal to:

$$6000° + 273° = 6273° \text{ approximately.}$$

If we take the temperature of the human body, about $37°C$, as the cosmic measure of Man, we will realize how close man is to the outer Darkness, and how great is the distance which separates him from the vivifying Light emanating from its Source, which is our Lord, Love-God and God-Love, the Sun of Truth.

Thus man is separated from the darkness of Zero degrees Absolute by $37° + 273° = 310°C$, while the distance which separates him from the sun is $6000° - 37° = 5963°C$ approximately.

In other words, in relation to the Source of organic Life on Earth, and therefore, to the source of his own life, man is situated at a thermic distance NINETEEN times greater than that which separates him from Zero degrees Absolute, that is, from the outer Darkness where all Life, all existence, and every vibration ceases for lack of the warmth of Love.

If we take the thermic distance of $310°C$ which separates man from the Nothingness as the characteristic measure of his state of evolution on the cosmic scale, we can understand that when he crosses the First Threshold, man 1, 2, or 3 will have nineteen similar stages to pass through before reaching and crossing the Third Threshold!

(9)

We might say that this is terrifying.

Yet, when the disciples asked the question: '*Who then can be saved?*' Jesus looked at them and said: '*With men this is impossible, but with God all things are possible.*'[23]

(10)

B esides the *positive* types of allegedly polar couples we have just studied, there are other types of partial, *negative* polarity of a pathological nature. These cases are numerous. Here, we will limit our description to an analysis of the only extreme case falling within this category.

This is characterized by a complete polarity of the motor centres, as well as of the negative parts of the two other centres, the positive parts of which are in a state of profound lethargy.

Only the heavy karmic burden of a past full of crime, of devouring passions, of violence, and of cold-blooded cruelty, accumulated in common through several incarnations, can lead to such a deformation of two Personalities and knit them together so closely.

As long as the two partners are alive, their activity is limited to the horrors of the crimes which fill the forensic news. But, in certain cases, the discarnate woman survives after death and takes on the demonic form of a *succubus*. The man, who is still alive, then combines the presence and strength of the two Personalities in his being. Let us note that, with the integral polarity of the two motor centres, and with the positive parts of the two other centres atrophied, the 'double-being' formed in this way has no doubts — and cannot have any. The total assurance he has of himself then doubles his strength, which becomes demonic.

This type represents the pathological phenomenon of the *negative androgyne*. Through a large usurpation of dual sexual energy, a black androgyne of this kind becomes extremely strong and wicked. Bringing together in him the two Personalities, closely united by strong negative passions; hate, jealousy, vengeance, and lastly a thirst for blood, this possessed man is a true danger to society.

This extreme case of the negative, pathological, demonic and bestial androgyne is the opposite of the angelic androgyne that can be achieved by man after he passes the Second Threshold. We mention it for this reason, and also to give the reader an idea of the profound meaning of the parable concerning the man of the Gadarenes who was possessed by

---

23. Matthew xix: 36.

nearly two thousand demons.[24] Bringing together two dark Personalities in a single body, this demoniac carried in himself:
987 + 987 = 1974 diabolical little 'I's.

24. Matthew viii: 32; Mark v: 13; Luke viii: 33.

CHAPTER XXII

(1)

In men, in common with all species of organic Life on Earth, attraction between the sexes has three forms. More exactly, it occurs in three groups of forms. These groups exist on three different levels of consciousness. For each individual, the first group from below to above — the largest — contains the sixty-six types of polarization that are possible between the twelve sectors of the motor centres in the opposite sexes.

If neither of the two other centres is involved, this kind of attraction only produces the temporary link of a free romance, or, in current language, an *affair*. Only the typical man 1, who is polygamous by nature, can find deep satisfaction in this. And these cases are rather rare as this is a purely physiological phenomenon as a result of the overproduction of Hydrogen SI 12 by both the masculine and feminine organisms.

For men 2 and 3, the constatation of whose psyche is more developed and refined, pure carnal love — when it occurs without even partial participation by one or two of the other centres — appears as the maximum expression of the bestial side of human nature. In such cases, Love merely takes the forms of *desire* and *pleasure*. Once physical desire is satisfied, the person 2 or 3 no longer feels linked to his partner. Instead, he often experiences a reaction, a feeling of having fallen, a kind of shame at having fallen under the sway of his own bestiality. We must say that this fall is real. However, for men 2 and 3, this is so only after they have reached a certain level of inner culture. Generally, without introspectively analysing the movements provoked by this fall — without even realizing it — such a person feels more or less quickly the need to flee from the subject of his ephemeral affair. Once the pressure of the overabundance of accumulated Hydrogen SI 12 is reduced — for it is this excess that breaks the balance of the forces of the Personality — the man returns to the habitual if still unstable balance of his psyche. This will then tend to be broken in another direction through the disgust that even a subconscious feeling of this fall produces.

This also explains the well-known phenomenon of the unfaithful husband who multiplies his attentions to his wife!

(2)

A completely different reaction may be observed in cases where, in addition to the engagement that is the result of the polarization of

sectors of the two motor centres, one of the three centres of their Personalities is *totally* absorbed in Love as a result of the total polarization of this
centre in both partners. Then an attraction of the psyche, which is much
stronger than purely physical attraction, becomes a factor in the relationship between the sexes. Psychology then makes its appearance alongside
physiology. This communicates a strength and a delicacy to the love-
relationship between the partners which is unknown in the previous case.

Here, we are referring to *human Love*, no longer bestial but giving birth
to true romance, not just to an affair. This true romance, still taking the
form of the *free romance*, is characterized by a more or less long period of
manifestations of tenderness, with a tendency towards permanence even
before the sexual act actually takes place. This situation usually leads such a
couple to one of the three cases, within the sixty-six cases that we are
studying, that are appropriate for *marriage*.

(3)

In this second group of cases, as in the first, the romance always starts
with a physical attraction. However, because of the integral polarity of
one of the centres, the *psychic Love* thus set in motion immediately takes
precedence over hylic or *carnal Love*. Enriched and transcended at the same
time, carnal love loses the character of a categorical imperative. The
strength of sexual attraction does not disappear, but it takes on a new,
functional character.

We may notice that in the case of purely hylic sexual appeal, the lovers try
to pass directly to love-play, quickly followed by the final act. On the other
hand, the appearance of Psychic Love acts as a brake on the carnal effects.
This is normal. Today, when these customs are considered rather old-
fashioned, lovers are called upon to observe a more or less long period
of abstinence called the *engagement*. And the true betrothed usually refrain
from sexual relations until their wedding night, in spite of their mutual
physical attraction, which may be very strong.

At first sight, it is curious to note that 'modern' girls who, before
marriage, change lovers as often as boys change mistresses, once they
have experienced Psychic Love, will often instinctively refrain from sexual relations with their fiancees during the engagement period.

Although this fact may be noticed, no one bothers to explain it. Most
people are content to defer to tradition and custom. Rarely does someone
understand the true role in psychic Love that is or should be played by the
betrothal. But, in esoteric work, if both of the couple take part, the
engagement, while changing slightly in form, plays a determining role.

(4)

Let us leave aside cases of conflict between carnal Love and an imaginary Psychic Love that often arise between a married couple after initial and reciprocal errors of judgement. These lead either to a rupture or, worse still, to a sometimes artificial and abnormal psychic and sexual coexistence.

This contemporary phenomenon is due to the fact that, if the polarization between certain sectors of the motor centre in a couple is real, the alleged *integral* polarization of one of the centres of their Personalities is imaginary. The cause of this is that in relationships between man and woman, much more than in other manifestations of life, we take our desires for reality, especially on the masculine side. This is always a direct or indirect result of the influence of the General Law.

In time, the original enthusiasm fades—in proportion to the hold of this illusion — and we begin to run into 'discrepancies' from the cherished image, which we have endowed with all its qualities.

In the cases where physiology ranks before psychology, we are sometimes faced with a phenomenon as bizarre as it is harmful: a strong sexual attraction retains its original character of a categorical imperative, but it is accompanied by a reciprocal aversion of the psyche, or by excessive jealousy when the illusion has disappeared in one of the partners but stays alive in the other. These are precisely the cases to be found at the root of crimes of passion.

We will set aside the whole scale of conflicts which arise from this mismatch within couples between the manifestation of carnal love and the psychic love which allegedly unites them, and also leave aside the whole scale of 'Gordian knots' which are thus created in life — a scale which forms the subject of psychological novels — since our concern is with human psychic Love.

(5)

On all planes, the objective sign of Love's participation is the creative spirit which animates the subjects for whom it has become an aim. Conversely, if we think we are in Love but objectively do not notice an increase in creativity on any plane, either in ourselves or in our partner, we can be sure that the relationship is based on anything but Love.

The so-called marriage of reason, like the whole scale of physical and psychic prostitution practised by men as well as women, presents a rich variety of different forms and manifestations of these aberrations.

(6)

The phenomenon of *true* psychic Love is more rare. Kindled by physical attraction, it can attain an intensity on the psychic plane that cannot be compared with any of the cases described above. It is not yet platonic Love, in the complete sense of this term, which is so widely misunderstood, but in the best cases it can approximate this and so produce positive effects.

Though rather rare, the phenomenon exists and is real in its essence. We can observe it especially in cases where the rich but latent creative spirit of the *man* is aroused to manifest in life in all its radiance under the psychosexual influence of a *woman*.

This happens in different degrees. Depending on the calibre of Personality of the partners, it can affect different planes: emotional, intellectual, and even motor.

Generally, when the nature of the man is only ordinary in his profession and among those around him, and the inspiring influence of his partner, although adequate and polar, remains hidden, the phenomenon becomes difficult to observe. This is why it is rarely dealt with in literature, which is preoccupied with the description and analysis of conflicts in the life of the psyches of men and women through the perturbing action of carnal Love. These conflicts produce either a tearing of the Personality, or the collapse of the unstable balance in which each of the partners lived before their fatal encounter.

With rare exceptions, the study of this psychic love, which has a positive effect in human beings who are not in any other way out of the ordinary, is not normally discussed. Thus, in order to find examples of this kind of Love and of the effects it can produce, we must look at biographies of remarkable Personalities, and only those biographies that are known to have a certain degree of truth and objectivity.

(7)

Psychic Love has this characteristic in common with carnal Love on the one hand, and with courtly Love on the other: it begins in spite of circumstances and even propriety. It cannot be 'channelled', and even less can it be 'mastered'. When it manifests it asserts itself with all the force of its objectivity, without asking for the agreement of the partners or the consent of those around them. It emerges in the full glory of its power and its absolute liberty. It remains as it first appears, without any possibility of compromise; its form and its strength marvellously adjusted to the latent needs as well as the creative possibilities of the couple. But their consciousness of its mission in life as well as of the domain in which it should be fulfilled generally remains most vague.

The appearance of Psychic Love is a kind of divine offer that carries with it adequate means for the practical execution of this mission. It is up to the couple to accept this offer, to grasp the profound meaning of its nature and the opportunity given by its appearance, and, finally, to find points of application in themselves that can be adapted to this divine force in order to respond usefully to its call.

This is generally far from easy. It is only rarely that psychic Love occurs in circumstances which provide opportunity for its application. Because of the karmic tare that weighs on each of the partners, this Love appears more like a disturbing force. That is why, more often than not, one of the partners, and sometimes both, will retreat before the vision of a struggle against inopportune circumstances. Instead of breaking with the circumstances, they prefer to break with Love!

We should not judge them. Of course, human frailty is no excuse to turn our back on the divine call. But we should not neglect the implacable fact that man lives bound by old Karma, doubled by what he has created in this present life.

But we must admit that the divine call — an expression of the Love of God, since God is Love — never intervenes to give us a command which is beyond our strength.

That is why, in their own interest and in the interest of those with whom they live, before they dismiss it as 'impossible', the partners who are in the grip of this psychic Love should minutely analyse their situation and look for an objectively just solution in relation to the Call. A *true* Call is only made when there is a possible solution to the situation, whatever that may be.

They must not adopt a solution blindly: in the first place, they must be convinced that they are really faced with a divine call and have not fallen into a trap laid by the General Law.

St John gave us the following indication, which should always be kept in mind:

Beloved, believe not every spirit, but try the spirits whether they are of God.[1]

(8)

Let us now study a few examples of how Psychic Love acts when, through the intervention of the feminine impulse, it awakens the wealth of the creative masculine spirit which, without this fertilization, would be condemned to remain in the state of unachieved or partially

---

1. John iv: 1.

achieved possibilities. Pushkin was certainly referring to Psychic Love, when he said:

All ages are subject to Love,
Its transports are beneficial!

Pushkin's wife was a beautiful coquette whose success at the Russian Court attracted the attention of Nicholas the First himself. But Pushkin was bound to her only by hylic Love, and in her company he did not find the feminine impulse of the psyche which would bring him the transports he was looking for. He was therefore forced to search for it elsewhere.

His poetic genius kept him under a strong, permanent pressure, creating in him the need to express himself. But the 'feminine fertilization' was missing — just as a woman born to have children needs 'masculine fertilization' on the hylic plane.

'How you bore me with your poems, Pushkin!' the beautiful Natalie, his wife, would say to him ... And the great poet—the Russian Dante, who was the chief creator of the modern literary language — found the desired influence in the company of Madame K., who had a refined, passionate nature, but who, from all appearances, was not even his mistress!

(9)

Professor Serge Voronoff, the famous innovator in questions relating to rejuvenation, made a deep study of Love and its psychological and physiological effects in correlation with his research in the biological domain. In his work on love and thought in animals and man, he wrote the following:

'Love is not only the attribute of youth and of the age that we call adult. The age where the senses are not yet appeased, the age to love, to create, to live in the joy of the body and the spirit, can be prolonged over the average usually regarded as adult.

'At sixty-four, Wagner conceived a passion for Judith Gauthier, poetess, and daughter of a poet. For him she personified Kundry, the burning mare prostrate at Parsifal's feet — the myth of the woman enslaved by the poet, of the sinner conquered by divine love.

O you, sweet warm soul, how inspired I was
in your arms.

he wrote to Judith (Guy de Pourtales).

'Thanks to this divine source of inspiration, love, Wagner at sixty-four created the most beautiful and most marvellous work that his genius ever produced: *Parsifal*.

'In 1823, at the age of seventy-four, Goethe fell madly in love with Ulric von Leventzow, a young girl of seventeen. His spirit enkindled, he became young again, and once more found in himself the secrets of his exaltation. He drew on this love for another joyous outburst, the passionate return to the lyrical springs of life. When leaving Marienbad to go and beg the Grand Duke of Saxe-Weimar to ask Mrs. Leventzow, on his behalf, for her daughter's hand, he was in such a state of passion, and of exaltation, that he wrote the *Elegy of Marienbad* at one stretch, and it may be considered one of his most beautiful pieces (Edmond Jaloux).

'In 1883, eighty and still sensitive to feminine charm, Victor Hugo gave his grandson, Georges, his most important piece of advice: "Love, look for love — love makes man better, Give joy and take it in loving as much as you can. One must love, my son, love well -all one's life!"

'And one year before, he wrote: "One has everything, yet one has nothing if one does not have love".'

Thus, concludes Voronoff, the psychic phase of love, the marvellous phase, the rising of desire, the rapture of the heart, the exaltation of the spirit, fills our whole being with a kind of felicity, of elation. This is all to the benefit of the individual, in whom it exalts the best qualities — whether or not this phase is followed by the physical phase of love.[2]

(10)

These examples were chosen by Serge Voronoff as appropriate to the main subject of his work, which was rejuvenation. He based his work on the principle that old age was a result of a decline in the functioning of the sexual glands, and he revived them, as we know, by means of grafting. Through this — in the language of 'Gnosis' — he was looking for, and in many cases, obtained, a reactivation of the first gamut of nutrition through an adduction of animal SI 12 — the nearest to man (chimpanzee). But, he probably did not know that animal SI 12, in even the best cases, only corresponded to the LA 24 of man, the Hydrogen of the motor centre, and not to that of the sexual centre. However, through this, he gave a new impulse to the motor centre in its instinctive function, and *indirectly* facilitated an increase in the production of SI 12 in the patient. In certain cases, the result was evident; in others, the grafting was a failure.

What is more, the positive result was always temporary, for the organism of the patient fights against a graft of heterogeneous tissue and it is resorbed in a more or less short period.

---

2. Serge Voronoff, *L'Amour et la pensée chez les bêtes et chez les hommes*. Paris, Fasquelle Ed., 1936, pp. 136–138.

(11)

The reader of 'Gnosis' must add the following considerations to what we have just said.

The scale of human Hydrogens belongs to the note LA of the Second cosmic Octave. That of animals, even those nearest to man, like the chimpanzee, belongs to the note SOL of the same octave, which is not of the same *cosmic* nature. Because of this, the SI 12 of the chimpanzee does not even correspond wholly to the human LA 24.

What is more, it is evident that complete rejuvenation cannot be attained simply by renewing the working of the first octave of nutrition. Besides, Voronoff and his pupils did not arrive at a complete renewal of the latter through the grafting that they practised.

In order to solve this problem, it would be necessary to revive the working of the second and third octaves in parallel and simultaneously. Voronoff did not take this necessity into account. He seems to have had some inkling of this, but he did not have access to the schemata we have reproduced here. However, he understood very well that, rising from the lower to the higher, the rejuvenating action on the plane of the psyche also originates in the sexual domain. He tried to prove this by quoting examples. These very same examples show—and this is essential— that the action of *sexual* rejuvenation can be produced on the psychic plane *without preliminary rejuvenation of the organism on the hylic plane*—as the cases quoted by Voronoff prove.

We can now draw the following tentative conclusions.

In certain conditions of agreement of types (66-3-1), the woman's sexual influence can make the man manifest a rush of creative spirit on the psychic plane. This can happen independently of the carnal relationship which may exist between the couple, but this, on the contrary, often reduces and sometimes prevents such a manifestation on the psychic plane.

This must be remembered. We have suggested this theory more than once from different points of view. At the present time, this kind of psychic relationship between the sexes is expected to become much more common, as it is the principal means of the reorganization of human society by a type of New Man.

But we must nevertheless say — we must even underline it — that this marvellous manifestation of the creative spirit in man under the psycho-sexual influence of a woman is subject to a basic condition: the man must possess in himself this creative spirit in a latent state, strengthened with his own original richness. If the man does not possess the creative spirit in potential, even the strongest psycho-sexual impulse from the woman will not produce any material effect — just as a carnal impulse from a man cannot fertilize a sterile woman.

Let us add the following: just as one particular woman produces a different effect of carnal attraction on different types of men, so, on the psychic plane, the creative spirit of a man produces a different psycho-sexual attraction on different women. To avoid any confusion of ideas, and to end our commentary on the cases quoted by Serge Voronoff, we must say that the latter necessarily chose his examples from among aged persons, since he was trying to rejuvenate worn-out organisms. The phenomenon of the fertilization of the creative spirit in a man through the psycho-sexual impulse of a woman retains its full potential whatever the ages of the partners.[3]

(12)

When researching in this domain, it is therefore necessary to be on one's guard and not slide into a confusion of planes:

Carnal Love has its *immediate* raison d'être in the corporeal reproduction of the species, and acts on the lower plane of consciousness;

Psychic Love has its *immediate* raison d'être in the production of moral values, and is realized on a plane of consciousness higher than the preceding.

The attentive study of the gamuts of nutrition shown in the *Enneagram* will give evidence of a strong interdependence between the action of these two aspects of Love; psychic and carnal — with a continuous variation in the percentage preponderance of one over the other, as their participation is always inversely proportional.

(13)

We must understand that if his Personality has become senile and has lost the vigour and elasticity of youth, it is materially impossible to 'rejuvenate' man by grafting or by other active means which aim at the rejuvenation of the patient's body. In the same way, we cannot 'rejuvenate' a Personality which systematically turns its back on the real 'I', believing itself to be the summit of life. But it is possible, with the support of this real 'I', not only to regain the vigour of youth, but also, through esoteric work, to develop the Personality up to the limit of its possibilities.

---

3. In the same work, Voronoff also quotes the case of Dante and Beatrice, as well as that of Petrarch and Laure. Ibid., pp. 139–145.

Thus, the problem of *rejuvenation*, which is that of *permanence*, can only be usefully resolved by appropriate action on the three planes: hylic, psychic, and pneumatic. As far as the physical body is concerned, it is a dangerous illusion to think that grafting, or the introduction of *animal* organs and cells into the *human* organism, is beneficial. This idea must be completely abandoned. Although in certain cases this method may produce a stimulating effect, it does not last, and we will now understand why it necessarily leads to a fall of the organism to a lower level than the one at which it was before the treatment.

It is possible that we may finally discover a more effective psychosomatic method of rejuvenation than Voronoff's grafting, though we would wish to pay homage to him for his role as a pioneer. What we would like to emphasize is that no results can be obtained in this domain by action limited to the hylic plane as practised today.

It is important that specialists who undertake research in this field keep this principle in mind.

(14)

Though psychic Love produces fruits that are more durable than carnal Love, the values created by this psychic Love also fade in time.

For psychic life in its totality, and on the whole scale of terrestrial human values, is manifested in time and has as its final limit the duration of a particular civilization; after that, centuries or sometimes millennia after the death of their creators, its products fall into Lethe.

Only the values acquired on the higher plane of human possibilities do not fade away with the passing of extinct civilizations: these produce spiritual Love, for pneumatic Love combines the supreme wealth of the permanent value that is its higher nature with all the marvels of hylic Love and psychic Love.

Symbolically, if we could place carnal Love on the steps of the celestial Temple and psychic Love in its nave, we would find spiritual Love hidden in the Holy of Holies, behind the sacred Veil. From there, as absolute Lord, it gives a raison d'être to each of its manifestations, whose meaning and mission it fixes and whose breadth and duration it regulates. Most men do not even suspect the true source of Love, whose expression on the physical and psychic planes offers them an irresistible attraction and supreme joys.

Here is a very ancient hymn preserved by Tradition for disciples engaged in esoteric work:

Our Lord is great and glorious.
He fills the Universe with his Love!
Thy love belongs to him;
The love of the soul is its salvation.[4]

Unfortunately, man does not know how to distinguish Love from passion, so he often takes the reflection for the source. One definition, not of Love, which is indefinable, but of its attributes, has been given by St Paul in terms which are as precise as they are meaningful. We have already quoted it in the two preceding volumes of 'Gnosis'.[5]

Because of its importance, we are quoting it for the third time:

Love, wrote St Paul, suffereth long, and is kind; Love envieth not; Love vaunteth not itself, is not puffed up, doth not behave itself unseemly, seeketh not her own, is not easily provoked, thinketh no evil. Rejoiceth not in iniquity, but rejoiceth in the truth; Beareth all things, believeth all things, hopeth all things, endureth all things. Love never faileth; but whether there be prophecies, they shall fail; whether there be tongues they shall cease; whether there be knowledge, it shall vanish away.[6]

If we meditate on this text, we will understand that a true abyss separates love from a 'loving' passion; yet we so often take the latter for love!

But passion's motivation is to *possess*, and this produces effects diametrically opposed to those described in St Paul's text.

The spirit of Love is to *give with no return.*[7]

II

(1)

Let us now go back to the question of spiritual Love in its practical aspect: this pneumatic Love which is ONE in its thousands of manifestations, Lord of our life. Can it be attained by man — and how — here below, in this very life?

All the studies in the 'Gnosis' series converge towards this final major aim, which encompasses all the possible aspirations of human beings and which, if it is once attained, opens the door to Permanence.

It is only with this Love that man passes from *existence* to *Life*.

It is with this that man can finally say with certainty that he is happy to have come into the world.

---

4. *The Golden Book.*
5. Vol. I, p. 193; Vol. II, p, 278.
6. 1 Corinthians xiii: 4–8.
7. An Indian text calls this 'undemanding love'. (Ed.)

Try to attain Love, taught St Paul.[8] This short sentence sums up the whole meaning of the inner and outer work of the disciple who has crossed the First Threshold and starts climbing the Staircase.

All through our work we have studied this problem in its different aspects and in every nuance, and we have particularly drawn the reader's attention to the special possibilities offered to the seeker of the Fifth Way, that of the Knight and the Lady of his dreams. Because this Way, which is the way of exception par excellence, is wide open to us now and for the remainder of the time of transition. This possibility meets the urgent need for the rapid formation of a new ruling elite formed of New Men, initiated into pneumatic Love, the one and only thing possible that can conquer the anarchy of a psychic life (which has been) abandoned to itself.

(2)

The disciple who chooses the *Fourth Way* has as a task to act as if his magnetic centre was already formed and passably developed, and must do so in all the circumstances of his inner and outer life.

Disciples—necessarily two—who choose the *Fifth Way*, the Knight and the lady of his dreams, whether they are so in *truth* or *honestly claiming to be so*, must endeavour to act in all circumstances of their inner and outer life *as if* they were already united in their consciousness of the real 'I', which is indivisible although bipolar, and ONE for their two Personalities and their two bodies.

Their task is more difficult and strenuous than that of the *sly Man*. For, right from the beginning, it demands a great conscious effort—in principle permanent — of self-mastery by both partners of the couple.

This demands precision in thought, without any 'displacements', and methodical treatment of negative emotions as well as the cultivation of positive emotions oriented — like the mental efforts — towards a carefully and sincerely chosen esoteric goal which is identical for both. They must not only satisfy the demand that they should not lie to themselves, but they must take even more care not to lie to each other in word or in thought, and this from the very day they make the decision to embark on the Fifth Way together.

On the other hand, if they fulfil these general conditions of conduct and work, as well as the specific instructions which have been given them, the very fact of walking together while endeavouring at each step to act *in the spirit of the bipolar 'I'*, will greatly facilitate their task.

From every point of view, the absolute sincerity demanded of them will form a solid basis for their relationship in all its connections. If this

---

8. 1 Corinthians xiv: 1.

essential condition is not fulfilled, it will give way immediately to a partial or temporary fall, which could even become final if relapses occur.

In this case the culprits will be thrown back below the First Threshold, and everything will have to be begun all over again.

(3)

In our study we have introduced the notion of couples *claiming to be polar*. The time has come to define this, but we think that the attentive reader of 'Gnosis' must have already formed some idea of this subject.

In our study of different cases of *partial* polarization, we mentioned the case of complete polarization of one of the three centres of the psyche in a couple. Among the three possible cases of this kind of partial polarization, it is necessary to distinguish one which has a special meaning and which opens up particular possibilities. This is the integral polarization of the two emotional centres of the couple, intensified by the polarization of both the emotional sectors — positive and negative — of their intellectual and motor centres, and even more, by a pronounced polarization of their growing magnetic centres.

The relationship between the partners in such a couple is very nearly that of a true polar couple. In these cases — reserved for humans of type 2 — the four sectors of their two intellectual centres, and even the four sectors of their motor centres, although they are not polar, will without much difficulty follow the movements ordered by the rest of the psychic system which is developing in the couple.

Under the hold of a strong, perfectly normal sexual attraction, marked by a sentimental shade of romantic tenderness due to the polarity of their emotional centres and with the whole of their psychism oriented towards the same esoteric goal, a couple with this makeup will sincerely think that they are a true polar couple. We will then see them step enthusiastically onto the Staircase in order to attain the Second Birth.

If two beings with this conformation meet when one or even both of them are below the First Threshold, then — like true polar couples — they will find themselves transported, and they will be immediately placed on the third step of the Staircase, that of Knowledge.

This immediate transportation to the third step of the Staircase is justified by the very fact of the couple's *polar consciousness*, although it does not correspond entirely to reality. Acquired spontaneously because of the complete polarization of their emotional centres, this consciousness kindles real *Faith* in their hearts just as it does for true polar beings. As for *Hope*, this will be acquired largely because of the polarization of the emotional sectors of the intellectual and motor centres, acting under the aegis of the growing magnetic centres.

In these conditions, the work of a couple on the third step of the Staircase, that of *Gnosis*, will be made much easier. Their task will then appear to them not as a *duty*, but as an urgent *need*, and it will be experienced with a joy that is already of a higher order.

(4)

The psychic state established in this way gives the couple the possibility of attaining and practising *courtly Love*. Even if it is not integral in its content and intensity, it will at least be sufficient to reach the commencement of the fourth step, that in which Love is all.

At this moment, the Knight and his Lady will begin to notice their non-polarity, or more exactly, their lack of integral polarization. If the third step, that of Knowledge, permits a certain dualism by the very nature of the process of acquiring *Gnosis* — since the way towards the truth necessarily passes through doubts — this is not the case on the fourth step. The progress of the couple on this step, the last stage dedicated to the acquisition of Love itself, demands — by its very nature — progressive identification of the partners (with one another), as they are called on *wholly* to become a *unity in polarity*.

Toward the end of the fourth step, this identification must become absolute so that they are not stopped at the decisive moment, just as the Guardian holds out his flaming sword to them.[9]

To summarize: the polarity *assumed* by the couple on the First Threshold and *established* on the first three steps of the Staircase, gives birth to *courtly Love,* which enables them to attain the fourth step. But from the moment that they reach this step, *Love in itself* must be progressively *lived*. Its nature is such that it can stand no compromise, nor any approximation. If the partners have made a mistake in considering themselves polar, they will quickly realize their initial error of conception.

(5)

As we have already said, this error does not entail any grievous results. The opposite is true.

Progress on this step, where the virtue to be attained is the androgynous consciousness, will progressively make the non-coincidence of the real 'I's of the partners evident. Thus, each of them will learn that his or her *true*

---

9. Vol. I, pp. 170–1.

polar being is not the one he or she sincerely believed they saw in the other partner.

Soon, this negative consciousness will become positive. The consciousness of the real 'I' whose light will progressively brighten the depths of their respective beings like the dawn will make them see the image of their *true* polar beings, which in each of them will surge up from the depth of their heart.

This image will at first be perceived as if through a misty glass, then, with their progress towards the Second Threshold, in a more and more precise and clear manner, and at last it will appear face to face in all its brilliance.

At that moment, the 'travelling companions' will understand that, by working together, they were in fact working for four.

III

(1)

It is still necessary to give some additional information which will be needed by true polar couples.

From the time they pass the First Threshold until the fourth step of the Staircase, the relative position of the partners remains practically the same as in the previous case. As we have already said more than once, it is only on approaching the Second Threshold that they will finally learn for certain whether their subjectively felt polarity will prove to be objectively real or false.

(2)

The first question to resolve is whether two polar beings can belong to two different human types? For example, can man 3 have as his polar being a woman of type 1 or 2? This is absolutely out of the question. The real 'I', which is ONE for the couple, implies an ideal bi-polarity. In the same way, the polarization between the two Personalities of polar beings, a double reflection of that of the real 'I', is also necessarily ideal. That is to say; the polarization between the equivalent centres of their psyches is *total*. More than this, even the physical bodies of the two polar beings are also rigorously polarized.

This is the meaning of the diagram, already shown in Volume II, which we reproduce in fig. 22 overleaf:

FIG. 22

This diagram is of Adam and Eve before their fall. It survives in potential in every couple of adamic polar beings, whether or not they recognize each other in life.

(3)

The second question asked of the Knight in search of his Lady-elect is how he can recognize her when they meet? How can he be sure he does not take a stranger for Her? One of the 66 or the 3? How to avoid passing her by? This question does not exist for the just, for in all circumstances, they see rightly. But for corrupt hearts—and in different proportions, this is the general case — the question is not so easily resolved.

The karmic tare leads to a deformation of the Personality until it no longer represents an ideal reflection of the real 'I'. This deformation, which is doubled as a result of the burden acquired in this life—for example, the professional deformation of the psyche—covers the Personality with a sort of *crust*. Because of this, unless the man is already well-trained in esoteric work, he sees everything through this screen, which deforms the true image of people and things. What is more, only through the deformations produced by their own crust can he perceive the Personality of the human beings he tries to understand.

We must add that the karmic tare of two polar beings is not and cannot ever be identical. In order to understand this, it is sufficient to re-read the pages in this work that describe the *Film*. In fact, by the autonomy of his life, every Personality produces a particular Karma. Among other consequences, one result is that two polar beings can be born, not at the same time, as should normally happen, but with a difference in time which in certain cases can be considerable. All this 'muddle' explains why polar beings so rarely recognize each other spontaneously at the moment of their encounter.

This confusion of facts also justifies the noble medieval tradition in which the Knight and his Lady-elect were willing to go through generally difficult trials before they were finally united.

(4)

But before speaking of trials — which will always remain the rule — it is necessary for the two beings gripped by vivifying Love to reach a sincere and almost absolute convinction of their polarity.

(5)

The karmic deformation of the Personality, we have said, always appears as a crust on the surface. Behind this crust, the psyche remains itself: more or less developed and more or less balanced. The exercise of constatation, methodically pursued, enables the man to discriminate between the elements of the acquired crust, which are heterogeneous by nature, and the 987 little 'I's which together form his Personality. Through introspective observation beyond the crust, the man will easily distinguish the human type to which he belongs.

This is important. But it is not yet sufficient to make the Knight, once he sees himself in this way, form a precise and ideal image of the Lady of his Dreams. For this, he will still have to make considerable conscious efforts.

(6)

In order to approach the problem better, we must go back to the fragment from the Golden Book quoted in the second volume, so we will reproduce it here:

Every man is born bearing within him the image of his polar being.
As he grows, this image grows within him;
It takes form and is filled with life and colour.
Man is not conscious of it. Yet it is his ALTER EGO,
The Lady of his dreams, his PRINCESS OF THE VISION.
In quest of her he must eternally go.
In Her alone, he will find a perfect echo of himself;
Of the most intimate, inexpressible movements of his soul,
For in their union, the limit between the I *and the* THOU *is obliterated.*
Since she is his SINGULAR, *his* LEGITIMATE SPOUSE.
And SILENCE *will then be the depositary of the fullness of their Love.*

We can now take another step towards penetrating the profound meaning of this text.

Man cannot see himself as long as he is identified with the whole: the Personality-Crust. For he is then identified — on the plane of waking consciousness — *with what is not, strictly speaking, himself*. By eliminating the crust through exercises he achieves an identification with his naked Personality, and in this way he acquires the possibility of proceeding to an *introspection of the second degree*. This will then allow him to distinguish within himself the image of his ideal polar being who, says the text we have just quoted, lives within him and, it says exactly, accompanies him night and day all through life from birth to death, just as an *ideal* image of him lives throughout life in his polar being, untouched by his circumstances.

At this point, the reader of 'Gnosis' will understand for himself what path to follow and where it leads: once freed from the obstacles to the introspection of the second degree, and starting from the 'I' of the Personality — now liberated from the crust — man can go on to gain the vision of his real 'I'.

In his epistle to the Ephesians, talking of marriage, and quoting the text of Genesis, St Paul discusses this question in the context of the relationship between Christ and his Church: '*For this cause shall a man leave his father and mother and shall be joined unto his wife and they two shall be one flesh.*'[10] And he adds: '*This is a great mystery.*'[11]

To come back to man's search for the image of his polar being in himself — this mystery consists of the real 'I', bi-polar in itself and ONE for the couple. In the man *it is turned to face his feminine side*, so to speak, and *in the woman it faces her masculine side*.

It is in this way that the Knight carries the *ideal* image of his Dream Princess in himself, and the Lady carries within her that of her Prince Charming.

The image grows in the man with his growth, says the text of the Golden Book. But it appears only *as a result* of the evolution of the Personality, and consequently it can attain all its fullness only at the end of the actual development of the Personality.

IV

(1)

What then is this considerable conscious effort that the Knight should make, during the introspection of the second degree, in order to

10. Genesis ii: 24.
11. Ephesians v: 32.

discover in himself—with astonishment—the *idealized* image of his Dream Princess?

Through the methodical practice of introspective constatation, man manages to distinguish within himself the crust of his own Personality. In other words, through this he finds the true 'I' of his Personality. Of course, this is not his real 'I', but neither is it the false 'I' of his Personality as it appears when man is identified with his 987 little 'I's *plus the crust.* Compared to the 987 little 'I's, the crust often takes a dominant place in the waking consciousness of man. When this dominance is very pronounced, it is easily perceptible; we then say of the individual that he is false, dissimulating or deformed. By liberating himself from the hold of the crust, the man becomes himself again — of course on the plane of waking consciousness, that of the 'I' of the Personality. We then say of him that he has an 'open mind'. Though there is nothing esoteric about them, these latter cases are quite rare in contemporary society.

(2)

The exercise of constatation by which man reaches this first considerable success on the way to *Know thyself* is an act of *passive* concentration.

However, to acquire in himself the vision of the ideal image of his polar being in this introspection of the second degree, man must practice *active* concentration.

If, from the day that man learns about the existence of polar beings, his heart is aflame with the ardent desire to find his, he must start work without further delay. He will realize that the situation is very complicated to unravel. Yet he must not be discouraged, but must keep in mind St Paul's words: *'For it is God which works in you both to will and to do of his good pleasure.'*[12]

Thus, if a man, young or old, burning with a valiant heart, becomes a Knight in order to follow the Fifth Way, (the same goes for women and young girls), he must henceforth *live for that* alone. To this end he must cultivate a double desire:

a) to merit the joy of recognizing in himself the image of his polar being, and

b) to merit the joy of recognizing her when they meet.

The general rule, which should be rigorously applied is: *'to attain the desired goal, it is necessary to think of it without ceasing.'*[13] This is the *active* concentration that is needed.

---

12. Philippians ii: 13.
13. The Golden Book.

Contrary to what one may fear, this permanent exercise is not an obstacle to other exterior activities, but it even considerably augments the capacity for work. It is not difficult to understand why: this is because, from the first day that he practices this active introspective concentration, the man turns towards his real 'I', which is the source of his life and strength, and step by step, day by day, he draws nearer to it.

So let us not lose sight of the fact that the door of the Fifth Way is now wide open due to the needs of the Time of Transition, to the rapid approach of the Era of the Holy Spirit, to the accelerated incarnation of the souls attached to our planet and, lastly, to the prospect of a struggle between the two terrestrial humanities. Because of this, Knights, as well as their presumed Ladies-elect, benefit more especially from divine grace: forever united in Truth and Life, they will enter into the bosom of the Lord in order to be immediately employed on a task in His service.

For today, as of old, *'the harvest truly is great, but the labourers are few.'*[14]

---

14. Matthew ix: 37; Luke x: 2.

EPILOGUE

More than once, in our work, we have drawn the reader's attention to the analogy that exists between the work entrusted to John the Baptist, who was the only Forerunner to Jesus, and the work that the best spirits must accomplish collectively during the present Time of Transition so as to prepare for the arrival of and make possible the establishment of the Era of the Holy Spirit on Earth.

This analogy goes very far. This is why the little knowledge that we have on the way John the Baptist carried out his mission — a mission which ended in failure—should be the object of profound meditation for all those who aspire to enter the ranks of the modern Precursor-Knights.

During these meditations, we should particularly keep in mind a fact which generally passes unnoticed, which is that *John the Baptist did not perform any miracles.*

While Jesus largely used miracles, starting with the one at the wedding at Cana in Galilee, and his Apostles followed Him closely, the Forerunner did not resort to them in any circumstance.

This fact is significant. The Precursor-Knights should not count on the aid of miracles in their task. The work should be accomplished by our own abilities. This is an ultimate test to which the whole of human society is now being subjected: will it prove capable, in responding to the Lord's call, of conceiving a new elite formed of New Men, who will be able to assume the responsibility of power in all humility in order to save mankind from the Deluge of Fire which is approaching from the side of Darkness, and so ensure the advent of the Era of the Holy Spirit which, if Love is victorious, will bring to the Earth the Light, the Truth, and the Life.

Geneva, 1963 — Athens, 1964

Translation completed
Newbury, MA, USA, 1993

INNER CHRISTIANITY

by Saint Theophan the Recluse

THE HEART OF SALVATION

translated by Esther Williams, introduction by George A.Maloney S.J. The life and teachings of Theophan the Recluse, one of the greatest and most recent of Russia's masters of the psychology of the inner life. Explains esoteric doctrines never previously published in English in ways comprehensible to the modern mind.

208 pages, paperback, $17.95 | £9.95   *ISBN 1-872292-02-X*

THE PATH OF PRAYER

– Four Sermons on Prayer. Translated by Esther Williams. A full introduction to the use of liturgical prayer as a method of spiritual development by the author of more than half the quotations in *The Art of Prayer*.

96 pages, paperback, $7.95 | £5.95   *ISBN 1-872292-14-3*
Hand bound, $10.95 | £8.95   *ISBN 1-872292-13-5*

by P.D.Ouspensky

THE COSMOLOGY OF MAN'S POSSIBLE EVOLUTION

Companion volume to Ouspensky's well-known *Psychology of Man's Possible Evolution*, definitive text only made available in 1989.

128 pages, paperback, £7.50   *ISBN 1-872292-01-1*

THE PSYCHOLOGY AND COSMOLOGY OF MAN'S POSSIBLE EVOLUTION

'Together for the first time:' a Definitive Limited Edition of both texts.

224 pages, hard cover, £14.95   *ISBN 1-872292-00-3*

These two books by P.D.Ouspensky were published in England by Agora Books at the request of certain of his senior pupils, and are not for sale in North America for copyright reasons. They are available in the UK from Praxis Institute Press, which is now continuing the main work of Agora Books internationally.

by George Capsanis,
Abbot of the Monastery of Osiou Gregoriou on Mount Athos

THE EROS OF REPENTANCE

Translated by Alexander Golitzin. A contemporary 'father' of the Greek Orthodox church – Igoumenos of a monastery that is more than 700 years old and now in the forefront of the new revival of Mount Athos – writes about the transformation of Eros in the monastic life.

96 pages, paperback, $6.95 / £4.95   ISBN 1-872292-04-6

by Eugraph Kovalevsky, Bishop Jean of Saint-Denis
Founder of the French Orthodox Church

A METHOD OF PRAYER
FOR MODERN TIMES

Detailed instruction on the application of the ancient methods of Eastern Orthodoxy under the conditions of modern life, an in-depth study of the Lord's prayer, and texts on the Lord's prayer from the early fathers.

144 pages, paperback $15.00, £8.95   ISBN 1-872292-18-6

Videotape

1000 YEARS ARE AS ONE DAY

Made for TV - sensitive 1 hour study of Mount Athos monastery. (Initially available only in North America)

$50

Audio tape

READINGS FROM THE PHILOKALIA

Selected by Gerald Palmer, read by Sergei Kadloubovsky, son of the other translator.

two tapes, four sides $19.95 / £12.00

Ask your bookseller, write for list and for details of correspondence course, or order direct from:

PRAXIS INSTITUTE PRESS

a division of Praxis Research Institute, Inc.
275, High Road, Newbury, MA 01951, USA
Tel: (508) 462 0563 Fax: (508) 462 2340
and China Hill, Brightling Road, Robertsbridge,
E. Sussex, England TN32 5EH. Tel: 0580 881137